STORIES OF CHANGE

STORIES
OF
CHANGE

*Narrative and
Social Movements*

EDITED BY
Joseph E. Davis

STATE UNIVERSITY OF NEW YORK PRESS

Published by
State University of New York Press, Albany

© 2002 State University of New York

Printed in the United States of America

For information, contact State University of New York Press, Albany, NY
www.sunypress.edu

Production by Cathleen Collins
Marketing by Fran Keneston

Cover photo courtesy of Hulton Getty Archive/Liaison.

Library of Congress Cataloging in Publication Data

Stories of change : Narrative and social movements / edited by Joseph E. Davis.
    p. cm.
Includes bibliographical references and index.
ISBN 0–7914–5191–7 (alk. paper) — ISBN 0–7914–5192–5 (pbk. : alk. paper)
1. Storytelling. 2. Social movements. 3. Discourse analysis, Narrative.
I. Davis, Joseph E. II. Title.
GR72.3 .S755 2002
303.48′4—dc21
                                    2001020146

10 9 8 7 6 5 4 3 2 1

Contents

Acknowledgments

This is a book about stories, but it also has a story of its own. While the details of this long and rather circuitous tale are not of general interest, I want to acknowledge and thank a number of colleagues who helped bring it to a happy ending with timely advice and support along the way. These include, most notably, Robert Benford, Donald Black, Edith Raphael Brotman, Gary Alan Fine, James Davison Hunter, Marcus Mahmood, Francesca Polletta, and Jeffery Tatum. I also want to express special appreciation to Brooke Lea and Jack Rossman of the psychology department at Macalester College, who were gracious and generous hosts during the summer months in which this book was completed. At SUNY Press, I am very grateful for the interest and enthusiasm that Dale Cotton, former acquisitions editor, expressed for the project, for the constructive comments of the three anonymous reviewers, and for the careful work of Cathleen Collins in bringing the book to completion. The Institute for Advanced Studies in Culture, my intellectual home at Virginia, provided research support, and Kristine Harmon, research associate, provided painstaking editorial assistance as well as help with the preparation of the manuscript. To Kristine and to the Institute, my sincerest thanks.

PART ONE

Narrative and the Sociology of Social Movements

ONE

Narrative and Social Movements

The Power of Stories

JOSEPH E. DAVIS

The past two decades have witnessed a great flowering in writing about narrative and the effort by a wide variety of scholars to incorporate it into their disciplines. The study of narrative in fiction has, of course, long been central to literary theory. More recently, however, narrative study has moved out of English Departments to take on new prominence in psychology, philosophy, semiotics, folklore studies, anthropology, political science, sociology, history, and legal studies. The "narrative turn" (Mitchell 1981) in so many fields of human inquiry, has, no doubt, many and complex causes. This development, however, is clearly part of a renewed emphasis in these fields on human agency and its efficacy, on context and the embeddedness of human experience, and on the centrality of language to the negotiation of meaning and the construction of identity in everyday life (see Hinchman and Hinchman 1997).

In specific areas of inquiry, however, both within and across these disciplines, a concern with narrative has often been slow to develop, and research on social movements is paradigmatic. Within sociology, for instance, there has been a resurgence of interest in narrative as a social act and form of explanation, on storytelling as a social process, on life histories and "accounts" as social objects for investigation, and on the narrative constitution of identity (see, for example, Davis 2000a; Griffin 1993; Maines 1993; Richardson 1990; Somers 1994). Yet, with respect to social movements, little of this interest in narrative can be found. As Gary Alan

Fine has observed, narrative "has barely been explored by social movement researchers" (1995: 133). For some, a neglect of narrative stems
from the continued sway of theoretical orientations that emphasize structural and interest-oriented explanations, to the near exclusion of
ideational factors. A certain resistance might also be explained by the
antipositivist and postmodern stance of some sociologists who promote a
focus on narrative. With a few notable exceptions (e.g., Benford 1993b;
Fine 1995; Hunt and Benford 1994; Polletta 1998a), even scholars who
have sought to reinvigorate movement research with increased sensitivity
to issues of agency, context, and language have tended not to directly
engage the concept of narrative. Neglect from this quarter is especially
surprising because social movements are dominated by stories and storytelling, and narrative goes to the heart of the very cultural and ideational
processes these scholars have been addressing, including frames, rhetoric,
interpretation, public discourse, movement culture, and collective identity.
The investigation of narrative in social movements is both warranted and
overdue.

Combining theoretical analysis with empirical studies of narrative in
specific movements, this volume argues that narrative is both a vital form
of movement discourse and a crucial analytical concept. It demonstrates
that studying narratives, their functions, and the conditions under which
they are created and performed adds to the growing "cultural turn" in the
study of social movements by offering analytical insights and understandings that extend contributions in the recent constructionist and new social
movement scholarship. The analysis of narrative, as the contributors
show, overcomes key limitations in the framing perspective and illuminates core features of identity-building and meaning-making in social
activism. It also sheds new light on movement emergence, internal dynamics, and public persuasion, and addresses cultural aspects of activism that
get short shrift in movement research.

Moreover, this book's empirical cases include movements that are
prominent on the American landscape and that have high rates of participation, but that typically have been regarded by social movement scholars
as too apolitical or individualistic to be considered social movements, and
therefore ignored. Unlike movements with an explicit focus on the state,
self-help and New Age movements, like many other "culturalist" new
social movements, have looser, more fluid structures and direct activism
toward far more diffuse and decentralized forms of social power. These
forms of collective action represent challenges to power relations that are

inscribed in social institutions and cultural practices, including aspects of everyday life. They engage what Anthony Giddens calls "life politics," a politics that concerns "issues which flow from processes of self-actualization in post-traditional contexts" (1991: 214). Studying movement narratives, as the case studies show, provides analytical purchase on unifying and oppositional elements not only in state-targeted movements but in these less overtly political movements as well.[1]

Stories of Change was conceived for all those interested in movements and the role that stories and storytelling play in them. Given the sociological orientation of the volume, however, theoretical developments and debates within that field form its backdrop. In order to provide some context, I begin by briefly reviewing the new theoretical emphasis on culture and the construction of meaning within social movement research. I then turn to the concept and the functions of narrative in social movements.

THE CULTURAL TURN IN SOCIAL MOVEMENT RESEARCH

Over the past twenty years, resource mobilization theory in its several versions (political, entrepreneurial, and political process) has been the dominant approach to the study of social movements. In this perspective, and in contrast with the earlier models of collective behavior it effectively replaced, social movements are viewed as "normal, rational, institutionally rooted, political challenges by aggrieved groups" (Buechler 2000: 35). They are studied in terms of conflicts of interest, like other more conventional forms of political engagement, and in terms of their organizational dynamics. Movement participants are viewed as rational actors, who are recruited and who choose involvement based on a straightforward cost-benefit calculus. Movements, however, unlike established special-interest groups, arise outside the polity and therefore must rely on noninstitutional means to achieve political influence and change. Thus, the cost of movement participation is higher than in conventional politics and so movements must typically provide additional "selective incentives" to recruit members. In explaining movement origins, resource mobilization theorists have argued that grievances per se have little explanatory value since they are always present and essentially a constant. The resources necessary to carry out activism, however, are variable and so group mobilization of resources (funds, talent, contacts, and so on), usually in formal organizations, is the key explanatory mechanism.

There have been many specific criticisms of resource mobilization theory (see, e.g., the review in Buechler 1993), but in particular, critics have in various ways focused on the perspective's failure to engage the cultural and symbolic processes that underlie collective action. As a response to these deficiencies, new perspectives have been formulated over the past decade and a half that directly challenge resource mobilization's rationalist, individualist, and instrumental/political assumptions, as well as its overemphasis on formal organizations and deemphasis of ideational factors. These perspectives—new social movement theory in Europe and the social constructionist approach in the United States—have laid new, in part renewed, stress on the role of ideas and identity, the symbolic and expressive, in the analysis of social movements (see, e.g., Jasper 1997; Melucci 1989; Morris and Mueller 1992; Laraña, Johnston, and Gusfield 1994; Johnston and Klandermans 1995a).[2] They have sought to reinvigorate movement study with a focus on culture, the construction of symbolic systems of meaning, and the larger social and historical context of movement mobilization.

The new social movement (NSM) approach originated in Europe in the 1980s. In general, NSM theory has two principal dimensions. One is a causal argument about the connection of contemporary social movements to broad structural changes in society as a whole—notably features of postindustrial society, including capitalistic markets, bureaucratic states, instrumental rationality, pervasive social control, and so on. While NSM scholars differ on the nature of the specific structural dislocations, the general approach concentrates on specifying the link between these dislocations and the resulting novel "morphological changes" in the structure and action of social movements (Melucci 1989). In short, this dimension of the theory is concerned with the relationship between movements and macrolevel social changes. The second dimension of NSM theory is an argument about features of contemporary movements (of the 1960s and after) that distinguish them from the working-class (labor) movements of the industrial period. A key task for NSM scholars has been to identify these features and to develop analytical tools to study them. Scholars argue, for instance, that NSMs, with a complex social base decoupled from the class structure, have an ideological outlook centered on autonomy and identity. NSMs emphasize quality of life and lifestyle concerns over economic redistribution and challenge the "structures of representative democracies that limit citizen input and participation in governance, instead advocating direct democracy, self-help groups, and cooperative styles of social organization" (Pichardo 1997: 415). As a result, these groups tend to structure themselves in a fluid, decentralized style, to emphasize the reflexive construction of collective identities and the moral meaning of everyday life, and to rely on cultural and symbolic forms of resistance at least as often as more conventional political activism. While these features are not unique to contemporary movements, they are characteristic of many and this dimension of NSM theory centers on the signal role of values, symbols, and sources of consciousness in these movements.

The social constructionist research on movements began to appear in the mid-1980s in the United States with the initial formulations of the "framing perspective." Unlike NSM theory, however, constructionism has been closer to resource mobilization, seeking to compliment its structural variables by drawing attention to the neglected relationship between mobilizing beliefs and ideas and identification with and participation in social movements. Scholars working from this perspective focus on the "signifying work" of movements to "frame" grievances and mobilize support. And they stress the importance of interaction, interpretation, and discourse in the framing process and in the building of collective identities (Gamson 1992, 1995; Johnston, Laraña, and Gusfield 1994; Snow et al. 1986; Snow and Benford 1988, 1992; also see Fine, this volume).

In the framing perspective, "collective action frames" emerge through an interactive and negotiated process as a group consciously fashions its grievances, strategies, and reasons for action by drawing on and modifying existing cultural beliefs and symbols. These frames are ways of understanding offered by the movement that "inspire and legitimate" movement activity, both in terms of the need for such activity and the desirability of undertaking it (Snow et al. 1986). In diagnostic framing, for instance, the movement defines the problem it seeks to address as well as the actors (groups or individuals) who are the cause of the problem. Prognostic framing involves the identification of possible remedies, and may include the delineation of appropriate tactics and strategies. In motivational framing, the rationale for activism is specified and a sense of agency to affect change and urgency to do so are called out (Snow and Benford 1988). Though subject to ongoing revision, as these frames are defined, they serve to guide collective and individual participant action. Frames, according to constructionist scholars, also serve as a persuasive tool for enlisting new participants. Movements seek to recruit outsiders through attempts at aligning movement frames with the personal experiences, interests, and beliefs of potential participants, and use a variety of frame alignment

processes beyond motivational framing (Snow et al. 1986). When successful, these processes foster a link between an individual's personal identity
and the collective identity of the group (Hunt, Benford, and Snow 1994).

In NSM theory and social constructionism, social movements represent more than collectively organized action: they also consist of collectively constructed and shared meanings, interpretations, rituals, and
identities. In attending to the strategic use of signs and symbols, and not
just structures and resources, these theoretical approaches have provided a
language for analyzing the social construction of collective action. They
have focused new attention on the internal cultural dynamics of movements. And they have led to a greater recognition of diffuse expressions of
social activism, and less programmatic and conventionally political agendas for social change. Contemporary movements, as NSM theory especially has emphasized, may or may not place their locus of activity within
specific organizations, state their goals programmatically, make clear distinctions between leaders and followers, or draw sharp lines between participants and nonparticipants. Even the individual and intimate relations
can be sites of movement activity, as in self-help movements and movements that engage in "identity politics." NSM theory and social constructionism, then, offer new ways of understanding contemporary movements'
symbolic and social-psychological dimensions (and, it might be added,
hitherto neglected features of older, more established movements), their
changing forms, and the specific social and historical conditions they
reflect and to which they respond.

In the introduction to a 1995 volume entitled *Social Movements
and Culture*, the editors suggested that the emerging emphasis on
frames, identity, and other symbolic-expressive processes may represent
a "paradigmatic shift" toward culture in the study of social movements
(Johnston and Klandermans 1995b: 3). Although subsequent events
have not bore this prediction out, such a strong statement from two
noted social movement scholars does suggest that the cultural turn has
had significant impact within the field. The emphasis on the cultural and
performative dimensions of activism has opened up new and productive
avenues of research and shed light on overlooked aspects of social movements and their dynamics. In addition to strengths, however, this scholarship has also had its limits. NSM theory (see the review in Pichardo
1997) and, to a much lesser extent, the framing perspective (see Benford
1997) have been the subject of critical attention. Many of these criticisms go

afield of this volume and so need not be reviewed here. But certain weaknesses are relevant because, I want to argue, attention to the concept of narrative and the stories activists tell would help to overcome them.

The relevant weaknesses, in brief, converge around a tendency in NSM theory to skirt the problem of meaning-making and in the framing perspective to overemphasize cognitive factors. While NSM scholars have emphasized the constructed nature of collective identity, they have not typically shown how activists themselves fashion their identities and interests. Similarly, among some of the most prominent NSM scholars, including Alain Touraine and Jürgen Habermas, there has been a tendency to overlay their own interpretations on those of activists, instead of seeking to understand how activists themselves make and modify meanings in specific settings (Jasper 1997: 72). As described in the literature, the concepts of framing and frame-alignment suffer from an overemphasis on logical persuasion and consensus of belief. In matters of recruitment, for instance, the framing perspective draws attention to the inherently moral claims of movements, but focuses on cognitive dynamics and provides little illumination of how specific moral responses are aroused. The perspective intimates the importance of emotions that mobilize and demobilize, yet concentrates on congruent and logical beliefs as organizing experience, building a sense of personal efficacy, and guiding action. Moreover, framing scholars have argued that the frame alignment process is precarious and depends on resonance with preexisting meanings in the wider culture, but tend to focus only on external threats to alignment and tend not to systematically explore the preexisting meanings. They have recognized that the framing and alignment processes are fluid and dialectical, yet have directed minimal attention to internal movement processes and the situated and negotiated nature of participant engagement and solidarity.

Beyond specific issues not well handled in current cultural approaches, there are additional cultural dimensions of social movements that tend to be neglected altogether in movement theory. In *The Art of Moral Protest*, for example, James Jasper suggests several such cultural dimensions and argues that each deserves substantive consideration. His list includes the influence of time and place—"the ways that we place ourselves in the world and in history" (1997: 70)—the symbolic significance of singular events and individuals, and the life passages and existential moments that help determine the meaning of life. Like morality, emotions, identity, internal movement culture, and so on, the study of narrative could also provide a window on these neglected cultural dimensions. Indeed, it seems fair to say that all cultural elements, all symbolic expressive aspects of movements, can be related to narrative and illuminated by its study. Culture is more than stories, of course; and not all cultural features of movements necessarily involve narratives. But, and this is my point, these features *might* involve narratives—be it vocabularies of meanings, expressive symbols, music, film, rules, rituals, histories, sacred places, or so on. Attending to stories is *one* way—but not the only way—to bring these crucial features of movements into the foreground and explore their context and explanatory significance.

To this point, I have argued that the cultural turn in social movements research has opened the way for, and would greatly benefit from, another development: a new focus on narrative as a social practice. In order to develop this thesis further, to illustrate more concretely the power of narrative for the study of movements, the concept of narrative itself must be explored.[3] What is a story? What makes a story a story? How does a story differ from other, nonstory forms of discourse?

THE CONCEPT OF NARRATIVE

According to the opening line of a book on narrative theory, "Everyone knows what stories are." And a fortunate thing it is because, the author continues, it has been extremely difficult, despite many efforts, to formulate a rule that unequivocally distinguishes "things that are stories from things that are not" (Leitch 1986: 3). Literary theory, where the most important work has taken place, offers diverse and divergent perspectives on how to define and analyze narrative. Modern approaches to narrative fall roughly into three clusters (see Martin 1986): the first treats narrative as a form or representation (a sequence of events; "plot" in the traditional sense) and focuses on principles of narrative structure; the second, exemplified in part by the French structuralists, treats narrative as a manner of speaking about events (a "discourse" produced by a narrator) and focuses on certain techniques of narration ("point of view"); and the third, exemplified in part by reader response theory, treats narrative as verbal acts in a social transaction highly sensitive to context, as something constructed "between" narrator and audience. This third approach focuses on the reader as an essential feature of the narrative situation. In addition to theoretical plurality, the boundary between narrative and other forms of discourse is simply not sharply marked off. Features characteristic of narrative, such as temporal sequencing, change, and closure may be found in other discursive forms (a sonnet, for instance, or an essay) and stories may be found that lack key narrative features. The relationship between stories and human experience can also be conceptualized in different ways. Among other possibilities, stories can be conceived as simply after-the-fact representations of the experiences they recount, as cultural scripts that supply guidelines for understanding and action, or as performances that create as well as comment on prior experiences. While recognizing that narrative is not a simple or fixed concept raises definitional challenges, it also highlights the generative complexity of narrative and the possibility of multiple analytic strategies. No single definition or approach exhausts its meanings.

In general, social scientists, concerned with nonfictional historical or social narratives, have emphasized the traditional meaning of narrative. Maines (1993), for instance, argues that narratives have three irreducible elements: events, sequence, and plot. Polkinghorne suggests that "narrative is a meaning structure that organizes events and human actions into a whole, thereby attributing significance to individual actions and events according to their effect on the whole" (1988: 18). Griffin notes that

> Narratives are analytic constructs . . . that unify a number of past or contemporaneous actions and happenings, which might otherwise have been viewed as discrete or disparate, into a coherent relational whole that gives meaning to and explains each of its elements and is, at the same time, constituted by them. (1993: 1097)

These offerings, and others like them, emphasize plot structure, the notion of narrative as an unfolding of "events" (meaning both human actions and experiences), and the central importance of time. In narrative, as contrasted with other discursive forms, past events are selected and configured into a plot, which portrays them as a meaningful sequence and schematic whole with beginning, middle, and end. In terms of efforts to identify a minimal universal narrative form, this is the basic description.

It is also one description that informs the meaning of narrative in this book. In the next section I will briefly elaborate on each of the characteristics that define the classical narrative form. At the same time, however, I also want to emphasize, with recent narrative theories, that (1) character and plot are interdependent, and both are dynamic elements of stories; and that (2) narrative is not only definable in terms of its structure but also in terms of its mode of presentation. Stories do not just configure the past in light of the present and future, they also create experiences for and request certain responses from their audience. They are fundamentally transactional, and this, in addition to their organizing operations, accounts for their discursive power.

Characteristics of Stories

Whatever their theoretical persuasion, most scholars of narrative would certainly agree with Donald Polkinghorne that narrative is "the primary form by which human experience is made meaningful" (1988: 1). In stories, whether of individuals or collectivities, the meaning of events is created by showing their temporal or causal relationship to other events within the whole narrative and by showing the role such events play in the unfolding of the larger whole. Narrative explanation works through "emplotment." Narratively, to understand an event, even to explain what caused the event, is to locate it within the temporal and relational sequence of a story, linking it with both previous and subsequent events over time. Further, once emplotted within a story, the character and function of that event in the development of the entire temporal sequence can be comprehended, and thus the meaning of the event defined. The order and position of an event within a story explains how and why it happened. In an important sense, then, narrative explanation operates retrospectively, since the events earlier in time take their meaning and act as causes only because of how things turned out later or are anticipated to turn out in the future (see Martin 1986: 74). Stories reconfigure the past, endowing it with meaning and continuity, and so also project a sense of what will or should happen in the future.

In order to understand this unique and powerful form of meaning-making, the place to begin with is the end. Stories are predicated on an "end" in a double sense. One sense is of a teleology, some valued endpoint that the sequence of events, the plot, displays. Stories are told to explain, to exhort, to persuade—to communicate a perspective on what happened in the very process of telling what happened. Perhaps, as Hayden White suggests, "every fully realized story" is in fact a "kind of allegory," which has as its "latent or manifest purpose the desire to moralize the events of which it treats" (1981: 13–14). In the personal experience stories recounted in this book, such as those of codependents, battered women, or drug court clients, the moralizing impulse seems clear enough. But if that goes too far for all stories, as some critics have suggested, then, at a minimum, we can say that informing the unfolding of a story is a "moral," a "point," a "theme" that provides its rationale as a unitary whole and for which, to some important degree, the story is told.[4]

The second sense of an end to a story, and related to the first, is that of a termination. The function of the ending is to bring closure to the chain of events set in motion by the beginning. The beginning of a well-formed story, according to Lionel Trilling, "is not merely the first of a series of events; it is the event that originates those that follow" (1980: 125). In a well-formed story, the meaning is immanent in all of the events from the beginning, and so beginning, middle, and end are closely and coherently linked. The story's denouement brings resolution to the action and typically provides or confirms the point of the story. Thus, the classic story moves from some initial event or situation through a series of conflicts or complications to a point of resolution and equilibrium at the end. However, this tidy pattern is by no means the only or even the most common possibility. Many stories accommodate ambiguity and resist closure, at least in the sense of providing a resolution. In chapter 3, for instance, Robert Benford describes social movement stories that leave the outcome open-ended, projecting different possible endings depending on whether collective ameliorative action is undertaken or not. Much the same indeterminacy can be seen in personal experience stories like those of the New Age participants interviewed by Michael Brown (chapter 5). Their self-narratives project a future, but because these narratives are continuously in process, made and remade, they remain necessarily unfinished. In these "endless" stories, a line of development is implied but closure is indefinitely postponed. Thomas Leitch, in a discussion of interminable stories, notes that

> Stories do not necessarily promise (although they may) that conflicts will be definitively resolved or the truth manifested once and for all; they promise only that something further will happen, or that there is something else to learn. (1986: 122)

Stories, then, may not reach a final resolution or state of equilibrium but always provide at least a premise or point of departure (and hence gain coherence as a unity).

The valued endpoint of a narrative guides the selection and evaluation of events for the telling; the plot makes the chosen events cohere. In constructing stories, tellers select some events for inclusion, while excluding other actions and details that do not serve to make the endpoint "more or less probable, accessible, important, or vivid" (Gergen 1994: 191). As Hayden White observes, "every narrative, however seemingly 'full,' is constructed on the basis of a set of events which *might have been included but were left out*" (1981: 10; emphasis in original). Further, since the selected events are not all of equal relevance to the endpoint, tellers evaluate events, giving greater prominence to key actions and turning points. Tellers then link the selected and evaluated events together along a temporal dimension so as to display the effect one event has on another, and to portray an interdependent and meaningful whole. The plot governs this ordering process.[5] Plot transforms a mere succession of events into a configuration (Ricoeur 1984: 65). E. M. Forster's famous example is suggestive. Of the following two sentences, according to Forster (cited in Martin 1986: 81), only the second is a plot.

1. The king died, and then the queen died.
2. The king died, and then the queen died of grief.

By adding cause and effect to temporal succession, the second turns time into a plot. Although skeletal in the extreme, the combination of temporal succession and causality endows the events with a narrative "design and intention"—to borrow a phrase from Peter Brooks's (1985: xi) definition of plot—that the first statement does not possess.[6]

In the classical narrative tradition since Aristotle, plot is the heart of narrative and is a representation or display of human action. Theoretically, action has priority; the consideration of character—regarded as a static element, along with setting—is subordinate. Although some argue that in modern narrative (notably the novel) the hierarchy is reversed with character, rather than action, having priority, theorists generally treat the relative emphasis on action/plot or character as a variable. The stress on one or the other varies in different kinds of stories. Recent theorists, notably structuralists, have also insisted that plot and character are inseparable, existing in a reciprocal relationship. Roland Barthes, for example, argues that characters are defined at least in part by their relation to the plot, while coming to understand the characters illuminates the significance of the actions in the plot (Martin 1986: 116–117). Character, in other words, is interdependent with plot, and so it, too, should be considered a dynamic element of narrative.

Characters have been defined as those story agents who are not simply a byproduct of the function they perform in the plot. Characters have qualities "neither required by nor expended in the action" (Leitch 1986: 149). They are not entirely predictable and convey some sense of depth and a capacity to change. In contrast to characters (or "round characters") are those agents (sometimes called "static characters" or "flat characters") who are more or less just a plot function (though, as Jerome Bruner [1986: 38] argues, story figures always convey at least "some inkling" of what they would be like in more general terms). In the battered women's stories cited by Bess Rothenberg in chapter 9, for instance, the victim (wife, girlfriend) is a character. As narrator (and thus authority), the victim describes episodes of abuse while also displaying her reactions, fears, desires, intentions, and so on, while the victimizer (husband, lover), on the other hand, is exhausted by his role in the plot as the causer of harm: he has no depth, no pangs of conscience, no capacity to grow. While displaying a wide range of complexity, characters exhibit a stability of identity. To be coherent as characters, they must behave characteristically (Fisher 1987: 47). Of course, characters in many stories do undergo a transformation, but when this happens, the story itself is typically told to explain the transformation, often in terms that maintain the character's consistency.

Characters are woven together from the depiction of various traits, including physical description, mental attitudes, actions, and interrelations with other characters. Yet to see characters as simply a bundle of traits is to miss something fundamental about their display. Characters are more than the sum of their traits. They are perceived as a unified *Gestalt*, not as a list of traits (Bruner 1986), and so we describe them as compelling, memorable, as having depth, and so on. In addition to the imputed traits and the development of the plot, something more is at work. This further element is not so much a quality of the story itself as it is of the transaction between teller and audience. Characters, like stories more generally, are meant to be apprehended in a particular way. We cannot understand the dynamism of either without considering the response that both are designed to arouse.

Stories as Social Transactions

So far I have argued that the narrative form is powerful because it configures experience by selecting and plotting events within a temporal order that infuses these events with significance and exploits them for valued ends. But stories are also powerful for another reason: because they are social practices. Stories involve two parties, a teller (or narrator) and an interpretive audience (listeners/readers), and well-told stories establish a relationship between the two. According to narrative theorists, this relationship is created by the teller's engagement of the audience's "narrativity," their ability to fill in connections that are required to make sense of the characters and events in the story. For the teller's part, engaging the audience's participation means filling out a "given pattern or idea by providing enough details to make the audience's narrativity necessary and rewarding" (Leitch 1986: 63). The teller's task, in other words, is to say "enough" but not too much. What is left out of a story and underspecified in characters is also critical to their success. According to the reader response theorist Wolfgang Iser, "It is only through inevitable omissions that a story will gain its dynamism." These omissions are crucial because they give us the opportunity "to bring into play our own faculty for establishing connections—for filling in the gaps left by the text itself" (1972: 284–285). A well-told story is a creative process that implies certain connections, speculations, and emotional reactions but avoids spelling everything out or attempting "to control an audience's emotional or psychological reactions too openly" (Leitch 1986: 36). On the contrary, the "unwritten" part of a well-told story stimulates the audience's creative participation and identification and invites them to supply what is unspecified yet required.

The story, then, is more than the text, for as Iser argues, the "text only takes on life when it is realized" (1972: 279). It is the reader/listener that "sets the work in motion," a process that in turn "results ultimately in the awakening of responses within himself" (1972: 280). By engaging the audience's narrativity, storytellers draw the audience into the story because the connections being made are the product of the reader/listener's mind and not simply a perception of what is written or heard. As a result, he or she can feel involved in events and care about characters even when they are, in fact, very far from his or her own experience (a point of obvious importance to social movements). And, of course, the same story can differently affect different reader/listeners. Iser calls the product of this creative activity the "virtual dimension of the text." The virtual dimension, he writes, "is not the text itself, nor is it the imagination of the reader: it is the coming together of text and imagination" (1972: 284).

In activating the audience's narrativity, the storyteller seeks to provoke a particular type of response. Although dealing with a larger class of speech acts than just narrative, the description of "tellable" assertions by the literary theorist Mary Louise Pratt nicely captures the kind of audience experience that storytellers aim to create. She contrasts assertions, whose primary purpose is to exchange information (e.g., answers to questions), with tellable assertions (such as stories) that "represent states of affairs that are held to be unusual, contrary to expectations, or otherwise problematic" (1977: 136). In making a tellable assertion, she argues, the speaker

> is not only reporting but also verbally *displaying* a state of affairs, inviting his addressee(s) to join him in contemplating it, evaluating it, and responding to it. His point is to produce in his hearers not only belief but also an imaginative and affective involvement in the state of affairs he is representing and an evaluative stance toward it. He intends them to share his wonder, amusement, terror, or admiration of the event. Ultimately, it would seem, what he is after is an *interpretation* of the problematic event, an assignment of meaning and value supported by the consensus of himself and his hearers. (1977: 136; emphasis in original)

Central to this interpretative consensus is identification between storyteller and audience. Reader/listeners who identify with the storyteller step into the story, recreate the world it presents, and retain the experience. They make, in short, the story their own.

Inviting the audience to join in the creative process, the storyteller fosters identification by stimulating recognition and empathy. According to the philosopher Walter Fisher, audiences assess stories according to principles of narrative coherence and fidelity. They ask about a story and its characters, whether they "hold together" and add up to a "reliable claim to reality." And they ask whether or not a story (or a character) is consistent with related stories (characters) that they already know and believe (1987: 194). On this account, for narratives to be persuasive, they must appeal to what audiences think they know, what they value, what they regard as appropriate and promising. Readers/listeners conceive of themselves in specific ways, and so if a story, as Fisher argues, "denies a person's self-conception, it does not matter what it says about the world" (1987: 75); there is no basis for identification with story or teller. This, he notes, is why the philosopher Alasdair MacIntyre is correct in observing that "the utterance of protest is characteristically addressed to those who already share the protestor's premises" (1981: 69; emphasis deleted). Rival movement activists talk past each other because their rival stories "deny each other in respect to self-conceptions and the world" (Fisher 1987: 75). If what a story communicates about the world is to be accepted, it must affirm not negate the self-conceptions that audience members hold of themselves.

Storyteller-audience identification is necessarily context dependent since it hinges on how successfully the teller accommodates the interests of the audience (Herrnstein Smith 1980) or delivers the rewards the audience has been led to expect.[7] Indeed, since stories are always produced and told under particular social conditions and constraints, historical, institutional, and biographical contexts are always critical to understanding the intelligibility, believability, and relevance of stories. The social norms and conventions operating in various cultural and institutional contexts govern when stories are told (expected, demanded, or prohibited), what kinds of stories can be told (rules of appropriate content), and how stories are told (rules of participation) (Ewick and Silbey 1995). For example, in chapter 7, James Nolan describes in detail the content rules that govern client narratives within the drug court movement. To be successful in court, and even apart from actual changes in drug-using behavior, clients must tell the "right story," communicating in their participant narratives the expected attitudes toward themselves and their therapy (they have a disease, are in need of treatment, and so on). Those who fail to tell a story in terms of these content rules can meet with serious consequences. The drug court, when contrasted with the criminal trial, also illustrates different rules of participation. In the drug court, the judge is defined as the principal audience, while in a criminal trial, as described by Jeffery Tatum in chapter 8, the participation rules assign the primary audience role to the jury. Further, the contrasting rules assign the storyteller role differently and specify differently who can speak, about what, and according to what forms of interaction.

Viewing stories as part of a social transaction draws attention to the role of the audience and to the social context in which stories are produced and experienced. These aspects of narrative, in turn, suggest some important ways in which stories are different from more expository forms of communication. Unlike prepositional arguments, which aim to make their claims concerning causality and truth explicit and therefore testable or debatable, stories invite their audience to an imaginative and emotional involvement, and employ techniques that are designed to control the responses and inferences the audience has to the story characters. Further, the underlying criteria used to determine event selection, causality, and significance is not directly displayed. In stories, as White observes, events seem to "tell themselves" (1981: 3). This makes stories difficult to test or challenge. Unlike prepositional arguments, one does not need specialized knowledge or theoretical sophistication to judge stories. According to Fisher, audience members do not have to be taught narrative coherence and fidelity; they culturally acquire these skills "through a universal faculty and experience" (1987: 75). Finally, narratives reach beyond logic and proposition, working not by deduction and reflection but by suggestion and identification. Stories appeal to the intellect to be sure, but also to emotion and imagination, to moral and aesthetic intuition, as well as logical reasons.

Group Stories and Self-Narratives

The storytelling process, as a social transaction, engages people in a communicative relationship. Through identification and "cocreation" of a story, the storyteller and reader/listener create a "we" involving some degree of affective bond and a sense of solidarity: told and retold, "my story" becomes "our story." While narratives may certainly be strategically used to strengthen a collective identity, as several of the chapters in this volume demonstrate, they can also be the basis on which social relationships are organized. Interpretive communities come together around stories, constituting and reaffirming themselves as groups with particular attributes (Carr 1986; Hinchman and Hinchman 1997; MacIntyre 1981). Collective memory is directly tied to story emplotment. This is no less true of social movements, as several of the chapters in this volume make clear. In chapter 2, for instance, Francesca Polletta, drawing on student's accounts of the 1960 Southern sit-ins to protest racial segregation, argues that narratives gave coherence and directionality to rapidly unfolding events, helped to constitute and sustain a collective identity, and configured emotions so as to provide incentives to high-risk participation. In chapter 10, Gary Alan Fine argues in detail that internal social movement culture is basically a storied process; the continuous telling of stories helps to foster, sustain, and guide movement participation and allegiance.

As collective identities are constituted by stories, so too, many scholars have argued, are individual identities (e.g., Bruner 1986; Kerby 1991; Ricoeur 1988; Somers 1994). In this view, identity is not some inner essence but rather an ongoing story that emerges in and through the selection and emplotment of experience. Individuals search for self-understanding by imposing narrative structure on their lives, an interpretive process that both looks back in time and projects into the future. The self-narrative configures key experiences into a meaningful whole, introduces a sense of coherence and temporal unity to one's development and future direction, and at the same time serves as the basis by which individuals represent themselves to others.

Conceiving of identity as a narrative focuses attention on the evaluative and goal-directed nature of self-understanding, as well as highlighting the importance of past and future. Self-narratives plot the type of moral agent the individual is, and his or her purposes and intentions. As the philosopher Charles Taylor (1989) has shown, individuals define their identity in reference to a moral horizon or framework. "To know who you are," he argues, "is to be oriented in moral space" (1989: 28). Moral space is a realm of questions about what is good, what is worthwhile, and what has meaning. In this perspective, identity cannot be detached from the individual's beliefs about what things have significance, from his or her fundamental evaluations with regard to questions of the good in life. Self-narratives reveal the value determinations and distinctions in the narrator's life "by selectively plotting only those actions relevant or tributary to certain central purposes" (Kerby 1991: 56). The past is interpreted in light of an anticipated future (more or less distant), the possible self that one might be or become.

Self-narratives, however, are not "free fictions," but influenced and structured by many types of preexisting narratives, from cultural myths to the stories of one's family (Ezzy 1998). The process of interpreting and "narratizing" personal experiences—"biographical work"—is artful, to be sure, but it is also constrained by the repertoire of stories available and sanctioned in one's context of action. As the sociologist Margaret Somers notes, "all of us come to *be* who we *are* (however ephemeral, multiple, and changing) by being located or locating ourselves (usually unconsciously) in social narratives *rarely of our own making*" (1994: 606; emphasis in original). Stories, even self-stories, are inherently social. We are selves, according to Taylor, only in relation to certain interlocutors, both those who were essential to our achieving self-definition, and to those who are now crucial to our "continuing grasp of languages of self-understanding" (1989: 36). We cannot be a "self" outside these "webs of interlocution," or as Somers (1994) calls them, "public narratives," for the language through which we articulate our moral frameworks and self-understandings is always relating us to others. Taylor notes:

> We may sharply shift the balance in our definition of identity, dethrone the given historic community as a pole of identity, and relate only to the community defined by adherence to the good (of the saved, or the true believers, or the wise). But this doesn't sever our dependence on webs of interlocution. It only changes the webs, and the nature of our dependence. (1989: 39)

Culturally and institutionally embedded narratives with which we identify, then, shape the construction of our self-story. And interpersonal networks, moral communities, and public institutions, including, importantly, social movements, both sanction and supply such narratives.

NARRATIVE ANALYSIS AND SOCIAL MOVEMENTS

As the foregoing discussion has suggested, viewing narratives as social acts, and not only as structures, highlights the functions they may accomplish for the individual or collective storyteller, the conditions under which they are constituted and performed, and the responses they call forth from their audiences. This perspective also directs attention to narrative variability. There are many possible narrative transactions, many purposes that storytelling might serve, and many effects stories might have (for more on narrative variability, see Fine, chapter 10). This multiplicity suggests that narrative—and here I draw on the typology of Ewick and Silbey (1995)— can be a focus of research in at least two ways. The first way is as an object of inquiry and explanation. In this approach, researchers study how stories are socially produced and function to mediate action and constitute identities. The second research approach treats stories as a method or means of studying social life. Researchers collect and examine narratives as a lens or window through which other aspects of the social world can be accessed or revealed. While these two approaches are not mutually exclusive, they do suggest different ways in which narrative analysis can play a role in research. Both approaches are represented in the following chapters. Exploring the conditions and strategies of narration within social movements, stories are shown to be a powerful vehicle for producing, articulating, regulating, and diffusing shared meaning. At the same time, authors demonstrate how narrative study can illuminate social movement emergence, recruitment, internal dynamics, resource mobilization, and public persuasion.

Within social movements, we can make an analytical distinction between personal and collective level stories, although these are never entirely separate and not uncommonly run together. At the personal level are the stories people tell about themselves, the self-narratives through which their experience and their selves attain meaning. These vary in their temporal range, from configurations of a whole life to stories of significant life passages, existential moments, and traumatic events. The battered women's accounts (Rothenberg, chapter 9), the final taped interviews with the decedents played at the Kevorkian trial (Tatum, chapter 8), the "histories" of codependents (Rice, chapter 4), and the "life stories" of New Age participants (Brown, chapter 5), are all examples of self-narratives. Self-narratives precede movement involvement but may be deeply influenced by another type of more delimited personal experience story, what Robert Benford (chapter 3) calls "participant narratives." In these stories, the protagonist is the movement participant, who relates his or her own (though sometimes others') movement-related experiences. Examples of participant narratives include the spontaneity accounts given by the sit-in students (Polletta, chapter 2), the "happy ending stories" of drug court clients (Nolan, chapter 7), and the testimonies of attendees at New Age workshops. All movements spawn such stories. They may be of only passing significance to the teller's deeper self-narrative or may be emplotted within that self-narrative and even become the basis for a comprehensive biographical rewriting (e.g., a conversion). For many movement participants, movement-mediated transformations in identity are one of the key legacies of activism (cf. McAdam 1988).[8]

On a collective level, Benford identifies "movement narratives," the collectively constructed stories and myths that movement participants tell about the movement itself and the domains of the world it seeks to affect. Instances of such narratives include the various myths espoused by peace movement activists (Benford, chapter 3), the "war stories" told by drug court judges, and the tales of spiritual crisis informing the activism of individual fundamentalist movements (Yates and Hunter, chapter 6). Along with participant narratives, with which movement narratives may overlap, these are the stories around which collective identities congeal. At a yet broader level than movement narratives are what Joshua Yates and James Hunter call "world-historical narratives." These are myths and legends that interpret and configure overarching historical transformations and developments, and contest competing sociohistorical narratives on the same scale. A shared world-historical narrative of modernity, Yates and Hunter argue, lies behind the more specific movement stories told in the various fundamentalist movements.

Beyond stories, personal or collective, which are narrated by individuals, we must also include the public narrative models or scripts that influence, condition, and control the narratives that actors tell. Two types can be identified. One is the "cultural stock of plots," or "cultural narratives" that Polletta and Rice describe. These are general or canonical narrative models that exist within any cultural setting, functioning to pattern and constrain the types of stories regarded as plausible and acceptable within that setting. The other type of narrative model is a more subculturally specific ideological structure framed by institutions and collective actors to embody particular ideals, anticipate a new order, and organize individual self-narratives. The therapeutic rationales proffered in CoDependents Anonymous and the drug court movement embed such narrative models. In the terms of these movement-provided scripts, codependents and drug court clients are expected to reinterpret and renarrate their self-narratives, thus "getting their histories straight" and telling the "right story." The New Age movement also provides narrative scripts, as Brown points out, but with its deep suspicion of power and radically nonhierarchical philosophy of social organization, it encourages a higher degree of self-reflexivity and, as a result, a less rigid emphasis on conformity to the script.

In exploring these various types of narratives and narrative models, the contributors show, as noted above, how narrative analysis can expand and enrich our understanding of many aspects of social movements. With

NSM theory and the framing perspective, narrative analysis as used in this book affirms the importance of values, symbols, and sources of consciousness. It too draws attention to mobilizing beliefs, ideas, and identities, and the interactive and negotiated nature of movement meaning-making and solidarity. It too focuses attention on internal movement dynamics and draws attention to diffuse expressions of social activism. It too provides a language for analyzing the social construction of collective action, a language that both overlaps and goes beyond the conceptual frameworks of these other theories.

At the same time, narrative analysis also addresses weaknesses in the existing approaches and highlights cultural dimensions of social movements that are undervalued in movement theory. The framing perspective, for instance, emphasizes—in fact overemphasizes—the role of clearly articulated and coherent reasons for movement activism. Narrative analysis, by contrast, illuminates persuasion and shared vision at more subtle, imaginative, and pre-prepositional levels. As movement scholars have emphasized, participants must do more than agree with a particular formulation of grievances or a rationale for engaging in ameliorative action, they must be *moved* to act, to take risks, to get involved. They must, in Doug McAdam's (1982) famous phrase, experience a "cognitive liberation." Participants' involvement is perhaps never simply logical and instrumental, but—and in many contexts more so—also imaginative, intuitive, and emotional. Through stories, participants, actual and potential, are called not so much to reflect on the merits of coherent arguments or self-consciously adopt an interpretive schema—which, as Polletta observes in chapter 2, follow activism in the early stages of mobilization—but to identify and empathize with real protagonists, to be repelled by antagonists, to enter into and feel morally involved in configurations of events that specify injustice and prefigure change. In their teleological plot structure, authority, and transactional nature, stories can embed moral messages, engage our moral imagination (answerable to the sufferings of others), and call forth powerful moral reactions. Similarly, with their personal immediacy and symbolically evocative renderings of experience, stories can stimulate strong emotional responses in hearers—such as sympathy, which can heighten common identity, and anger, which can spur or increase the motivation to work for change. Through stories, participants are called to take an evaluative stance toward unjust social conditions, affirm the virtue of the oppressed (Couto 1993), confirm the rightness and efficacy of movement involvement, and imagine together an alternative social order. This mobilizing work does not mean that stories supplant frames or render them unnecessary. But it does suggest that in many contexts of action, stories precede frames, stories make frames compelling, and stories overshadow frames in mobilizing power and as a political resource.

Beyond the persuasive and imaginative functions of stories, narrative analysis illuminates other internal movement processes as well. I have already drawn attention to the power of stories to both create and strengthen movement community and collective identity. Movements come to imagine and know themselves in the stories they tell about themselves. In addition to enabling, however, stories also constrain. As amply documented in this book, narratives can formulate, control, and represent models of appropriate behavior and affect display, accounts of experience and legitimate motive, and normative moral understandings. Moreover, stories can encode models of what is normal or expected by providing examples of violations and the consequences of nonconformity. Telling stories according to movement-sanctioned models opens up possibilities, then, but it also closes off alternative configurations and mutes dissident voices. This preemptive potential means that narratives, whether intended as such or not, can function as mechanisms of internal social control (see Benford, chapter 3). By controlling narrative constructions and selectively sponsoring storytelling, movements can exact internal compliance and reproduce existing frames of meaning. All such control efforts vary widely within and across movements, of course, but since narratives are difficult to challenge, they can be particularly subtle and effective instruments.

The resistance of preexisting stories to challenge and change also has important implications for movements or nascent movements in their interaction with the broader society. In their efforts to transform values and institutions, movements struggle against preexisting cultural and institutional narratives and the structures of meaning and power they convey. Movements do this, in part, as the cases in this book suggest, through the construction and telling of oppositional or "counternarratives" (Steinmetz 1992; see also Ewick and Silbey 1995, who speak of "subversive stories"). Battered women's accounts, drug court stories, peace movement myths, and so on, are all forms of oppositional stories, each an alternative at odds with or precluded by preexisting and dominant social narratives. Still, these counternarratives do not float free of the larger structures of cultural and institutional meaning. Counternarratives modify existing beliefs and symbols and their resonance comes from their appeal to values and expectations that people already hold. Thus, even when a movement narrative defies a dominant social narrative, it remains subject to other narrative expectations in the wider culture, which constrain and even foreclose movement understandings and courses of action. For example, the 1960 student sit-in narratives, as Polletta shows, galvanized protest in terms of moral conviction, but this story line was incompatible with canonical plots of political and strategic motives and so circumscribed these possibilities.

Yet another area in which narrative analysis offers theoretical promise is in understanding the role of identity in movement building. In recent years, movement scholars have invested considerable effort in taking identity into account as a movement resource. The politicization of identity by the social movements of the 1960s and 1970s, for instance, inspired an immense body of research on the constitution of collective identities and the political implications that result from group struggles to self-characterize and claim social franchise. Study in so-called identity politics has focused primarily on identifications based on race, ethnicity, nationality, gender, and sexuality, though definitions of identity in such new social movements as animal rights and environmentalism have also been investigated. In this work, scholars have emphasized that identity is structured by, or constituted by, difference (Davis 2000b). Far less attention, however, has been given to the ways in which social movements themselves help to fashion identities and provide social recognition for these alternatives. Conceiving of identity as a narrative suggests that "we learn how to self-narrate from the outside, from other stories, and particularly through the process of identification with other characters" (Currie 1998: 17). Rather than prioritizing categorical or ascribed identities, a narrative approach emphasizes a dialogical subjectivity and the storied transactions and relationships within which identity and difference are negotiated and renegotiated. As several chapters in this volume illustrate, through their narratives and narrative models, movements provide new sources and means of identification and recognition. Movements provide characters and a defining moral community, for instance, through which members can reconfigure themselves as moral agents of a particular type and sensibility. They provide and honor accounts for stressful life events that order and explain those events and so serve to restore a sense of biographical coherence and direction. They make available and recognize public narratives and symbolic representations for the construction and legitimation of newly visible and empowering subjectivities.

Finally, narrative analysis also illuminates additional cultural features of movements that are underplayed or neglected in other approaches. Perhaps the most important of these additional features are events and time. The narrative form centers on the interpretation and emplotment of events and places the temporal dimension central to understanding and explanation. Much social movement theory emphasizes broad structural variables and downplays the importance of events in accounting for movement mobilization and protest. Narrative analysis, by contrast, shows how key events—be they sit-ins, nuclear accidents, or court decisions—are interpreted and made the basis for action through stories. In the same way, movement theory has tended not to give much explanatory significance to movements' thematization of history or the temporal unfolding of events. Yet, as Yates and Hunter show, it is precisely the sense of impending judgment or catastrophe, arising from a particular narrative of sacred history, that informs fundamentalist activism (the "warriors of rainbow" Indian legend that inspires Greenpeace's urgency regarding the imminent demise of life on the planet would be another example). Or, as Polletta demonstrates, in the stories students told of their lunch counter sit-ins, they characterized their experience in an historical and collective voice as "tired of waiting"—waiting for generations to be treated with dignity.

* * *

The study of narrative is overdue in social movements research. Narrative is a powerful concept, illuminating the interplay of agency and social structure, and storytelling, like movements themselves, specifies valued endpoints and stimulates creative participation. In the moral, emotional, rhetorical, and social control work of social movements, stories play a significant role. The promise of a narrative turn is to open up new and productive avenues of research and underscore aspects of social movements and their dynamics too often neglected. The point is not to "anoint narrative," as Fine notes, by privileging it over other theoretical approaches and methods. Social movement theory has been beset by enough such overreactions. We need to broaden, not narrow, our theoretical and methodological base. Toward this end, narrative analysis offers great promise.

NOTES

1. There are many definitions of the concept of social movements. With one caveat, the following synthetic definition proposed by Diani will

serve for the purposes of this volume: "A social movement is a network of informal interactions between a plurality of individuals, groups and/or organizations, engaged in a political or cultural conflict, on the basis of a shared collective identity" (1992: 13). The caveat concerns the distinction between "political" and "cultural," which is sometimes applied to movements themselves. There are political movements and there are cultural movements, a distinction that mirrors the old collective behavior separation of "expressive movements" (concerned with cultural and personal transformation) from "instrumental movements" (concerned with political and institutional change). Making this distinction, however, carries the potentially misleading implication that cultural conflict or cultural movements do not have political effects (Buechler 2000). They do; as Melucci (1989) in particular has argued, "cultural" forms of activism, forms that resist diverse and highly decentralized forms of power, also involve a political dimension (also see the discussion of self-help movements as social movements in Taylor 1996).

2. The symbolic interactionist version of collective behavior theory also emphasized the emergence and construction of new meanings. Social constructionism represents a recovery of this older approach. For a brief overview, see the discussion in Gusfield (1994). Beyond constructionism and NSM theory, a large literature on persuasion and social movements has appeared in the field of communications over the past two decades (see Stewart, Smith, and Denton 1994). Unfortunately, movement scholars in other disciplines, including sociology, seem to have largely ignored this body of work.

3. In this book, the terms "narrative" and "story" refer to the same phenomena. It should be noted, however, that in some perspectives, especially those influenced by structuralist literary theory, they are distinct concepts: the "story" refers to the sequence of events before the events are put into words, while the "narrative" or "narrative discourse" refers to the actual discourse that recounts the events. In the perspective taken here, there is no such thing as a prediscursive story. "A story," as Thomas Leitch, puts it, "is not what a narrative presents, it *is* a narrative" (1986: 17; emphasis in original).

4. Of course, one can tell a story that makes no point at all. However, as William Labov notes: "Pointless stories are met (in English) with the withering rejoinder, 'So what?' Every good narrator is continually warding off this question; when his narrative is over, it should be unthinkable for a bystander to say, 'So what?' Instead, the appropriate remark

would be 'He did?' or similar means of registering the reportable character of the events of the narrative" (quoted in Pratt 1977: 47). See below for more on the issue of listener/reader response.

5. Plots, however, including culturally-given plots, are not simply imposed on events. As Paul Ricoeur (1984) argues, emplotment involves a synthetic process, a fitting together through the comparison and revision of both events and plot structure.

6. There are many definitions of plot. Brooks's full definition is "the design and intention of narrative, what shapes a story and gives it a certain direction or intention of meaning" (1985: xi). For somewhat different definitions, see, for example, Ricoeur (1984) and White (1981).

7. The literary theorist Wayne Booth (1988: ch. 6) argues that storytellers offer a gift or benefit to readers/listeners and uses the metaphor of friendship to describe the relationship that tellers seek to create with audiences. He distinguishes between different kinds of friendship and different kinds of rewards that tellers promise.

8. Of course, when people narrate their experience and in what context are both crucial. Experiences that were meaningful or defining at one time may be more or less so in light of later reflection and subsequent experiences. And self-narratives are not univocal. Depending on the audience and the norms and conventions operating in the particular social context, individuals may tell different stories about themselves, selecting and evaluating different events in the service of somewhat different valued endpoints.

TWO

Plotting Protest

Mobilizing Stories in the 1960 Student Sit-Ins

FRANCESCA POLLETTA

On February 1, 1960, four black students from Greensboro Agricultural and Technical College purchased a few items in the downtown Woolworth and then sat down at its whites-only lunch counter. Told that they could not be served, they remained seated until the store closed. They resumed the sit-in the next day and the next, joined by other students from A&T and then from surrounding colleges. The Greensboro sit-in touched off a wave of similar demonstrations around the South. By the end of February, the sit-ins had spread to thirty cities in seven states; by the end of March, fifty-four cities in nine states. By mid-April, fifty thousand people had taken part in sit-ins (Carson 1981; Chafe 1980).

Students described the demonstrations as unplanned, impulsive, "like a fever" and, over and over again, as "spontaneous." Nearly forty years later, we know, as did the students themselves, that there was a good deal of strategic planning behind the "spontaneous" demonstrations (Morris 1984)—just as we know that Rosa Parks was a longtime NAACP activist before she refused to give up her seat on a segregated bus and precipitated the Montgomery bus boycott (Garrow 1988), and just as we know that Betty Friedan was a labor organizer concerned with issues of race and gender long before she wrote her account of awakening from the somnolent myth of feminine domesticity (Horowitz 1996). Why, then, these "myths of immaculate conception" (Taylor 1989)? Why do activists so often represent protest as sprung from the head of Zeus, ignoring or

31

sometimes downright denying the planning that preceded it? Why do they cast themselves not as strategic actors but as swept up by forces over which they have no control? And why do they do so even in communications with each other, where one would rather expect testimonies to the power of calculated and coordinated action?

In an earlier examination of students' contemporaneous accounts of the 1960 sit-ins as they were occurring, I found that students told *stories* of the sit-ins—remarkably similar stories—and that the sit-ins' spontaneity figured in many of them (Polletta 1998a). Spontaneity meant not a lack of planning, however, but independence from adult control, moral urgency, and action by local initiative rather than bureaucratic maneuver. Students narrated the sit-ins to make sense of them. But since narratives simultaneously explain and evaluate, account for the past and project a future, students were also constituting an action-compelling collective identity as they narrated it. In addition, the *failure* of the sit-in stories to fully explain the sit-ins endowed them with mobilizing power. The word "spontaneity" means both voluntary and instinctual (involuntary)—contradictory meanings contained in the same word. In the sit-in narrative, "spontaneity" functioned as a kind of narrative ellipsis in which the movement's "beginning" occurred and the nonnarratable shift from observer to participant took place. Drawing on the narrative theory of De Man (1979) and Miller (1990), I argued that the sit-in story could not fix the motivation for participation (just as no story can fix origins, whether of humankind or of collective action), and so required its own retelling. And since the story was a true one, retelling it required reenacting the events it related. The sit-in story's mobilizing power thus lay in its engaging inability to specify the beginning of mobilization. Analyzing movement narratives responded, I argued, to an important gap in theories of movement "framing": their neglect of the discursive processes that occur before formal movement organizations with clear recruitment objectives have been established.

In this chapter, I return to the 1960 student sit-ins and draw on additional narrative materials in order to respond to two additional weaknesses in framing theory. One is its neglect of emotions in protest. Recruitment depends on appealing to people's good sense but also to their passions—if the two can even be separated (Barker, forthcoming). I argue that stories are better equipped than other discursive forms to elicit emotions and, just as important, to attach those emotions to particular courses of action and targets. In the sit-in narratives, black students' "apathy" was reinterpreted as the repression of political aspirations, and thus transformed into a motivation for action. Students were not apathetic; they were "tired of waiting" for the rights denied them. In this and other respects, the sit-in stories invoked familiar dichotomies—apathy versus commitment, spontaneity versus discipline, instrumental versus expressive action—in order to plot transitions from one to another.

Yet novel meanings always contend with more conventional ones. As the sit-in narratives were told and retold, narrower meanings of key terms came to dominate. The sit-ins, and direct action generally, came to be viewed as expressive rather than instrumental and as spontaneous rather than disciplined. As a result, some of the sit-ins' instrumental possibilities were foreclosed. Elucidating this process responds to a second gap in framing theory: its neglect of the cultural constraints on framing. Conceptualizing frames exclusively as persuasive devices used to further instrumental movement tasks misses their role in defining what even counts as instrumental. Tracking movement narratives over time shows how the same events can lead "naturally" to more or less conventional conclusions about the scope of strategic action.

FRAMES AND NARRATIVES

Since Joseph Davis identifies key elements of frames and narratives in chapter 1, and since I have compared the two in detail elsewhere (Polletta 1998a, 1998b), I focus here on only one element of narrative: plot. I show how the operations and functions of plot help to account for (1) narratives' importance to recruitment efforts before the establishment of formal movement organizations; (2) their utility in stimulating mobilizing emotions; and (3) the processes by which narratives foreclose strategic options as well as open them.

Hayden White's (1981) definition of narratives as "chronicles invested with moral meaning through emplotment" highlights their dependence on plot. Plot organizes the events in a story, and makes the events "unfold" rather than simply follow each other. Plot involves "an initial situation, a sequence leading to a change or reversal of that situation, and a revelation made possible by the reversal of situation" (Miller 1990: 75). The story's "end" is also its end in the sense of purpose or *telos*; all stories have a moral. Plot gives stories a projective dimension as well as a configurational one, and the two are inseparable. By contrast, frames have three separate components: a "diagnosis" of an unjust situation; a "prognosis" for how to effect change, and a "call to action" (Snow and Benford 1988; Benford and Hunt 1992a). In stories, prognosis and call to action are *built into* the diagnosis. Skillfully told, an account of events makes any other denouement, any other course of action than, say, protest, unimaginable.

Plots are derived from a cultural stock of plots. Their canonical quality makes narratives recognizable: we interpret unfolding events as tending toward tragedy or triumph, or we recognize a story of self-discovery or human fallibility. This explains our tendency to turn to stories when we encounter phenomena that are unfamiliar or threatening (Polkinghorne 1988; Bruner 1986; Sarbin 1986). A. E. Michotte found that when presented with small colored rectangles moving on a screen, viewers constructed elaborate narrative plots:

> "It is as if A's approach frightened B and B ran away." "It is as if A, in touching B induced an electric current which set B going." "The arrival of A by the side of B acts as a sort of signal to B . . ." "It is as if A touched off a mechanism inside B and thus set it going." (quoted in Sarbin 1986: 13)

Observers often laughed at the rectangles' movements. Like them, we rely on narrative to make phenomena intelligible. Stories contain the disruptive within a familiar form.

Plots' canonical character also limits the kinds of stories that can be told. Framing theorists do recognize some cultural limits on framing. Successful frames resonate with extant "stories, myths, and folk tales" (Snow and Benford 1988: 210), and "ideology, values, belief systems" (Gamson 1988: 220). But that still leaves plenty of room for rhetorical maneuver. "Every coin has two sides; every argument has its opposite arguments," Klandermans observes (1992: 84), suggesting the multiplicity of coexisting, often contradictory value positions that can be mobilized. The "theme" of "technological progress" on which nuclear power proponents have relied has always coexisted with an Emersonian hostility to technology, Gamson points out, a countertheme mobilizable by antinukes. "There is no theme without a countertheme" (1988: 220). By contrast, theorists of narrative recognize much firmer limits. They differ on just how many plots there are, and just how universal they are. But they agree that stories not conforming to a cultural stock of plots typically are either not stories or are not intelligible. The oppositional stories constructed by activists thus must contend with the resonance of conventional narratives—narratives, for example, that reduce protest to the ephemeral, the nonrational, and the apolitical.

If stories are compelling in part by their familiarity, a story that is so familiar as to be entirely predictable would be unengaging. It would be the moral without the story. Narrative necessitates our interpretive participation and requires that we struggle to fill the gaps to resolve the ambiguities (Iser 1972). Successful stories' dependence on ambiguity contrasts with frames' supposed dependence on a "clear" specification of agents, antagonists, and targets (Stoecker 1995: 113), and a "clearly interpretable" rationale for participation (Snow and Benford 1988: 203).[1]

These features of narrative—their configurational and projective dimensions, engaging ambiguity, and canonicity—help to explain their role in fledgling movements. Under conditions of what Oberschall (1989) calls "loose structure," characterized by sporadic rather than formally organized protest, uncertainty about the costs of participation, and multiple and dispersed ideological spokespeople, movement discourse will be as much about making sense of unfolding events as about directing them. Narrative makes such events coherent in a way that also provides a compelling rationale for participation. Stories' conferral of directionality on events helps to constitute and sustain collective identities, especially during periods of change. They maintain the stability of the self and group, and, through a trope of reversal, connect the group under conditions of oppression and under conditions of liberation. An activist may be trying to make sense of what is happening around her more than trying to mobilize participation, but when she tells a story of the collective "we," she is helping to bring it into being. At the same time, stories' failure to fully "explain" protest may call for more stories, and more actions to recount.

Storytelling probably figures prominently among activists' recruitment strategies on account of plot's capacity to configure emotions. This represents a blind spot in framing analyses, as well as social movement theory more broadly. With exceptions (Gamson 1992, Benford and Hunt 1992a), sociologists have ignored the role of anger, indignation, outrage, shame, and love in mobilization (see Goodwin, Jasper, and Polletta 2000; Jasper 1998). As Scheff observes: "Descriptions of nationalist movements note [their] passion, indeed the very pages crackle with it. But these descriptions do little to conceptualize, analyze, or interpret it" (1994: 282).

How do activists inspire passion in potential recruits? And how do they link passion to some kinds of action and not others? How do they convince people, fired up about cruelty toward animals, that they should act on their outrage not by punching a passerby wearing mink but by joining a nonviolent demonstration? It is hard to imagine that simply instructing people to be angry or outraged or courageous would stimulate those emotions. One might have better luck describing one's own anger and outrage, hoping to create through empathy the same kinds of feelings. Or one might tell a story in which emotions are not even named explicitly but are elicited in listeners by the poignancy or outrageousness of the events chronicled. Professional actors learn to conjure up the emotions they need to perform not by trying to replicate emotions' physical markers, nor by imitating someone who is happy or sad or fearful, but by remembering—trying to relive—a tragic or fortunate or frightening event in their own past, or an event that occurred in a movie or book. Similarly, for the rest of us, narratives supply a guide to our own feelings, a kind of emotional propaedeutic.

Why is this the case? Theodore Sarbin (1995) challenges the standard psychophysiological definition of emotions as perceived perturbations within the body. Rather, anger, grief, jealousy, love, and so on are names for narrative plots, he argues: plots gleaned from parables, fairy tales, songs, poems, films, and other pervasive forms. He quotes a man's explanation for murdering his wife during a bitter argument in which she had compared his sexual prowess to that of a clandestine former lover: "I felt the anger rising inside me and I exploded. I couldn't stop myself" (1995: 215). Rather than viewing the man as a "passive object 'in the grip' of an emotion," Sarbin argues that "agentially he had gripped a familiar narrative plot, a plot in which an exquisite insult to his masculine identity required a retaliatory answer" (216). We know that anger calls for revenge, shame for redemption, embarrassment for moves to restore dignity. Emotions are thus configured by canonical plots, plots that are "part and parcel of a culture's mythology" (217; see also Lofland 1985; Hochschild 1979; Jasper 1997).

But this does not mean that individuals' self-understandings and emotions are simply reflections of powerful narratives "out there." For one thing, there are many plot lines; the same events can be fit into any number of them, with very different emotional outcomes: a story about "injustice" can elicit feelings of stoic acceptance rather than a determination to act. An effective story—a story that mobilizes—probably heightens feelings that people already have about particular issues, or reinterprets the sources of those feelings, or attaches them to new issues or lines of action. In a climate of interpretive ambiguity, such as that which characterizes fledgling movements, it may be easier to put new emotional glosses on old stories. On the other hand, the activist's task is made more difficult by the fact that we modern Westerners tend to think of emotions as being opposed to rational action. We often speak of being "overwhelmed" or "eaten up" by an emotion, being in its "grip" or at its "mercy." These phrases all suggest that our capacity for conscious, deliberate, coordinated behavior is weakened by strong emotions. Emotions galvanize action, we tend to believe, but action that is often counterproductive or destructive. Activists have to elicit passion but also modulate and channel it.

The widespread assumption that passion and rationality are opposed is a cultural belief that activists have to work with and around. In other words, dominant emotion cultures—rules for experiencing and expressing emotions (Hochschild 1979) and beliefs about how emotions work (Thoits 1989)—influence activists' ability to use emotional appeals effectively. Movement narratives reveal the workings of additional cultural constraints. As I noted, framing theorists do recognize that successful frames conform to the "larger belief system" (Snow and Benford 1988: 207) and "ring true with existing cultural narrations" (210). They have used the concept of "master frames"—"Black Power," say, or "civil rights"—to show how activists' persuasive appeals, as well as their selection among available tactics, are shaped by these larger ideological templates (Snow and Benford 1992; Tarrow 1998). But theorists have treated master frames as deliberately chosen worldviews, which can be embraced or suspended depending on leaders' perceptions of strategic imperatives. A master frame constrains tactical options, insofar as it figures as one more strategic consideration—along with balancing the demands of an external environment and an internal movement constituency—that leaders must take into account. What is missing is a recognition that activists' own criteria for strategic decisions are shaped by prevailing ideological frames.

Narratives' canonicity points to one way in which conventional understandings of protest and politics may enter into and constrain activists' strategic decision-making (narratives constrain challenge in other ways; see Polletta 1998b). Activists' very understandings of "strategy," "interest," "opportunity," and "obstacle" may be structured by the oppositions and hierarchies that come from familiar stories. Analysis of strategic deliberations within movements should reveal the presence of these conventional narratives. Analysis of movement narratives over time may show more capacious interpretations ceding to more conventional ones.

"SPONTANEITY" IN THE SIT-IN NARRATIVES

The very first accounts of the Greensboro sit-in were not narrative in form. An editorial in the Greensboro Agricultural and Technical College *Register* used an explicitly persuasive mode: "You as students can believe me when I tell you this will benefit every one of us who sit at the Woolworth counter." The piece emphasized not the transformation that is characteristic of narrative, but continuity. "The waitress ignored us and kept serving the white customers. However, this is no great surprise to me because I have been exposed to segregation at lunch counters for 15 years and the situation is predominately unchanged."[2]

In the next days and weeks, however, as students from surrounding colleges joined the Greensboro protest, and then launched their own sit-ins, a narrative evolved. Student accounts circulated in flyers and handbills, campus newspaper articles and letters to the editor, and sit-inners' speeches to student groups. After the Student Nonviolent Coordinating Committee (SNCC) was formed at a sit-in conference in April, stories submitted by sit-in groups appeared in its publication, *The Student Voice*. Students' writings on the sit-ins displayed a strikingly similar form. They recounted events occurring on their campus in chronological order, with a beginning, middle, and end. They detailed a key transformation and the revelation made possible by that transformation, and conveyed a normative prescription, a moral.

Did student writers emphasize the injustice of the situation, define themselves against clearly specified antagonists, and assert their capacity to bring about the changes they sought, as framing theorists would anticipate? No. The injustices they described were often vague: denial of "the humane aspects of the American dream" and "equality and dignity"; the injustice of "a passively immoral society." Sit-inners pitted themselves against "apathy," whose status as "situational" rather than "individual" (Klandermans 1988: 179), and as political rather than personal, is debatable. Students acted, powerfully and transgressively, with immediate, real consequences. And yet the students were simply the carriers of a force beyond them. The sit-ins came from nowhere—"boom." Narrators were as likely to deny conscious agency as to assert it, as when one group of students launched a demonstration: "This was a surprise (and shock) not only to the whole town but to themselves as well." "*No one* started it . . . ," a sit-inner insisted—his claim denying collective identity altogether. Students attributed the sit-ins not to a newfound sense of collective efficacy, but to forces over which they had no control. Rather than planning, they emphasized spontaneity.[3]

Journalists and academic observers at the time echoed students in describing the protests as unplanned and impulsive, spreading "without outside advice or even contact between schools except by way of press and radio news" (Fuller 1960: 13) "in the manner of a grass fire" (Oppenheimer 1989: 40; see also Zinn 1964; Matthews and Prothro 1966). But as Aldon Morris demonstrated twenty years later, these characterizations were wrong. The Greensboro sit-inners were members of an NAACP Youth Council and had close ties with people who had conducted sit-ins in Durham in the late 1950s. After the sit-in began, a network of ministers, NAACP officials, and the radical pacifists who had earlier trained Martin Luther King in techniques of nonviolence, swung into action. They contacted colleagues to spread the news, trained students in sit-in techniques, and persuaded adults to support the protests. The church was the linchpin of student activism, Morris argued, supplying leaders and guidance, training and inspiration. "To understand the sit-in movement, one must abandon the assumption that it was a college phenomenon" (1984: 200). Of course, calling the sit-ins "spontaneous" deflected charges that they were planned by outsiders—meaning communists. For that reason, some adult leaders described as "unplanned" the demonstrations that they themselves had coordinated (Killian 1984). But why would students themselves draw attention to—indeed, celebrate—the sit-ins' spontaneity? In communications out of the public eye, presumably aimed at mobilizing fellow students, why would they not assert the collective efficacy of protest? Why not claim that they had brought about the action they envisaged?

Consider the students whose flyer described their sit-in as "the result of spontaneous combustion," then chronicled the planning that had preceded it. They emphasized, however—and this seems to be the point of using the term "spontaneous combustion"—that "there was no organizational tie-in of any kind, either local or national." But they also acknowledged, "in order to make the story complete," that members of the sit-in organizing group had previously received a "Letter to Christian Students" from the National Student Christian Federation urging them to seek ways to participate.[4]

Students' characterization of the sit-ins as spontaneous, even as they acknowledged planning them, suggests that spontaneity meant something other than unplanned. In fact, it meant several things. It referred, first, to

the sheer power of moral protest. Sitting-in was motivated by an imperative to act now that brooked no compromise. One simply put one's body
on the line, without debating its ideological potential or waiting for
instruction from higher-ups. "The fact that the protest broke out
overnight and spread with fantastic speed said simply this: the Negro,
despite the thoughts of too many whites, is NOT content . . . And *nobody*
could escape this." A piece in the *Student Voice* opened a story of one student's effort to launch a sit-in: "It is really strange—to do things alone.
Sometimes we have no alternative." Descriptions of protest "burst[ing],"
"breaking," "exploding," "sweeping," "surging," "unleashed," "rip[ping]
through the city like an epidemic," of students "fired" by the "spark of
the sit-ins," of "released waves of damned-up energy," of a "chain reaction"—all suggested an unstoppable moral impetus. "The spirit reached
the boiling point at 11:00 a.m., March 10, 1960," wrote Philander Smith
College students in Little Rock, Arkansas. For Vanderbilt students, the
"current wave of demonstrations is the spontaneous ground swell of the
profound determination of young Negroes to be first-class citizens."[5]

Second, "spontaneity" referred to a generative break with adult
forms of protest. "Our impatience with the token efforts of responsible
leaders was manifest in the spontaneous demonstrations which, after February 1, spread rapidly across the entire South," said Nashville sit-inner
Marion Barry. "Spontaneous" meant free of the caution, slow-moving
consultation, and sheer timidity that students saw in adult protest. Com-
mending the formation of a new black periodical, SNCC wrote to its editors, "There is no longer a way to rationalize gradualism. It did die on
February 1, 1960, in Woolworth's of Greensboro. It will die again and
again when every individual rises to his responsibility."[6]

"Spontaneity" also described the emotional experience of the sit-ins.
Students applauded their comrades' discipline, calm, courage, and determination. Their "only prayer" was to "have the strength, knowledge, and
fortitude that these students exhibited." Students described the "spirit of
love" with which sit-inners had confronted their enraged white antagonists. But their accounts of the sit-ins also conveyed a sense of *fun.* They
emphasized not the sober religiosity and seriousness characteristic of pacifist and Quaker nonviolent witness, but rather humor, excitement, and a
giddy sense of triumph. Editors of a college newspaper wrote, "Here were
two harmless young people sauntering through a store . . . stalking them
in true dragnetness were no less than half a dozen police officers, while
customers and managers hovered in corners as if the invasion from Mars

had come!" A Knoxville College writer composed an "Ode to a Lunch Counter":

> Little lunch counter with your many stools
> And your nervous pacing manager fools
> How do you feel amid this confusion and strife?
> Do you object to a change inevitable in life? . . .
> If you could only speak and tell us what you have in mind
> It's almost certain that your suggestions would not be unkind.
> 'The trouble,' I'm sure you'd say, 'certainly is not my fault,
> And this stupid mess should be brought to a screeching halt.'

None of the stories represented the sit-inners as enraged, cynical, or calculating.[7]

Yet the sit-inners did frequently describe themselves as "tired": they were tired "of waiting for the American dream to materialize," "tired of un-American discrimination," "tired of moving at an ox-cart pace," tired of "wait[ing] for the course of time to supply us those rights we as first class citizens of this our America deserve." They had "'taken it' since the day we were born," and the sit-ins were the result of their impatience. "After 95 years of discussions, delays, postponements, procrastination, denials, and second-class citizenship, the Negro of today wants his full citizenship in his day." After "nearly a hundred years" of living "without pride and honor," the sit-ins "serve[d] notice that the Negro, particularly of the South, no longer accepts second class citizenship."[8]

The narrative formulation of "tired" has several interesting features. It merged the individual with the collective: I protest because "I" have waited for generations to be treated with dignity. "Our biggest influence has been inside—all those years of second-class citizenship." Moreover, the motivation conveyed in this formulation was a simple one. You didn't have to have a sophisticated agenda or ideology in order to protest; you just had to be impatient and unwilling to "stifle" your "feelings any longer." And impatience was familiar to most adolescents. The notion of "tired" is also interesting for another reason: it was often paired with a characterization of students before the sit-ins as "apathetic." The sit-ins had destroyed "the myth of student apathy," had dealt "a death blow to apathy" and to students' "false robe of sophistication and unconcern." "No longer may students be called the 'Silent Generation.'" Being "tired" and being "apathetic" both suggested passivity and inaction. Yet being "tired of waiting" issued in radical action.[9]

The narrative thus reconfigures apathy *as* being "tired of waiting." The only thing that distinguished those who were laying their bodies on the line from those who were lying around in their dorm rooms was that the former had come to recognize their apathy as nothing more than repressed desires and aspirations that had been too long denied. It wasn't that they were apathetic, it was that they were "weary with waiting."[10] In that sense, said students, "we had been ready to do something like this for a long time" (quoted in Walzer 1960: 114). Indeed, "we have been planning it all our lives" (Fuller 1960: 13). Rather than exhorting students to shake off their apathy—an injunction that most students probably associated with the familiar calls to vote for student council, to come to the debate club, or to volunteer—the narrative endowed apathy with a transformative *telos*:

> Time was when our elders, those who in their school days dreamed radical dreams, wondered what disease was responsible for the apathy that was apparent among today's college students. Three months ago, they ceased from wondering about the apathy and began marveling over the radicalism . . . the students say— and it is reasonable to believe them—that they are tired of waiting for the humane aspects of the American dream to materialize.[11]

Other emotional transformations figured in the sit-in narratives. The "butterflies" of apprehension ceded to "joy" in demonstrating.[12] Students in North Carolina, said journalist Michael Walzer, "told one story after another about . . . minor but to them terribly important incidents in the buses, in stores, on the job. The stories usually ended with some version of 'I ran out of that store. I almost cried . . .'" (1960: 119). The sit-in narrative transformed a too-common story of humiliation into one of triumph.

Narratives of the sit-ins, in which spontaneity denoted a break with adult gradualism, a moral rather than political strategy, a joy in action, and an unstoppable force, motivated students to engage in time-consuming and dangerous activism. Students narrativized what was happening in order to make sense of it, but also to signal its significance. "The sit-ins," SNCC Chairman Charles McDew said in October 1960, "have inspired us to build a new image of ourselves in our own mind" (1966: 57). Along with a new identity and accompanying moral obligations, the sit-in stories created a replicable experience of emotional transformation.

INSTITUTIONALIZING SPONTANEITY

How compelling were the sit-in narratives? By September 1961, seventy thousand people had participated in the demonstrations (Oberschall 1989). In addition, the challenges created for the fledgling SNCC by the sit-in narratives suggests their potency. Spontaneity, emblematic of students' independence and their unique contribution to the movement, became an organizational commitment which both animated and constrained strategic action. Students called for coordination but were resistant to direction, wanted the movement to speak to the nation but were wary of leaders, wanted to expand the scope of protest but distrusted adult advice. At a college workshop sponsored by the radical educational Highlander Center in April 1960, just before SNCC's formation, seventy-five students discussed "the spontaneous origin and spread of the sit-ins" (Horton 1989: 242) and complained about adult interference. They were determined that no organization should temper or control the protests. Participants at SNCC's first and second conferences delineated only a modest role for their own organization in which it was "made quite clear that SNCC does not control local groups."[13]

SNCC's administrators found themselves repeatedly compelled to defend the organization's very existence to its members and supporters, and specifically to reassure them that organization would not stifle the "spontaneity" of the movement. SNCC's Jane Stembridge responded directly to a donor's concern: "We believe that the spontaneity will not die and the coordination will speed the coming of genuine equality." She and chair Marion Barry told another supporter, "The purpose of the Coordinating Committee meetings is not to control the movement, but to make an attempt at coordination of efforts in order to strengthen the thrust of the movement." In funding appeals, newsletters, and speeches, SNCC leaders represented the group as an extension of the spontaneity of the sit-ins, and of the values of moral imperative, local autonomy, and radicalism that spontaneity connoted.[14]

Many of the SNCC staffers interviewed by sociologist Emily Stoper in 1965 said they joined SNCC because they "did not want to be held back by the bureaucratic slowness or mature restraint of the NAACP or even SCLC" (1989: 92). It was precisely students' capacity to move fast that was responsible for the remarkable scope and scale of the demonstrations, they believed. They would be disciplined, nonviolent, fair-minded, loving—but they would not go slow. Spontaneity was by no

means contrasted to effectiveness; to the contrary, spontaneity was instrumental—*and* expressive. At this point, the conventional oppositions
between spontaneity and organization, and between instrumental and
expressive action, simply did not hold. However, spontaneity's more capacious meanings would eventually be threatened by its more conventional
ones.

In SNCC, this occurred in the summer of 1961, as members debated
moving from direct action desegregation efforts—the sit-ins and the freedom rides that followed them—to voter registration. The previous
summer, SNCC volunteer Bob Moses was persuaded by renegade NAACP
activist Amzie Moore to plan a voter registration program in Mississippi.
At the same time, several other SNCC leaders were offered support by the
federal government if they committed the organization to voter registration activities (Carson 1981; Zinn 1964; Garrow 1988). The idea still met
with fierce resistance within the group. Detractors were wary of the federal government's support and worried about co-optation. They also saw
electoral politics as "immoral," and as antithetical to the moral protest
that had animated SNCC's activism thus far (Stoper 1989). An organizational split was averted only through the intervention of adviser Ella
Baker, who persuaded them to form direct action and voter registration
wings, an arrangement that was soon abandoned in favor of a concentra-
tion on voter registration.

The episode demonstrates the institutionalization of the sit-in narrative: the values of moral imperative (versus political maneuvering), local
autonomy (versus bureaucratic hierarchy), and youthful urgency (versus
adult direction) that were thematized by the sit-in narrative had become
organizational commitments. It also shows spontaneity's polyvalence of
meaning ceding to a conventional understanding of protest. The implicit
association of direct action with moral imperative that underpinned the
sit-in narrative worked the other way too: direct action was represented
by SNCC workers as *non*-political and as *non*-strategic.

However, SNCC workers' abandonment of direct action was motivated more by their realization that in the Delta region of Mississippi,
where any kind of activism provoked stark repression, "voter registration
was direct action." Moreover, local Mississippi activists made clear to
SNCC organizers their lack of interest in desegregation efforts; they
sought political power. A tendency to view direct action as nonstrategic
by definition was much more pronounced among the white New Leftists
who would take SNCC as their moral exemplar.

For northern white students after the sit-ins, says New Left historian Paul Buhle, "everything now started with the Blacks" (1987: 224). Students on northern campuses were impressed by the sit-inners' courage, but also by their unabashed sense of moral purpose. They expressed a utopianism that was neither ascetic nor retreatist but joyfully *acted* on. "The movement didn't simply demand, it did," recalls SDS leader Todd Gitlin. "By taking action, not just a position, it affirmed the right to do so; by refusing to defer, it deprived the authorities of authority itself. How did you 'join' the movement? An old-fashioned question from unhip reporters and Congressmen, to which the answer was: you put your body on the line" (1987: 84). A determination to act for one's ideals—now, and without calculation or compromise—was a challenge not only to the tough realism of contemporary liberalism but to that of its left critics. Indeed, postwar liberalism owed its success in large part to its "ability to appropriate the 'hard-boiled' pragmatism of ex-radicals," historian Christopher Lasch observes (1965: 289). Pragmatism, "facts," a resolute anti-utopianism, and a muscular realism—these were the buzzwords and orientations along the political spectrum.

The sit-ins defied all that. University of Michigan student Tom Hayden saw them as "risky, shoot for the moon affairs," and as the beginnings of "a revolution that would reduce complexity to moral simplicity" (quoted in Miller 1987: 52). He joined a tiny group of student Leftists, newly named Students for a Democratic Society, who had set out to build a white northern counterpart to the black student movement. Their manifesto, written two years later, was infused with their commitments to action over long-winded deliberation, and to moral urgency over political expediency. "We cannot stomach the politician morality," Hayden wrote in a first draft of the Port Huron statement:

> We are too tightly confined to specialized roles to understand and take up the citizen's role which might integrate us as participants in society's total progression. We are instead as spectators; no—not even that—we are as strangers, living in the caverns of the community of man, sometimes overhearing, but never fully understanding, what the other fellow is doing.

The key was to participate, to *act*, Hayden insisted: "Participation animates the abstract ideas of freedom and responsibility, and ensures that morality has meaning in the practical life of men."[15]

Hayden and other SDS activists were unashamed of their admiration for the black student movement. But they were not shy about identifying what they saw as its limitations. The sit-ins were admirably "moral," but not yet properly "political," they argued. SDS founder Al Haber criticized black and white activists in 1960 for remaining focused on direct action, which was "non-political" (1966: 40). "A moral aspiration for social equality, unaccompanied by a political and economic view of society is at best wistful . . . and, at worst, politically irresponsible," Hayden wrote in his draft of the Port Huron statement. A year earlier he had applauded SNCC's shift from sit-ins and freedom rides to voter registration on those grounds. SNCC's "new emphasis on the vote heralds the use of political means to solve the problems of equality in America, and it signals the decline of the short-sighted view that 'discrimination' can be isolated from related social problems." "The moral clarity of the movement has not always been accompanied by precise political vision," he went on, "and sometimes not even by a real political consciousness." Another SDS leader wrote in 1962, "The focus of action on Negro campuses in the non-violent protest movement has been largely 'non-political.' "[16]

The sit-ins—and, more broadly, direct action—were thus viewed as immediate, expressive, and powerfully moral—all meanings associated with "spontaneity"—but also as *non*-political and *non*-strategic. This perception endured for the rest of the decade. Staughton Lynd's was a minority position when he asked in 1966, "Why should it be assumed that direct action is 'moral' rather than 'political'? If enough people act, or if the act is of a particularly strategic kind, there is a political impact" (1966). Lynd was a longtime pacifist and well-schooled in the Gandhian techniques of direct action that pacifists had developed before and after World War II. While often trained by those pacifists, black student sit-inners had transformed direct action: they had put it on a mass scale, stripped it of its somber religiosity and asceticism, and made it exuberant. But sit-inners also made clear the discipline, training, and preparation preceding their actions. As the story of the sit-ins was retold, those features dropped out. As a result, Stewart Burns remarks in his history of the 1960s, "In the New Left and the peace movement, typically, civil disobedience was not carefully organized, guided by clear principles, or adequately prepared for by nonviolent training; it was frequently spontaneous" (1990: 181). Partly responsible for this change was the antinomy between spontaneity and strategy, on which conceptions of direct action came to rest. The conventional story line that has people acting out their moral commitments in emotional and impulsive protest eclipsed one in which people act emotionally, morally, *and* in politically instrumental ways.

CONCLUSION

Activists do more than tell stories. They storm barricades, negotiate with allies, plan demonstrations, march. Likewise, movement talk consists of discourses other than narrative, including referential, expressive, and persuasive modes (cf. Polkinghorne 1988: 31). In what circumstances, then, do movement activists tell stories rather than, say, make causal arguments, expressive pleas, or lists of costs and benefits?

I have argued that narratives are a common form of discourse in movements' fledgling stages, before the establishment of formal organizations or before their monopolization of micro-mobilization tasks. In what Oberschall calls a "loose structure," protest is sporadic, resources are uncertain, ideological voices are multiple, and the "collective" in collective actor is still tenuous. Narratives' endowment of events with coherence, directionality, and emotional resonance provides not only an explanation for events but rationale for participation.

The black students who launched the sit-ins, then kneel-ins, wade-ins, and pray-ins, and who founded SNCC, departed from the existing civil rights organizations not so much in long-term goals (integration) nor even in strategy (nonviolent resistance) as in militancy and organizational form. The sit-ins were represented as a break with the incomplete engagement and gradualism of adult leaders (spontaneity denoted a moral imperative to act), a break with the action-impeding bureaucracy of mainstream civil rights organizations (spontaneity denoted local initiative), and a break with the sober asceticism and discipline of prior direct action (spontaneity denoted a joy and freedom in action). Narratives of the sit-in helped make normative a physically dangerous, unpleasant, and personally risky form of activism.

To be sure, representing the surge of student protest as spontaneous delegitimated charges of outside planning by left-wing groups. Tying SNCC to the sit-ins legitimated it as an organizational expression of the sit-ins. However, my account suggests that this kind of instrumentalist view is limited. Rather than simply persuasive devices deployed by strategic collective actors, narratives helped to constitute new collective actors.

Multiauthored, in formal and informal settings, they made participation normative. After a formal movement organization was consolidated, the sit-in narratives shaped internal contests over legitimate strategies.

If narratives proved so mobilizing in this case, then should activists always tell stories rather than use other discursive forms? Is narrative always an effective framing device? More research is necessary to answer the question, of course, but one can imagine several reasons why people may *not* respond to narrative pitches made by formal movement representatives. Insofar as activists are perceived as "experts," storytelling probably conflicts with what is expected of experts, namely logical, well-evidenced, and clearly specified arguments. Insofar as activists are perceived as representatives of organizations, their personal stories may be viewed as toeing an organizational line rather than as authentic self-expression and may be discredited on that basis.

Further research should evaluate narrative's role in the dynamics of collective action other than mobilization. Again, why do activists tell stories? They probably do so to sustain and strengthen members' commitment. Movements in which the goal is self-transformation as much as political reform may see personal storytelling *as* activism. Narratives undoubtedly figure more in movement decision-making than classical rational models would have us believe (see Meyer and Rowan 1977 on the role of ritual and myth in strategic deliberation). Veteran activists may stake claims to authority by demonstrating their superior knowledge of the movement's history. They may legitimate and evaluate drastic transformations in agenda or strategy by telling stories that configure past decisions in a broader narrative of enlightenment. Stories are not only legitimating but evaluative; they are *lenses* through which opportunities and obstacles, costs and benefits, and success and failure are assessed (see King 1986; Voss 1996; Polletta 1998b). Jo Freeman argues that "past experiences" constrain the resources available to movement groups for action (1979: 177). But experience is filtered through discursive frames, among them stories. Narratives' dual character—both strategically deployed and constitutive of people's understanding of strategy, interest, and identity—is evident in their relationship to emotions. Stories are used strategically by activists to elicit emotions, say, the righteous indignation that propels someone into a march, or the anguish that generates financial contributions. At the same time, people make sense of their experience, and respond to it emotionally, based on familiar narratives.

The stories that are told about *past* movements are a way to trace movements' longer-term cultural impact. More difficult to capture than legislative or policy outcomes, changes in cultural understandings—inside and outside mainstream political institutions—may be equally or more important than formal outcomes (although not necessarily so; see Polletta 1997). Contests over the public memory of movements both show people's instrumental efforts to adapt insurgent pasts to current purposes, and hint at the limits of such efforts. I show elsewhere (Polletta 1998c) that African-American congressional representatives in the 1990s frequently told the story of the civil rights movement—an episode of *extra-institutional protest*—in a way that effectively legitimated their own *institutional* positions. At the same time, a clear bifurcation of legislative and commemorative occasions in congressional discourse, with invocations of the civil rights movement relegated to the latter, has limited black representatives' ability to use such invocations to legitimate redistributive policies. Examining narratives of insurgent pasts can usefully connect work on social movements with the collective memory studies which have, until recently, concentrated on national pasts rather than dissident ones (see Olick and Robbins 1997 for an overview).

The fact that movements' legacies are often the subject of symbolic contest (Mendel-Reyes 1995; Kohl 1995) suggests the power vested in authoritative stories. Here, as in other phases of protest, the task is to show not only when, why, and how effectively activists use narrative forms to persuade and challenge, but to show how familiar stories set the very terms of strategy, identity, and interest.

ACKNOWLEDGMENTS

Thanks to Joseph Davis and two anonymous reviewers from SUNY Press for valuable comments, and to the many archivists who helped me locate and search campus newspapers, especially Ms. Kathy Jenkins of Howard University's Moorland-Spingarn Research Center, Ms. Tanya Moye of Atlanta University's Robert W. Woodruff Library, and Ms. Ledell B. Smith of Southern University. Research was supported by a grant from the Columbia University Humanities and Social Sciences Council.

NOTES

1. Gamson suggests that although the identity of the "they" in an adversarial ("us and they") frame may be elusive ("In the pursuit of cultural change, the target is often diffused throughout the whole civil society and the they being pursued is structurally elusive"), the "we" must be clearly specified ("In sum, frames with a clear we and an elusive they are quite capable of being fully collective and adversarial") (1992: 85).

2. Agricultural and Technical College *Register* 5 February 1960.

3. "Sitdown Protest in Pictorial Retrospect," *Shaw Journal* May 1960; "Justifiable Recalcitrance," *Shaw Journal* March-April 1960; "The New Freedom," SNCC, reel 4, #108; Carson 1990: 23; "A Report on the Student Direct Action Movement at Penn State as of March 31, 1960," SNCC, 44, #22; "Call for Unity in Struggle for Freedom," Howard University *Hilltop* 7 March 1960.

4. "A Report on the Student . . . March 31, 1960," SNCC, 44, #22.

5. Speech to National Student Association by Jane Stembridge, SNCC, 44, #1280–1283; SNCC newsletter entry, 1960, SNCC, 5, #190; Jane Stembridge to Lillian Lipsen, 18 August 1960, SNCC, 4, #207; Sample Fund-Raising Letter for Student Nonviolent Coordinating Committee, SNCC, 3, #785; Bennett 1960: 35; Carson 1990: 23; Carson 1990: 22; Carson 1990: 20; Bennett 1960; "Drama of the Sitdown," *Shaw Journal* March-April 1960; "Students Continue Woolworth Picket," *Hilltop* 8 April 1960; "Up Against the Obstacles," NA, ND, SNCC, 4, #980; "This Is Important," NA, ND, SNCC, 44, #113.

6. The Student Nonviolent Coordinating Committee to Mr. Bill Strong, 31 July 1960, SNCC, 1, #207.

7. Sandra Battis to Editor, Fisk University *Forum* 30 September 1960; "Newsletter to Congressmen," August 1960, SNCC, 1, #291; "Column from Cambridge Correspondent," SNCC, 62, #130 (ellipses in original); "Ode to a Lunch Counter" by Robert Booker, *Aurora* June 1960.

8. Edward King to Dear Friend, 12 September 1960, SNCC, 4, #920; H. David Hammond to Editor, *Hilltop* 8 April 1960; Dykeman and Stokely 1960: 10; Frank Smith and Olin Grant, NT, Philander Smith College, Little Rock, Arkansas, 12 March 1960, SNCC, 4, #977; Joan Burt to Editor, *Hilltop* 31 May 1960; Letter to the Editor, *Aurora* April 1960; "Justifiable Recalcitrance," 1960; "Students Applaud Demonstrations," *Hilltop* 23 Mar 1960.

9. Joan Burt to the Editor, 1960; "This Is Important," SNCC; *Hilltop*, 7 March 1960; ". . . to Mr. Bill Strong," SNCC; "Congratulations Sit-Inners," *Hilltop* 30 September 1960; "The New Freedom," SNCC, 4, #108.

10. Marion S. Barry to Honorable Byron L. Johnson, 22 August 1960, SNCC, 1, #285.

11. "Sitdown Protest in Pictorial Retrospect," 1960.

12. Henry Thomas report, ND [July 1960], SNCC, 5, #170.

13. Excerpts from tape of College Workshop, 1–2 April 1960, Highlander Papers, box 78, folder 9; Minutes of SNCC Meeting, 25–27 November 1960, SNCC, 1, #780.

14. Jane Stembridge to Mrs. Schreiber, 18 July 1960, SNCC, 4, #189; Marion Barry and Jane Stembridge to Mr. Lawrence Gundiff, 7 July 1960, SNCC, 1, #29.

15. Hayden, "Manifesto Notes: A Beginning Draft," 19 March 1962, SNCC, 9, #1088.

16. Hayden, "Manifesto Notes," SNCC; To SDS, From Hayden Re: Race and Politics Conference, ND [1961], SNCC, 9, #1142; Robb Burlage, "For Dixie with Love and Squalor," ND [1962], SNCC, 9, #1144.

THREE

Controlling Narratives and Narratives as Control within Social Movements

ROBERT D. BENFORD

As the essays in this volume demonstrate, narrations constitute a pervasive and influential form of activity for collective actors across a wide array of social movements—be they concerned with politics, religion, or lifestyle. My interest in this chapter is not with the form or content of such stories; nor am I concerned with how collective action narratives are constructed and disseminated. Rather, I focus on the recursive relationship between narratives and social control within social movements.

Once a set of movement narratives has been constructed, social movement actors seek to sustain them. That is, they actively, often strategically, collude to uphold various aspects of the movement's narratives, in part by preventing alternative or competing narratives from being constructed and disseminated. While most movement adherents routinely engage in various activities directed toward controlling the story that is told about the movement, the narratives themselves function as internal social control mechanisms, channeling and constraining individual as well as collective sentiments, emotions, and action.

In this chapter, I offer a preliminary conceptual elaboration and analysis of the relationship between narratives and social control *within* social movements. This framework is grounded in research of and experiences in various social movements.[1] I begin by distinguishing between two generic types of collective action stories—participant narratives and movement narratives. Next, I discuss the concept of social control before turning to a theoretical discussion of the concept's utility in understanding social movement dynamics. Then, after delineating several peace movement narratives, I identify and illustrate individual and collective processes that are constrained by movement narratives and which in turn serve to reproduce movement stories. I conclude by suggesting some additional theoretical considerations, including various contexts that are likely to affect the relationship between narratives and social control within social movements.

GENERIC TYPES OF COLLECTIVE ACTION NARRATIVES

There are two generic types of narratives discernable within social movements: participant narratives and movement narratives. *Participant narratives* refer to the stories that individual participants tell about their (and sometimes others') movement-related experiences. Movement actors and their opponents fashion and tell stories: stories about encounters with unjust authorities (Gamson, Fireman, and Rytina 1982; McAdam 1988), stories expressing moral outrage in response to suddenly imposed threats to their welfare or way of life (Ĉapek 1993; Jasper 1997; Walsh 1981), stories recounting how and why they became involved in the movement (Hunt and Benford 1994; Polletta, chapter 2), stories of empowerment in the course of participating in movement activities, and stories highlighting who they are and who they are not (Hunt and Benford 1994; Rice, chapter 4; Taylor and Whittier 1992). These various participant narratives or "bundle of stories" contribute to the construction of a group's "idioculture" and are among the interpretive materials from which movement narratives are fashioned (Fine, chapter 10).

Movement narratives, by way of comparison, refer to the various myths, legends, and folk tales, collectively constructed by participants about the movement and the domains of the world the movement seeks to change. Participant and movement narratives are closely linked in much the same fashion that individual interpretive frames and collective action frames are aligned (Snow et al. 1986) and personal and collective identities overlap or fuse (Hunt and Benford 1994).

Movement narratives are distinctive from most other narratives in a fundamental way. Whereas the temporal structure of most narratives includes a singular beginning, middle, and end, movement narratives suggest alternative middles and endings.[2] Typically, at least two middles and two endings are portrayed in movement narratives. One middle and one ending are offered as the logical flow of events that will unfold if no collective ameliorative action is undertaken. This *status quo story* is then contrasted to an alternative approach for dealing with what movement actors see as the problematic set of conditions, an alternative middle that they posit (or at least hope) will lead to a different, more desirable, ending.[3] Thus, movement actors seek to insert themselves, individually and collectively, into an extant narrative (the status quo story) to bring about change, to create a new narrative.[4]

For present purposes, what is most relevant regarding this feature of movement narratives is that it tends to amplify social control issues. As Maines (1993: 21) notes, "Narratives and narrative occasions are always potential sites of conflict and competition as well as cooperation and consensus." Social movements are replete with such "narrative occasions." Movement opponents espouse narratives that conflict with movement stories (cf. Meyer and Staggenborg 1996). Within movements, disputes erupt between various factions regarding appropriate representations of past and present conditions as well as over alternative futures (Benford 1993a). In consideration of these and a host of other movement dynamics, it stands to reason that issues of narrative control are paramount in mobilizing and sustaining support for most social movements.

SOCIAL CONTROL WITHIN SOCIAL MOVEMENTS

Social control is one of sociology's oldest concepts. It has been employed in almost every substantive area of the discipline[5] and is frequently included in micro- as well as macrolevel theories or models. Social movement scholars have contributed to this rich intellectual tradition as well. However, nearly all such explicit treatments of social control focus exclusively on the effects various *extra*movement organizations or actors (e.g., agent provocateurs, media, police, the state, countermovements, "deprogrammers" and other opponents) have on movement outcomes (such as participation/withdrawal, mobilization/demobilization, success/failure) to the neglect of attempts to control the course of social movements from *within*.

The omission of systematic analyses of *intra*movement social control processes is surprising in view of the wealth of empirical evidence from a variety of contemporary movements, including the civil rights (McAdam 1982; Morris 1984), black power (Gerlach and Hine 1970; Haines 1988), women's (Buechler 1990; Freeman 1975), animal rights (Jasper and Nelkin 1992), student/antiwar (Gitlin 1980; Heirich 1971; Sale 1971), peace (Kleidman 1993; Meyer 1990), and antinuclear (Nelkin and Pollak 1981; Price 1982) movements. Data presented in each of these case studies suggests that social movement actors collectively devote considerable effort to maintaining the socially constructed order of their movement and/or movement organization, to shaping the direction of the movement or Social Movement Organization (SMO), to regulating or influencing the tactics employed by other SMOs affiliated with their movement, to controlling the actions of individual adherents, and, by implication, to sustaining movement myths and other movement narratives. Explicit recognition of these processes as attempts at *social control* is nonetheless lacking in each case.

In fact, except for Lewis's (1972) and Zurcher and Kirkpatrick's (1976) brief empirical observations on the topic, and Turner and Killian's (1987) description of modes of intramovement social control, acknowledgment of the role of social control *within* movements has been confined to scholars of new religious movements, cults, and communes (Beckford 1981; Kanter 1968; Lofland 1966; Richardson 1983; Robbins 1979, 1984). Much of this literature is devoted to identifying processes and causes of conversion and to debunking "forced conversion" (Schwartz and Isser 1981), "coercive persuasion" (Schein, Schneir, and Barker 1961), "brainwashing" (Sargent 1957), and "thought reform" (Lifton 1961) explanations of participation in "deviant" cults or new religious movements. While sifting through this vast literature yields some insights more generally applicable across social movements, much of it is so narrowly focused that it precludes theoretical extensions to political and lifestyle movements. The inordinate amount of attention devoted to the causes of conversion has left other domains and modes of internal social control relatively unattended. Moreover, public acceptance of "brainwashing" explanations (an interesting narrative in its own right) inspired a number of scholars to concentrate on external social control forces and processes such as those of the "deprogrammers" (Robbins and Anthony 1978, 1982; Shupe and Bromley 1980, 1983). In short, like the scholars of secular movements, students of religious movements have failed to outline thoroughly and analyze systematically intramovement control.

The processes of internal control within social movements take a variety of individual and collective forms. In this chapter, I focus on the narratives of social movements as both a mechanism and object of control. One of the fundamental conclusions elaborated below is that the social control dynamics between a movement's adherents and its stories are recursive. At the same time adherents engage in efforts to control, sustain, and reproduce movement stories, they are in effect being controlled by the narratives. This recursive relationship is perhaps most clearly illustrated by examining a movement's most sacred narratives: myths.

MOVEMENT MYTHS AND SOCIAL CONTROL

All social movements construct myths. By myths, I refer not to the popular use of the term as a false belief, but rather to the anthropological notion of a myth as "a sacred narrative explaining how the world and people came to be in their present form" (Dundes 1976: 279). Roucek (1978: 154) elaborates:

> Myth is an indispensable component of all ideologies. It is a highly symbolic account or story of a supernatural or extraordinary event within a culture or subculture, and is continually retold and contemplated for its wisdom, philosophy, inspiration, or practicality. As Pareto pointed out, myth is a system of ideas, very often utopian, that is set up to inspire action.

So conceived, myths are powerful intramovement social control mechanisms.

Several myths were widely accepted within the U.S. peace movement during the 1980s and early 1990s (Benford and Hunt 1992b; Hunt 1991). These sacred narratives operated in various combinations to inspire action and constrain individual and collective behavior.

Utopian Myths

One of the peace movement's most sacred myths posited an *utopian* vision of a harmonious world. This myth sustained participation for many activists in the face of a continuous stream of contrary evidence. Bolstered by tales of "peaceful" societies and claims that war and preparation for it are inherently "unnatural" behaviors, the myth allowed "the group an escape from the hard facts of reality in the vision of a glorious future" (Roucek 1978: 154). The glorification of charismatic leaders and accounts

of their heroic nonviolent struggles in pursuit of perpetual peace served to
legitimate movement tactics that might otherwise have appeared to be
ineffective if not useless.

Civil disobedience training sessions I observed, for example, often
began with tales regarding the effectiveness of nonviolent direct action
campaigns of other movements such as the abolition, Nazi resistance, civil
rights, and women's movements. These legends typically took the form of
David and Goliath tales, recounting how "ordinary people" such as Rosa
Parks overcame insurmountable odds for the cause of peace and justice. In
a similar fashion, peace movement literature invoked utopian images of an
eventual victory of the forces of good against evil. An excerpt from a Red
River Peace Network (RRPN) pamphlet is illustrative of scores of similar
documents I analyzed:

> Today people are crying for peace stronger than at any other
> time in history. We are speaking out and taking action because
> WE LOVE THIS PLANET. If we bring faith, commitment and
> hard work to this movement of concerned individuals, the scales
> will tip and a new era of human development will follow. We
> can save the planet from nuclear destruction, but only if we each
> do our part, however small, and do it now. Our planet is too
> wonderful to lose to the insanity of the forces of hate and fear.
> The force of love and hope is more powerful; powerful enough
> to release us and our beloved Earth, our home, from the grip of
> the nuclear menace. (1995)

Power of Nonviolent Resistance Myths

As the foregoing illustration suggests, the peace movement's utopian
myths gave rise to other myths such as the *power of nonviolent resistance*
myth, a narrative that was widely accepted and espoused by a significant
segment of the U.S. peace movement. This narrative took spiritual and
secular forms. Faith resisters, for example, engaged in sometimes dramatic
acts of civil disobedience (e.g., overt resistance to status quo stories) based
on an avowed faith in religious beliefs. To obtain the utopian ending of
"peace and justice" required that the story's protagonists follow sacred
commandments, adhere to the dictates of moral obligations, and make
personal sacrifices. One faith resister explained:

There seems to be a bit of confusion concerning one's ultimate commitment to a cause. We mistakenly equate willingness to die for a cause with willingness to kill for a cause. . . . Now for the punch line: Christ taught us to die for a cause; he did not teach us to kill for a cause.

The power of the nonviolent resistance myth was reinforced by participants' narratives. One testimonial from a confrontation between the Coast Guard and protesters piloting a small boat in a futile attempt to stop a Trident submarine's departure is illustrative of this type of narrative:

> A scene I witnessed on the Lizard of Woz [the protesters' boat] was that of Eve and Ted saying repeatedly to a Coast Guard officer, holding a pistol to Ted's back, that they loved him. I joined them in that, and we said the Lord's Prayer while kneeling by the officer. Did we love our Coast Guard brother deeply enough? Not enough to disarm him; perhaps enough to prevent a shooting. The pistol in Ted's back was cocked, and the finger on its trigger shaking. Had the trigger been pulled, I believe Eve would even then have loved the Coast Guard officer.

The secular variant of the power of the nonviolent resistance myth emphasized civic duty and the moral obligations of citizens. The following excerpt from a statement read to the press by a representative of a civil disobedience affinity group as they began their human blockade of a railway just beyond the gates of the Pantex nuclear weapons assembly facility typifies this variant:

> Our decision to blockade this railroad track was not an easy one. The trains that carry components into and nuclear weapons out of Pantex deliver the potential for an unprecedented catastrophe. . . . We realize we risk arrest and more by blockading the tracks. This willingness to make personal sacrifice is central to the power of civil disobedience to awaken the hearts and minds of our fellow citizens to the seriousness of the nuclear issue. This nonviolent action is offered by the Red River Peace Network as an opportunity for conscientious resistance to preparations for nuclear war . . . carried out in the spirit of love and reconciliation. . . . to call attention to

the threat posed by nuclear weapons and to encourage all of us to take personal responsibility for preventing nuclear war.

As I will show below, myths such as the power of nonviolent resistance functioned to control individual and collective sentiments, actions, and emotions.

The Myth of the Grassroots

Perhaps the most often invoked and widely believed myth pertained to claims about grassroots participation and mobilization. The central theme of this myth is that a critical mass of individuals has the potential to be mobilized to restructure existing social conditions and relationships. Mass participation, the *grassroots*, has the power to build a more just, democratic, and peaceful world. Most peace movement organizations I studied tended to refer to their group and the movement as "grassroots." An excerpt from Austin Nuclear Weapons Freeze Campaign instructions to door-to-door canvassers illustrates this collective identification:

Mobilization Target: You can't fight city hall!
Freeze Canvasser: We believe that organized people can and will
beat organized money! That's the power of a grassroots
movement like ours. By involving people from over 300
congressional districts around the country we are able to
mount an incredible amount of pressure on our representatives. Politicians listen to two things, money and votes. By
pooling our resources we are able to succeed in whatever we
are fighting for. That's why you should join. The more
people involved, the more strength our organization has.

The Myth of Political Correctness

Another myth that appears to be honored extensively, albeit not universally, within the peace movement is the "myth of political correctness."
Soon after beginning the study, I noted that there seemed to be a great
deal of taken-for-grantedness among adherents regarding appropriate
beliefs, opinions, feelings, and values concerning a myriad of issues,

including nuclear weapons, conventional weapons, military intervention, draft registration, nuclear power, the environment, apartheid, civil rights, women's rights, gay rights, animal rights, Palestine, abortion, capital punishment, gun control, jobs, and poverty. Although bitter disputes erupted within the movement regarding which issues ought to be addressed and linked during a given campaign or event, the single-issue advocates tended to agree substantively with the multi-issue supporters.

Activists referred to the movement's general ideological position on issues as "politically correct" without ever articulating criteria for arriving at positions on social problems or causes. Presumably, the common thread weaving the movement's ideological cloth together were life-affirming values and respect for human dignity and self-determination. But having established a common denominator does not render the question of political correctness nonproblematic on a number of issues where strong contradictory cases have been made (such as Palestine, abortion, animal rights). Moreover, when the myth of political correctness was perceived to contradict other movement narratives such as the power of nonviolent resistance, confusion arose regarding which narrative should take precedence. Members of the Texas Mobilization for Survival (TMS), for instance, debated whether or not to support a November 29th Coalition action because of concerns regarding the member groups' support for the Palestinian Liberation Organization (PLO).

> TMS Male Member X: Well, I'm kind of ignorant on what's been happening over there [in the Middle East], but I wonder whether or not the November 29th Coalition condones violence. Don't they support the PLO? And don't they employ terroristic tactics?
>
> TMS Female Member A: Well there are factions of the PLO that run the spectrum. And the November 29th Coalition does not endorse violence. . . .
>
> TMS Male Member Y: The terrorists have been ousted from the PLO. They didn't attempt to assassinate the diplomat, which was Israel's justification for the invasion [of Lebanon].
>
> TMS Female Member A: I think we must show our opposition to the Israeli invasion with U.S. guns. I don't have any problem attending an event with a placard explaining why

I'm there even if I disagree politically with some of the other supporters.

Despite some blemishes in the myth of political correctness, peace activists generally employ it as an influential control mechanism. On numerous occasions, I observed participants admonishing others for using expressions such as "lady," "handicapped," and "killing two birds with one stone" because they were imputed to be antithetical to peace movement values of human dignity and nonviolence. The most easily recognizable taboo in the U.S. peace movement was a prohibition against violence in all social interactions. Although not all U.S. peace movement participants considered themselves pacifists, most shunned violent practices. In addition to forums that expressed antiwar and antimilitarism views, workshops and discussions frequently addressed violence associated with parenting, formal education curriculum, children's games, popular media entertainments, protest, gay bashing, women battering, and police harassment of people of color, to name but a few issues. To do or say anything that challenged the practice of nonviolence—the underpinning of a harmonious world myth—drew immediate and sharp reactions.

The myth of political correctness served as a tool of ideological socialization and often functioned to control participant narratives. A wide array of adherent behaviors from dietary practices to interpersonal relations to recreational activities were also affected by the myth of political correctness. For instance, on my first day in the field I learned that some of my personal habits at that time—watching football and eating meat—were considered "politically incorrect." Thus, myths serve to control participants' interpretations, feelings, and actions, including their own stories. These effects, in turn, contribute to the reproduction of movement narratives.

ADHERENT CONTROL: KEEPING THE TROOPS IN LINE

The effectiveness of an SMO's programs, mobilization campaigns, collective actions, and narratives can hinge on the extent to which the group operates in a concerted or coordinated fashion. Hence, the social control of adherents is ubiquitous and necessary in all movements. Social movements have borrowed from their social milieu an extensive repertoire of social control tactics. At this individual level, movement narratives function to control participant's interpretive frames, vocabularies of motives, feelings and affective displays, and actions; these in turn function to sustain movement narratives.

Interpretive Frames

The role of ideas, attitudes, beliefs, and values in social movement participation and mobilization has been a long-standing concern of social movement scholars. However, only recently have scholars turned systematically to the issue of the processes and mechanisms by which movements attempt to affect cognition, such as grievance interpretation, often considered prefatory to taking part in movement activities and campaigns.

Much of this work is based on Goffman's (1974: 21) notions regarding "frames," which are conceived of as "schemata of interpretation" that enable individuals to "locate, perceive, identify, and label a seemingly infinite number of concrete occurrences defined in its terms." Frames render events meaningful and thus serve "to organize experience and guide action, whether individual or collective" (Snow et al. 1986: 464). Moreover, frames are inextricably linked to narratives inasmuch as they are the interpretive screens through which the past, present, and future are filtered and subsequently imbued with meaning and significance. I will elaborate and illustrate this topic below under a discussion of collective action frames, a particular type of interpretive frame. For now, it is important to note that all movements seek "to affect interpretations of reality among their intended audiences" (Benford 1987: 1). A movement's effectiveness in realizing the alternative ending proffered in its change narrative will depend in part on how successful it is in affecting and controlling individual interpretations.

Vocabularies of Motives

One way framing activity contributes to intramovement control is by espousing and cultivating a specific type of participant narrative—a "vocabulary of motives" (Mills 1940). These linguistic devices "function as prods to action" (Snow and Benford 1988: 202) by supplying adherents with compelling reasons or rationales for participating in SMO activities. Among those "compelling reasons" research has identified as necessary to affect adherent mobilization are vocabularies of motive concerning (1) the severity of the problem, (2) the urgency of the problem, (3) the efficacy of taking action, and (4) the propriety of taking action (Benford 1993b). Each of these vocabularies can be conceptualized as participant narratives that are grounded in and reinforced by movement narratives.

Peace movement organizations reward the espousal of the foregoing rationales, and discourage adherents from voicing motives deemed as inconsistent with movement stories. An excerpt from my field notes recorded during a 1986 antiapartheid demonstration on campus illustrates the process:

> A woman in the process of being arrested for "illegal assembly" [one of 182 arrested on this occasion] responded to a reporter's questions regarding her motives by stating, "It's what's happening!" Upon continuing to indicate that she was participating because it was exciting and "the thing to do," one of the protest organizers pushed his way between her and the television camera and interrupted with: "That's not the main reason why we're out here. We're here to protest U.T.'s [the University of Texas] eight-hundred and fifty million dollar investment in companies that do business in South Africa!"

Clearly, from the perspective of the antiapartheid protest organizer, the woman's expressed motive was deemed frivolous and risked undermining the movement's more serious narrative. The activist reacted by espousing a "good reason" for engaging in an act of civil disobedience, one that supported the movement's utopian, grassroots, and nonviolent resistance narratives regarding conscientious citizens engaged in artful moral protests (Jasper 1997) for the purpose of abolishing the apartheid system by persuading others to join in an economic boycott. This encounter, a form repeated on many other movement occasions, suffices to illustrate how controlling vocabularies of motive functions to sustain movement narratives—and thus participants' movement-related feelings and actions.

Emotions

Overlooked in most scholarly treatments of movements are the intense emotions, dramatic tensions, and heightened sense of expectancy associated with collective action (Benford 1997; Benford and Hunt 1992a; Jasper 1997; Zurcher and Snow 1981). Furthermore, social movements often engage in what Hochschild (1979: 561) refers to as "emotion work": deliberate attempts to "script" (Zurcher 1985), "orchestrate" (Zurcher 1982), "stage" (Snow, Zurcher, and Peters 1981), "manage" (Hochschild 1979, 1983), or otherwise control emotions.

Affective control depends in part on implicitly teaching people how they should feel in a given situation of a certain type—when to evoke and when to suppress particular feelings. These "feeling rules" (Hochschild 1979: 566) are socially constructed in the course of movement participation and become legitimated and solidified as participants recount their and others' emotional responses to various movement-related encounters. Movement activists attempt to orchestrate and manage affective orientations toward events or objects that they deem consistent with the movement's narratives. Though social movements often attend to the superficial issue of how people should *appear* to feel, especially when the objective is primarily one of managing the impressions of bystanders, antagonists, and/or targets, if they are to have substantial impact on their adherents, movement cadre must devote considerable effort to how people should actually *try* to feel. The recounting of movement "atrocity tales" (Bromley, Shupe, and Ventimiglia 1979; Hunt and Benford 1994), "war stories" (Fine 1995; Hunt and Benford 1994), "disillusionment anecdotes" (Hunt and Benford 1994), and narratives expressing "moral outrage" (Jasper 1997) serve to keynote and reinforce appropriate feelings associated with movement activities.

Actions

Most intramovement social control efforts, regardless of the level or domain, are ultimately directed toward affecting the behavior of specific individuals. For interorganizational control to be effective, for instance, the behavior of specific individuals, though acting on behalf of a group, must in some fashion be influenced, altered, or constrained. Likewise, attempts to control the affective and cognitive states of adherents are typically assumed to be prefatory to controlling their actions.

Control over participants' actions not only pertains to sustaining movement or SMO norms elaborated in movement narratives or eliciting conformity from the rank-and-file, but to logistical and technical behavior as well. At the very least, this involves the development of an informal division of labor within a given SMO, whereby specific individuals tend to perform specialized tasks consistent with the organization's strategy. The extent to which adherents' movement roles are monitored and regulated by activists varies across SMOs. But even within the most decentralized groups, movement narratives tend to function to constrain, facilitate, and coordinate adherent behavior.

A massive civil disobedience (CD) action organized by peace activists in June 1982 illustrates these dynamics well. As with most movement CD actions, all adherents who intended to participate were required to take part in a four-hour "nonviolent direct action training workshop." At the Austin workshop I attended (duplicated at over 150 locales across the United States), trainees were indoctrinated by Texas Mobe and War Resisters' League activists in the philosophy and history of nonviolent direct action in a number of ways: veteran activists provided numerous participant and movement narrations, each of which were punctuated with explicit references to the "moral" or "lessons" of the story; they taught us appropriate role-specific responses to various situations through a series of "role-playing" exercises; they briefed us on the logistical details of the plan and event site; and they gave us a forty-page *Blockade the Bombmakers Civil Disobedience Handbook* as our field manual. The manual scripted the dramatic enactment of civil disobedience, as well as providing participants and media representatives with a series of narratives that in essence constituted a narrative history of the New Left. In short, the training session linked the planned action (future) to the past and the present, identified villains and heroes/heroines, described the setting, and provided details regarding the plot.

During a second meeting, members of the "affinity group" (which named itself the "Texas Disarmadillos") chose general and specific roles to play during the action (the arrestee, support, legal observer, media spokesperson, runner, vibes watcher). The night before the action, the Austin affinity group met in New York City with other affinity groups from Texas to coordinate, review, and rehearse their roles. With few exceptions, the protesters behaved in compliance with their predesignated roles and the overall story—despite the fact that there were a number of unanticipated occurrences, including the use of physical force by several arresting officers.

On the rare occasions when an adherent was believed to have violated fundamental movement norms, such as those proffered in the movement's nonviolence narratives, they were given the "cold shoulder," if not completely ostracized from the group. For example, in the summer of 1985, just prior to an annual pilgrimage to Pantex, a disarmament activist (who was not affiliated with any of the groups examined in this study) removed several feet of track from the railway artery serving the nuclear weapons assembly plant. After his arrest, his spouse approached activists and adherents at the Pantex peace encampment for support for her husband's actions. The camp's participants shunned her, ostensibly because they felt that her husband had breached basic nonviolent principles. They withheld their names and addresses she requested for a mailing list and refused to accept a document she attempted to distribute that her husband had written in defense of his actions. The harsh reaction of the members of the Pantex peace encampment to the lone protester's actions can be more adequately understood when consideration is given to the notion that he had not simply violated norms; he had threatened to undermine the movement's most sacred narratives of nonviolence.

COLLECTIVE CONTROL: MAINTAINING THE PARTY LINE

The recursive relationship between narratives and movement adherents not only operates at an individual level, but at a collective one as well. A variety of collective processes recently identified by movement scholars as central to social movement mobilization dynamics fit well within the narrative paradigm. Three of these—collective action frames, collective identities, and collective memories—are constructions of, if not elements of, social movement narratives. Consequently, each plays a crucial role in social control processes associated with narratives.

Collective Action Frames

Collective action frames constrain and are constrained by movement narratives. As previously suggested, framing refers to movement "signifying work," activity wherein SMO adherents or activists "assign meaning to and interpret relevant events and conditions in ways that are intended to mobilize potential adherents and constituents, to garner bystander support, and to demobilize antagonists" (Snow and Benford 1988: 198; Benford and Snow 2000). Thus, "activists employ collective action frames to punctuate or single out some existing social condition or aspect of life and define it as unjust, intolerable, and deserving of corrective action" (Snow and Benford 1992: 137). In short, they are rhetorical processes that function to inspire, legitimate, and control collective action by elaborating various elements of movement narratives.[6]

Movement activists seek to influence and control the quality of the frames being proffered (Benford and Snow 2000). Indeed, every peace and justice movement organization studied actively sought to control its framing activities. They did so in a variety of ways: several established rules regarding the content of public messages, banners, and literature; a few appointed committees to monitor framing activities; and most selected one or two spokespersons whom they designated as the only ones permitted to discuss movement-related issues with reporters and other media representatives.

Austin disarmament activists were often divided on the issue of *frame control*. Some felt that it constituted "censorship" and thus contradicted the justifications traditionally offered by the movement in defense of its public demonstrations. Others argued that it was necessary to restrict its framing activity in order to prevent some individuals from damaging the movement's "image" represented in prevailing narratives.

The topic of frame control arose most frequently in the context of organizing large demonstrations. Occurrences associated with the 1985 Pantex Peace Encampment illustrate movement attempts to affect frame control as well as suggest ways in which the other mechanisms of intramovement control operate. Approximately one month prior to the Pantex demonstration, two members of the Revolutionary Communist Party (RCP) attended a Red River Peace Network (RRPN) planning meeting. Members of RRPN, the coalition which organizes the annual pilgrimage of several hundred disarmament adherents to the gates of the nuclear weapons facility, requested that the RCP members "stay away" from the peace encampment. The RCP members responded that they intended to participate in the event. Subsequently, RRPN representatives composed a "disclaimer"—the thrust of which reiterated their commitment to nonviolence and distanced their organization from the RCP—to be issued, if deemed necessary, to media representatives covering the Pantex demonstration.

A few days later, RRPN led a training session for those who had volunteered to be "peacekeepers" at the encampment. After outlining the schedule of planned activities for the event as well as the rules and procedures to be followed, the trainers dealt with potential violations of the script. They indicated that RCP members might attempt to disrupt the event, and perhaps even try to transform the peaceful demonstration into a violent confrontation. The role-playing scenarios the trainers organized for the peacekeeping trainees reflected these concerns. One scenario depicted the RCP people burning an American flag. The peace-keepers were instructed to surround the RCP members if they initiated a confrontation.

When a group of eight to ten people identified as members of the RCP arrived at the peace encampment, twenty-five to thirty peacekeepers converged nearby. At one point the peacekeepers and the alleged RCP group stood on opposite sides of the road glaring at each other. In response to this less-than-cordial welcome, the new arrivals decided to pitch their tents a few hundred meters beyond the boundaries of RRPN's encampment. Most of the so-called communists turned out to be "punkers" who denied affiliation with the RCP. The punkers voiced dis-satisfaction with the manner in which they had been treated. They said they felt like they had been discriminated against on the basis of their physical appearance. Expressing objections to the structure and rules RRPN had established for the encampment, the punkers referred to the peacekeepers, who wore pink T-shirts, as the "pink police" and the "pink pigs."

Rumors pertaining to the punkers and the RCP were rampant throughout the camp. RRPN members gathered in small groups and dis-cussed what they had heard about the unwelcome visitors and their inten-tions. One persistent rumor was that the punkers/communists were planning a civil disobedience action the following morning, and that it might take the form of trespassing on Department of Energy property or perhaps a "die-in" at the plant's employee entrance. Rumors that the punkers/communists had brought weapons with them also flourished.

Soon after the punkers arrived in camp, RRPN's coordinator called an emergency meeting of the "On-Site Decision-Making Committee," the encampment's governing body, to discuss what to do about the RCP people. The media co-coordinators proposed that the "disclaimer" be issued to the press immediately. They expressed concern regarding the "image" of the RRPN, an image that had, in their opinion, been carefully constructed over a two-year period. The image that had been fostered, they noted, was one of "rational, moderate, reasonable citizens" who were concerned about the threat of nuclear war.[7] The media co-coordinators contended that the presence of the

RCP members and the punkers would tarnish that image. One of the two cited a situation in which media cameras had been aimed at Bishop Matthieson until a punker approached wearing a Reagan mask, at which point the cameras all turned toward the punker.

A committee member suggested that the group should not worry about the punkers tainting the group's image, that "people will be able to distinguish between us and them" because of the punkers' distinctive appearance. "I never thought I'd find myself on this side of the generation gap," mused one committee member who was in his late thirties. Several argued that the media, the community, and the police would not differentiate between "us and them." Two members, both experienced activists from the 1960s, argued against issuing the disclaimer, stating that the punkers and RCP members "have every much a right to be here as we do." Another pointed out that the disclaimer would be a mistake because the media would play up the story of infighting and divisions within the camp.

One of the media co-coordinators responded that she had heard that the punkers were planning "an unauthorized act of civil disobedience."[8] A veteran activist replied that RRPN should not issue a disclaimer "even if they do CD, as long as it's clean." When someone asked what she meant by "clean," she said, "I mean as long as the CD were nonviolent, we should not distance ourselves from their action." Another member argued that "we would look ridiculous taking a stand against their CD when we're going to be engaging in CD the next day."

The committee decided to withhold the disclaimer from the press, apologize to the punkers, and try to elicit from them their actual intentions. The rumors proved to be false, at least according to the testimony and subsequent behavior of the punkers. Despite the apparent short-term success of RRPN's various social control efforts, the repressive style of the specific tactics employed left a bad taste in the mouths of a number of participants. For many, it was their final pilgrimage to Pantex. From their perspective, the heavy-handed attempts to protect and sustain one of Red River Peace Network's narratives—the narrative of ordinary people seeking nuclear disarmament—ironically undermined another movement narrative—the story of a progressive, democratic community open to new ideas and alternative lifestyles.[9]

Collective Identities

The foregoing illustration suggests that collective identity issues were also at stake. Collective identity refers to the "qualities and characteristics attributed to a group by members of that group" (Hunt 1991: 255). Collective identities are socially constructed through storytelling. As movement actors recount stories—participant narratives or movement narratives—they offer attributions about themselves and their movement or group (Hunt and Benford 1994). In this way, they construct and reaffirm their "collective character," a component of collective identity that "fosters a sense of unity" and includes the various sets of "behavioral, cognitive, and moral traits" that they impute to their movement or movement organization (Hunt 1991: 255). In the course of imputing traits about their own group, which they typically frame as the narrative's "protagonists," they also make negative attributions regarding movement opponents, the story's "antagonists" (Hunt, Benford, and Snow 1994; cf. Benford and Hunt 1992a).

Having carefully constructed a clear demarcation between the "good" folks and the "bad," movement adherents seek to preserve those distinctions. If it is suddenly revealed that the antagonist is actually good or that the protagonist is really not all that good, the movement story lacks "narrative fidelity" (Fisher 1984, 1987) and thus loses its "resonance" (Snow and Benford 1988). With these considerations in mind, it is apparent why collective identity is often the object of intramovement social control efforts.

Returning to the controversy that erupted at the Pantex Peace Encampment, some RRPN activists expressed concern that the presence of either "communists" or "punkers" in their midst would undermine their collective identity claims of "ordinary citizens." The presence of such characters would play into the hands of movement antagonists whose own narratives portrayed the protesters as being, at best, "weirdos" (such as "punkers") and, at worst, enemy "sympathizers" (such as "communists"). Hence, to maintain the collective identity represented in key movement narratives, several activists advocated and carried out a variety of controlling tactics ranging from gossip to ridicule to ostracism.

Collective Memories

The final element I wish to note as playing a crucial role in social control processes associated with narratives are collective memories. The term "collective memory" refers most simply to a "social memory" (Swidler and Arditi 1994: 308; cf. Halbwachs 1980; Schudson 1992; Schwartz 1991). Collective memories are essentially constructed and reconstructed narratives of the past. "In order not to forget that past," according to

Bellah et al. (1985: 153), "a community is involved in retelling its story, its constitutive narrative, and in so doing, it offers examples of men and women who have embodied and exemplified the meaning of the community." The content of narratives about the past are the subject of intensive social control efforts, typically reflecting extant power relations. Elite attempts to control the past do not necessarily go uncontested. Indeed, because collective memories are central to collective identities, they are often the subject of intense disputes, as illustrated in the mid-1990s by a spate of war museum controversies. Social movements typically play a significant role in disputes regarding whose collective memories will be preserved[10] and thus which character attributions will be culturally validated.

Once a social movement organization has constructed a particular rendition of the past, its adherents seek to preserve it through the telling and retelling of participant and movement stories. When a participant's narrative contradicts a movement myth or other movement narrative, adherents will seek to redirect the participant back onto the proper narrative path. The following excerpt from my field notes of a 1993 statewide March Coordinating Committee meeting illustrates such attempts to control collective memories:

> [A University Mobe member] expressed pessimism regarding the prospects of overcoming the nuclear threat by pursuing nuclear disarmament: "Sometimes I have doubts about it, especially trying to prevent nuclear war. When you look back at history . . . previous attempts to prevent war have failed."
>
> [A Veteran Texas Mobe activist] retorted: "We can change history! We're going to win this! We stopped the Vietnam War! Our protests *did* make a difference then and they can make a difference now. We've got Reagan on the run."

The foregoing encounter also underscores how controlling the past can have a potential impact on action in the present and thus affect opportunities to impact the future.

CONCLUSION

In this chapter, I have offered a preliminary sketch of the relationship between narratives and social control *within* social movements. In so doing, I hope to stimulate further theory construction and research on the recursive dynamics between movement narratives and control. Because this was an initial excursion into some unfamiliar territory, my own narrative of the expedition is no doubt subject to challenge and revision. Moreover, I have also omitted discussions of a number of important issues of relevance.

Perhaps the most obvious omission pertains to the analytical issue of context. Specifically, what conditions are likely to affect the relationship between narratives and social control within social movements and how? Although answers to these questions remain to be addressed, extant literature would seem to offer some fruitful suggestions. For example, it seems reasonable to suggest, à la Berger and Luckmann (1966), that narratives are more fluid and subject to revision during the early days of a movement's or movement organization's emergence. But once the movement or group has begun to solidify some of the elements of its organizational infrastructure, its narratives will become objectivated and reified as well. Henceforth, an official or quasi-official "party line" will take shape that adherents will seek to sustain by employing the various social control mechanisms discussed above.

Space does not permit further discussion of these and other contexts that are likely to modulate dynamics associated with movement narratives and internal social control. However, I would like to offer a partial list of possible factors, derived from social movement literature, that would appear to warrant future consideration. They include the following conditions: a movement's or SMO's temporal location within a cycle of protest; the presence or absence of a master frame and the narrative's relationship to it; extant popular narratives from the wider culture; mobilizing structures, social movement organizational structures, and organizational infrastructures; political opportunity structures; and the actions and narratives of countermovements. Each of these would seem to play a crucial role in controlling movement narratives and narratives' capacity to control.

ACKNOWLEDGMENTS

A version of this chapter was presented at the annual meeting of the Midwest Sociological Society, Kansas City, April 1998. I am indebted to Joseph Davis, Bill Gamson, Tim Gongaware, Scott Hunt, David L. Miller,

Michelle Hughes Miller, Carol Mueller, Francesca Polletta, Hugh Whitt, anonymous reviewers, and members of the University of Nebraska's Deviance and Social Control Study Group for comments on earlier versions of this chapter.

NOTES

1. The bulk of the data was derived from a multimethod field study of the nuclear disarmament movement. From mid-1982 through mid-1986, I collected data on eighteen peace and justice organizations. Nine of the social movement organizations (SMOs) were local, six operated at the national level, and three were local or regional coalitions of peace and justice organizations. The principal method of data collection involved intensive and extensive participant observation. I participated in the activities, meetings, and campaigns of five of the local disarmament groups and all three coalitions. I was accepted in each of those SMOs as a person concerned with the purposes of the organizations and as a researcher gathering data about their activities. Detailed field notes were taken and recorded fully within twenty-four hours after taking them. Data from the remaining four local organizations were gathered using observational methods. I spent approximately 2,100 hours in the field, and the study yielded 961 pages of field notes. I conducted formal, intensive interviews with twenty-one core activists of the twelve local and regional SMOs. Additionally, I interviewed 132 rank-and-file members during the course of participation. Finally, I collected, coded, and analyzed approximately 1,400 movement-generated documents (memos, newsletters, fliers, speeches, press releases) of all eighteen SMOs (including the six national groups). For additional details regarding the methods employed and the specific fieldwork roles I derived during the course of the study, see Benford (1987).

2. In this sense, movement narratives are similar to other stories of change, such as those associated with collective attempts to affect attitudes, feelings, behavior, or social conditions.

3. Limitations of space preclude a thorough discussion of the various theoretical and methodological implications of simultaneously fashioning and sustaining at least two narratives.

4. These observations apply not only to social movements but to countermovements as well. The only difference is that the extant narrative

posited by countermovements is one of a middle that has already changed toward an undesirable end. Countermovement actors thus seek to insert themselves in the middle of that story for the purpose of obstructing or reversing the changes in order to yield the ending they desire.

5. Gibbs (1989) contends that control could and should be considered as "sociology's central notion," one that would bring "maximum coherence" to the discipline.

6. Collective action frames are distinctive from narratives, in that frames constitute the socially constructed means by which elements of the broader narratives are understood. Movement stories are fashioned in part out of such cultural understandings. For further elaboration on the relationship between collective action frames and narratives, see chapters 1, 2, and 10 in this volume.

7. In order to sustain its prevailing narrative, RRPN had carefully controlled slogans, banners, and press releases during the preceding summer's encampment. Confrontational signs and messages attacking Pantex employees had been forbidden. Restrictions were relaxed somewhat for the 1985 event after several RRPN supporters complained that the 1984 controls had been too repressive.

8. At first glance, the phrase "unauthorized act of civil disobedience" might seem to be an oxymoron, inasmuch as all acts of civil disobedience are against authority and therefore "unauthorized." However, from a narrative perspective, this phrase makes sense. In essence, the woman was saying that the rumored act of civil disobedience planned by the "punkers" would violate the movement's narrative and thus was not appropriate.

9. Ironically, the first of nine published and posted RRPN norms ("Discipline of the Pantex Peace Camp") read: "Our attitude will be one of *openness and respect towards all people.*" (Red River Peace Network 1985: 2; emphasis added).

10. Various social movements and other interest groups actively lobbied to affect exhibits at Smithsonian's Air and Space Museum, the Holocaust Museum, the Lawrence Livermore Laboratory Museum in California, Bradbury Science Museum in Los Alamos, the Strategic Air Command Museum near Omaha, the War-Dead Memorial Peace Prayer Hall in Tokyo, and the Neue Wache War Memorial in Berlin (Benford 1996).

PART TWO

Analysis of Narrative in Social Movements

FOUR

"Getting Our Histories Straight"

Culture, Narrative, and Identity in the Self-Help Movement

JOHN STEADMAN RICE

> [N]arrative history of a certain kind turns out to be the basic
> and essential genre for the characterization of human actions.
> —MacIntyre, *After Virtue*, 2nd Ed.

As the opening epigraph suggests, this chapter will discuss narrative as a fundamental resource for achieving a coherent understanding of human action, both at the individual and, since there is an inescapable tie between the two (Mead 1934, 1978), the communal levels. Narrative's overarching significance in social life is perhaps nowhere more clearly and forcefully demonstrated than in the recent proliferation of the identity-related groups and organizations that fall under the larger rubric of New Social Movements (NSMs). Using data derived from my research on one such group, this chapter examines the role of narrative in CoDependents Anonymous (CoDA).

CoDA was and is but one of a plethora of self-help groups formed in the 1980s and 1990s that were modeled (albeit often very loosely) on Alcoholics Anonymous (AA) and its Twelve-Step program of recovery from alcohol addiction. The proliferation of this particular genre of self-help group, as I have argued at length elsewhere (Rice 1996; see especially chapter 2), constituted what can fairly be described as a "codependency movement" (see also Bethune 1990; Greenberg 1994; Kaminer 1992). That movement, in turn, can readily be subsumed within NSM theory and research, which assigns a prominent role to culture in the development of movements, placing special emphasis on culture's status as a source of and resource for collective symbolization and identification (see Johnston and

Klandermans 1995a, 1995b; Laraña, Johnston, and Gusfield 1994). The resources that CoDA provides its members—as do similar groups—are a life narrative for the organization of identity and the "communities" that provide the social recognition in and through which, as Peter Berger puts it, "identity is socially bestowed [and] socially sustained." (1963: 98).

Several interrelated points will guide this analysis. First of all, I take both collective and individual identity to possess a narrative character. That is, there is a narrative structure to individual identity, and this structure is derived from collective—cultural—narratives in relation to which, and *only* in relation to which, the story of an individual life can be rendered anything other than purely idiosyncratic (Bruner 1987; MacIntyre 1984; Rice 1992). The story of an individual life—and the coherence of individual identity—depends, for its very intelligibility, on the stories of collective identity that constitute a culture. Herein lies a significant link between and among the sociology of culture, social psychology, and social movements: the widespread public appeal of identity-oriented NSMs stems from their role in making possible alternative forms of individual and collective identity, particularly during a period in which culture has, to some significant degree, lost its capacity to effectively carry out this task. NSMs accomplish this not insubstantial result by offering to their members alternative narratives for making sense of their lives. These stories—whether accurate or inaccurate, sublime or ridiculous (and these, as we will see, are important considerations)—facilitate the creation of collective identity and the social relationships that embody that identity, thereby making particular kinds of individual identity possible.

CULTURE, NARRATIVE, AND THE ORGANIZATION OF IDENTITY

Save among the most dedicated solipsists, it is axiomatic that cultures and societies organize individual identity. The term for this organizing function, of course, is socialization, which—as any introductory sociology textbook tells us—comprises a lifelong process of social interaction, defined by the exchange of significant symbols (Cooley 1964; Mead 1934, 1978). In the course of interaction, neophytes learn not only language but also systems of classification, meaning construction, and moral differentiation. Most salient for present purposes is that the components of culture into and by which we are socialized also possess a narrative character, providing accounts of the collectivity's history—stories chronicling how and why we, as a society, came to be as we are, and of what we will or aspire to be in the future.

The intrinsically narrative character of cultures issues from the central characteristics of narrative itself—of which, for the purposes of this analysis, it is helpful to emphasize three: *description, explanation,* and *thematic unification.* A narrative, of course, is a story, a "writing up" and/or retelling of significant events and figures in an individual's or collectivity's lived experiences.[1] This retelling is by and large a descriptive task, a public accounting of what happened, when and where it happened, who was involved, and why it was and is significant.

As Arthur Danto (1968) has pointed out, however, narratives always do more than describe events: indeed, they impose an order on lived experience, establishing, *inter alia,* a temporal sequence *to* those events and, in doing so, simultaneously propose at least rudimentary cause-and-effect relations between and among them. By positing an order of occurrence to the events they describe, narratives proffer explanations: the described events play themselves out across time, one following logically (even if sometimes unexpectedly) from another, such that a prior event is portrayed as a necessary antecedent in the overall chain of events. This temporal order, therefore, works retrospectively, accounting for present circumstances—where I am (or we are) now—as the outcome of prior events.

The conventional name for collective narratives is, of course, history. The history of a people is possessed of precisely those descriptive, explanatory, and thematically unifying components that constitute any narrative. Themes such as freedom, progress, and justice, for example, comprise the symbolic foundations of culture, but they are at the same time fundamental components in the (grand) narrative histories of Western republics, representing ideas and ideals to which those societies aspire, and against which present conditions are always assayed.[2] The ideals constitute the collective *telos*: they are the ends, in relation to which all that has come before, all that is, and all that is yet to come must be and are understood.

The foregoing points bring us full circle, harkening back to MacIntyre's observation that narrative is the "basic and essential genre for the characterization of human actions" (1984: 208). Narrative is the basic and essential genre at both the collective and the individual level, since cultural narratives serve as the bases for the organization of individual identity as well.[3] As MacIntyre puts it, "the story of my life is always embedded in the story of those communities from which I derive my identity" (1984: 221). Jerome Bruner also emphasizes the narrative tie between cultural and individual identity, noting the following:

> One important way of characterizing a culture is by the narrative models it makes available for describing the course of a life. And the tool kit of any culture is replete not only with a store of canonical life narratives (heroes, Marthas, tricksters, etc.), but with combinable formal constituents from which its members can construct their own life narratives. (1987: 15)

Given this "cultural shaping" of the types of self that it is possible to be, Bruner continues, it is inevitable that "we [individuals] also become variants of the culture's canonical forms" (15; on the contextual nature of identity, see also Berger 1963; Berger and Luckmann 1966; Frank 1961).

As with the broader cultural narratives from which such "autobiographical narratives" derive (Bruner 1987; Denzin 1990; Rice 1992), the narrative character of individual identity is reflected in both our own and others' understandings of our actions. Because narrative thematically unifies and explains a life, it becomes possible to sensibly account—to myself and others—for why I take *this*, rather than some other, course of action: I do so because I aspire to this, rather than some other, goal, or—alternately—because I was subject to this, rather than some other, experience or set of experiences in the past. The point here is that people describe, explain, and make overall sense of what they are doing now—whatever that may be—by way of a narrative that imposes a unifying order to the events of their lives. These explanations, these narratives of one's life, are, as we have seen, drawn from the fount of available cultural narratives. Without cultural narratives, the coherence of individual identity is imperiled, if not impossible.

NARRATIVE, IDENTITY, AND CULTURAL CHANGE

Cultural values and social structures are, of course, not monolithic (Halton 1992; Turner 1967, 1974). The values that come to define a people—and so too the stories that document the collective realization and/or pursuit *of* those values—have, throughout history, periodically been matters of public contention and conflict. These "crises of legitimacy" ushered in, and have continually punctuated, the modern era (Durkheim 1965; Hunt 1984; Turner 1974). Just as cultural values and social structures are not monolithic, neither are collective narratives eternally persuasive. Indeed, the birth of the modern age testifies to precisely this point. By the late eighteenth century, the core ideals underlying the European feudal and monarchical system had been thoroughly (if not universally) repudiated, supplanted by the Enlightenment values of freedom, reason, progress, democracy, and so on. New narratives were created and required—narratives that took as their starting point the inequities and inadequacies of the feudal and monarchical system, the innate human capacity for reason, the virtues of democratic governance, and so on. These core premises came to be formulated in, and thematically unified by, an historical narrative of collective progress "necessarily" brought about by revolution (Hunt 1984, 1988).[4]

One need not be a postmodernist to recognize that, over the course of the past thirty years, "traditional" collective narratives have suffered a fundamental crisis of legitimacy. The Lyotardian (1984) perspective—that this crisis reached critical mass in the 1960s and 1970s—was and is embodied in the anti–Vietnam War movement; the multiple manifestations of the Civil Rights movement (race, ethnicity, gender, sexual preference); the youth culture or "countercultural movement," more generally; as well as in the birth of NSMs. This article is plainly not the venue for sorting out all of the developments leading up to or issuing from the cultural and societal upheavals of that tumultuous era (see Gitlin 1987 for a thoughtful insider's analysis of the youth culture; for a no less thoughtful, but much more critical analysis, see Collier and Horowitz 1989). What *is* of immediate pertinence for the purposes of this analysis is the steadily shrinking range of collective narratives in and since that era. It is important to be clear about the latter point: it is emphatically *not* the case that narrative *per se* has lost its significance in social life and in coherently characterizing human action (Fine 1995; Goodman 1978; Kerby 1991). Rather, it is more accurate to describe what has occurred as a demonopolization, if you will, of large-scale collective narratives, and an accompanying proliferation of alternative narratives of both collective and individual identity.

As a voluminous body of research now demonstrates, psychotherapeutic discourse has been a key source of, and a key symbolic resource for, a plethora of these alternative narratives. The widespread public acceptance of a therapeutic worldview over the past thirty years has been characterized as the *Triumph of the Therapeutic* (Rieff 1966): a development embodied in the rise of the *Psychological Society* (Gross 1978), populated by *Psychological Man* (Boyers 1975), a person living by *New Rules* (Yankelovich 1982), and possessed of a thoroughly "therapeutic attitude" (Bellah et al. 1985), in which the principal justification for pursuing any course of action is the degree to which it satisfies the individual's overall sense of personal satisfaction and well-being. This *Shrinking of America* (Zilbergeld 1983) has engendered and is embodied by *The Fall of Public Man* (Sennett 1976), and by *The Master Trend* of "free agency," in which "the interests of the individual take precedence over the needs of the family, the rights of an organization, or the power of the state" (Russell 1993: 27–28).

As this last observation indicates, a profoundly anti-institutional orientation lies at the heart of therapeutic culture, the core premise of which is that the self must not be subordinated to externally imposed and collective demands. This orientation, in turn, underscores why these cultural changes have often been characterized as "revolutionary" in nature (Inglehart 1991; Martin 1981; Rieff 1966): they have literally entailed a reversal in how millions of Americans think about and try to organize the relationship between self and society. Whereas a generation ago, people were much more inclined to see the self as of secondary importance to society, in the past thirty years those inclinations have been inverted: social norms and proprieties are now seen (by many, but by no means all, Americans) as antithetical to psychological health (Russell 1993; Veroff, Douvan, and Kulka 1981). It has become all but customary to see the cultural and societal shaping of identity in negative terms—to view cultural control of identity as "repressive" and stultifying, as a denial of one's "true self" grounded in a conformist and authoritarian culture.

This anti-institutional orientation is rooted in the discourse of "human potential," or, as I have called it elsewhere (Rice 1992, 1994, 1996), "liberation psychotherapy"—a neo-Freudian discourse embodied in a potpourri of clinical and theoretical modalities, all of which, despite superficial differences among them, are guided by two core assumptions: (1) that virtually all psychological sickness is the product of cultural/societal control of the self (as in, "repression"), and (2) that humans are by nature a benevolent, beatific, and constructive species.

These two assumptions underlie all liberation therapy discourse. Consider, for example, the following observations by Abraham Maslow—the creator and principal exponent of the notion of *self-actualization*, a term that plainly assumes the existence of an *actual* self (existing prior to and independent of cultural influence) that can, under the right circumstances, be brought into being (see Maslow 1964, 1968, 1970). Maslow asserts—as he did throughout his career—that every person, *under good conditions*, will make good choices. As the emphasized lines in the following passage indicate, it is clear that by "good conditions," Maslow means "in the absence of collectively-imposed expectations or demands."

> "Good conditions" can be defined in terms of a good free-choice situation. Everything is there that the organism might need or choose or prefer. *There is no external constraint to choose one action or thing rather than another. The organism has not already had a choice build* [*sic*] *in from past habituation, familiarization, negative or positive conditionings or reinforcements, or extrinsic and (biologically) arbitrary cultural evaluations. . . . In other words, 'good conditions' means mostly (entirely?) good conditions permitting truly free choice by the organism.* This means that good conditions permit the intrinsic, instinctoid nature of the organism to show itself by its preferences. It tells us what it prefers, and we now assume these preferences to express its needs, i.e., all that which is necessary for the organism to be itself, and to prevent it from becoming less than itself. . . . [T]his free-choice 'wisdom' is easily destroyed in the human being by previous habituation [and] cultural conditioning. (1964: 97–98; emphasis in original)

In short, Maslow is arguing that the integrity and health of the individual self depends on negating, and/or being liberated from, the "extrinsic" requirements of collective identity. Free from cultural repression ("previous habituation [and] cultural conditioning"), the self ("the organism") can express its innate ("instinctoid") morality and needs.

What is particularly important to recognize in Maslow's assumptions about the self and society—and these are representative of all liberation psychotherapy—is that they comprise the foundations for an alternative narrative of identity. Drawing on these assumptions, people whose present lives are marked by unhappiness, disappointment, or confusion about who they are or how they arrived in their present circumstances, can quite readily pull together a life narrative. This narrative *describes* their present state as psychologically troubled, *explains* those troubles as the product of cultural repression of their "true selves," and *thematically unifies* their past and present experiences.

ENTER CODEPENDENCY

For the purposes of this analysis, the significance of liberation psychotherapy's rise to a position of cultural dominance is twofold: on the one hand, it has become one of the principal factors contributing to problems with identity; on the other hand, and more than a little paradoxically, it has also—and at the same time—become the principal cultural symbolism for both characterizing and ostensibly resolving problems with identity. Both of these functions are essential to understanding codependency's emergence.

The role that liberation therapy plays in contributing to identity problems stems from its profoundly anti-institutional orientation. Promulgating the message that any and all cultural control of the self is a pathogenic force, liberation psychotherapy partakes of what Rochberg-Halton has called "the 'fiction' of modern individualism" (1986: 38), asserting that a stable identity can exist outside of, and thoroughly autonomous from, social and cultural influence and context. As Rochberg-Halton explains, "The meaning of uniqueness, individuality, and originality always resides in and for the common good, the cultivation of the community, both within and outside the individual person" (39). The assertion that a pre- or suprasocial self is possible is a fiction because *"this separate 'I,' the 'private I,' if you will . . . has no separate existence of its own"* (38; emphasis in original).

Although liberation therapy provides people with a ready-made narrative of personal identity, it simultaneously calls for actions that make that identity all but impossible for the individual to maintain. Because it portrays the relationship between self and society as exclusively adversarial, and equates psychological health with the individual's freedom from collective expectation, the liberation therapy narrative exhorts its adherents to separate themselves from the communities in which individual identities are derived and maintained. Moreover, to the extent that those communities are themselves no more and no less the embodiment of collectively held understandings of how one ought to live, the repudiation of those understandings logically leads to the destabilization of the communities themselves. After all, the narrative explicitly identifies psychological sickness as a function of individuals' willingness to stay in (or inability to leave) a relationship (friendship, kinship, marriage) that is constraining or emotionally unsatisfying, to abide by religious injunctions that curtail the realm of free choice, or simply to abide by banal social norms for daily interaction. As we have already seen, a wealth of evidence has pointed both to the widespread public embrace of these therapeutic ideals *and* to the accompanying destabilization of social institutions—especially those institutions in and through which individual identity is created and maintained. It is in this context, and in response to the problems that context creates, that codependency was born.

As a symbolic mechanism for assaying and dealing with identity problems, liberation therapy is embodied in and expressed by the emergence of codependency and the groups organized around the codependency discourse. Before examining that role in greater depth, however, a brief clarification is necessary. Although the term *codependency* was coined to identify a psychological "condition," it is better understood as a distinctive way of talking about self, society, and the relationship between the two. The creators of the codependency discourse have long claimed that "95 percent" of the U.S. population suffers from the condition (see Bradshaw 1988: 172; Schaef 1986: 14, 18; Whitfield 1986: 24). Plainly, such a claim is not a serious attempt at diagnosis, but rather the articulation of a cultural critique. In using the term *codependency*, therefore, I understand it not so much as a "condition" but as a cultural critique and a narrative of identity.

Describing and Explaining "the Condition"

Beginning in the mid-1980s, codependency's creators—a handful of people, all of whom were themselves members of Anonymous groups and were employed as counselors in the addiction treatment industry, including John Bradshaw, Melody Beattie, and Anne Wilson Schaef—reported that they had encountered over the past two-plus decades a disturbingly large and apparently growing number of people with all manner of serious life problems. These problems included the drug and alcohol problems with which these counselors were familiar, along with incest, physical and sexual abuse, extensive sexual adventuring, compulsive gambling, eating disorders, excessive spending, emotional volatility, and so on. The counselors took it upon themselves to make sense of this proliferation in both the number and type of problems they confronted in their work. The concept and narrative of codependency was the result.

In formulating codependency, its creators shared two characteristics. First, as I have demonstrated at great length elsewhere (Rice 1996), all were liberation psychotherapists. Second, all were immersed in the Twelve-Step addiction recovery subculture. It is important to note that in both liberation psychotherapy and the Twelve-Step subculture, understandings of personal and social problems are highly individualized. Cultural transformations and social structures simply play no role. Not surprisingly, with this baseline orientation, codependency's creators produced a narrative that reduces the diffuseness of experience and the panoply of problems addressed to a single "condition"—"codependency"—which is portrayed as both an addiction and the cause of all other addictive behaviors. The list of behaviors said to be manifestations of the "disease" of codependency includes not only alcoholism and drug addiction, but also spouse abuse, eating disorders, sexual abuse, promiscuity, and a lengthy list of other life problems (Beattie 1987; Bradshaw 1988; Whitfield 1986).

Since the range of problems covered by codependency went well beyond dependencies on mind-altering substances, in defining life problems as addictions, the creators of codependency needed an altogether new conception of addiction. This new conception they called "process" or "activity" addiction.[5] As Anne Wilson Schaef explains,

> A process addiction is an addiction (by individuals, groups, even societies) to a way (or the process) of acquiring the addictive substance. The function of an addiction is to keep us out of touch with ourselves (our feelings, morality, awareness—our living process). (1986: 24)

In addition to this new concept of addiction, codependency's creators also developed a causal model of addiction that takes as its bedrock the concepts of the "true self" and "repression." This causal model represents an explanation for the way that people's lives have gone.

The addiction model of codependency offers a "horror story" (Fine 1995) in which people's sickness (their addiction) is the product of their socialization—and hence, repression—by a sick society. Punctuating the "horror," repression is framed as "abandonment" and "abuse." John

Bradshaw, perhaps the most strident advocate of this logic, maintains that conventional society is based on what he calls a "poisonous pedagogy"—a system of conformist rules that "glorif[ies] obedience, orderliness, logic, rationality . . . [and] power." For Bradshaw, the entire social and cultural order embodies and perpetuates this "poison." "Many of our religious institutions offer authoritarian support for these [rules]. Our schools reinforce them. Our legal system reinforces them. . . . *[They] are carried by family systems, by our schools, our churches, and our government*" (1988: 166–167, 8, 187; emphasis in original). Defining socialization as abandonment and abuse engenders an inevitably long list of abusive practices. Bradshaw, for example, argues that families abandon and abuse children by "not modeling their own emotions for their children . . . not being there to affirm their children's expression of emotion . . . not providing for the children's developmental dependency needs . . . [and by] not giving them their time, attention and direction" (3).

In the addiction model, the true self, by contrast, is the "inner child" who—in accordance with liberation therapy—both possesses and represents the essential benevolence of human nature. The inner child, one reads in all codependency treatises, is "spontaneous, expansive, loving, giving, and communicating . . . expressive, assertive, and creative. . . . It is healthily self-indulgent, taking pleasure in receiving and being nurtured" (Whitfield 1986: 10). To recover from codependency is to get in touch with and learn to freely express this inner child.

"BECOMING" CODEPENDENT

In many ways, codependency simply reiterates what are by now widely accepted therapeutic ideas and ideals. But by fusing those ideas and ideals with themes from the discourse of addiction, the narrative of codependency enables the formation of groups possessed of a shared understanding of themselves and their lots in life. This is the principal source of CoDA's appeal. People first come to CoDA with a set of disappointments, dissatisfactions, and confusions. In CoDA meetings, these "newcomers," as they are called, encounter friendly and supportive people who also have stories of broken relationships, uncertain and impermanent ties to others, and doubts about themselves. Going to the meetings is one way to deal with such problems: there is always someone with whom to talk, to share ideas, to commiserate. In a confusing and discouraging world, these are indeed attractive features.

Those who come to CoDA for access to a set of social relationships learn that the surest way to maintain these relationships is to become a member—and the surest way to be a member is to "become" codependent: to begin to talk about, and understand, one's life as fellow codependents do. Becoming codependent is a process of conversion. It is not necessary, nor is there adequate space in this context, to discuss the conversion process in depth (see Rice 1996, chapter 6), but a brief illustration will be helpful. At the beginning of CoDependents Anonymous meetings, those in attendance introduce themselves to the group. The introduction is generic: a first name and, almost always, the accompanying self-identification: "And I'm codependent."

At one meeting, a woman introduced herself saying, "Hi, I'm Linda, and I'm just here to listen and find out whether I think this fits me or not." Eschewing the customary "and I'm codependent," Linda identified herself as a newcomer. Asked if this was her first CoDA meeting, Linda said, "No, I've been to two or three other meetings with Susan, there," nodding in the direction of a woman seated across from her. "She's the one that first told me she thought I might get something out of this." Several people said, "Welcome," and the meeting leader added, "We usually suggest that you come to at least six meetings before you make up your mind if CoDA's for you, or not."

The meeting progressed as usual, with members eventually taking turns telling their personal versions of the codependency story to the group. When a young woman documented her woes with her "emotionally unavailable" husband, Linda, the newcomer, began nodding her head. Her nods grew increasingly vehement as the woman continued, and she began to shift about in her chair. After the young wife's story wound down, the designated group leader said, "Linda, you seem to have heard something you could relate to." She responded,

> That's me. What she said, that's me. That's my husband. That's our marriage. God! To a "tee." Wow. And I've been muddling along, thinking I was the only one. Well, no—I mean I knew I wasn't, all you've got to do is look around. There's a lot of people that feel the same way. But, you know? Nobody to really talk to about this stuff. Stuck in a lousy relationship, no clue what to do about it. That gets really lonely. I mean, if what

you've all been saying is what you mean by codependency, well hell, I'm as codependent as it gets. You're going to be seeing me around here a lot from here on out, I can tell you that.

On this occasion Linda took a first step in the process of becoming codependent. This is a step all CoDA members must take. Linda did not talk of her problems as the product of childhood abandonment and abuse, or as the "symptoms" of an addiction—she did not yet use the narrative for the emplotment of her own experience. But by identifying with another's version of the narrative she had moved in that direction.

Whether Linda and other newcomers go on to talk about their lives in the requisite ways depends on whether they hear something they can "relate to" or identify with. In all probability many will, for the most common themes in CoDA—failed marriages and broken relationships, as well as their concomitants, single parenthood, isolation, confusion—are familiar refrains in contemporary American life. Hearing members discuss their own problems, and seeing them treated with kindness and empathy, Linda decided to come back; as she said, if trouble with marriage "is what you all mean by codependency . . . you're going to be seeing me around here a lot."

But there is a good deal more involved with what it means to "be" codependent than simply having a troubled marriage. Ongoing access to the supportive relationships that newcomers like Linda find at CoDA meetings requires "becoming" codependent, and this is a process demanding members' ability to talk about themselves and their lives in and through the narrative of codependency.

GETTING OUR HISTORIES STRAIGHT

Conversion entails working to make one's life story conform to the narrative of codependency. In CoDA, the members call this "history work," or "getting our histories straight." Ann's remarks illustrate the point:

> I've done a lot of work on my history—which they talk about in CoDA: "Get your history straight." I thought my history was fine, but then I started to work on it, and I realized that I don't have one recollection of my mother or father spending any time with me; there was a lot of abandonment. The abuse was very

subtle in my family, because the messages from my father . . .
were that you were the best, . . . but the way I interpreted them
was . . . that you could always do better, and that somehow
what you did gave you your worth.

Before coming to CoDA, and deciding that she wanted to be a member,
Ann "thought [her] history was fine." But the codependent's life story,
predicated as it is on the experience of "abandonment and abuse" in
childhood, demands that she do some history work and uncover some
instances of abandonment and abuse. If she is to have access to the ongoing social support that CoDA provides, she needs to emplot her experience on the model of codependency in the requisite fashion.

Ann's was not an isolated anecdote. Indeed, CoDA members frequently alluded to their efforts to assure that their biographies conformed
to the codependency narrative. Mary, in the midst of a discussion of her
adult problems with drugs and alcohol, reported that she knew those
problems stemmed from her abuse as a child. She knew this, moreover,
even though

> I don't have a lot of memories of childhood. I have sporadic
> memories. I've been told that the reason for that is that they're
> either too scary or too painful to remember, and that when it's
> time, the memories will come.

History work, as the term implies, entails reinterpreting one's biography in light of present circumstances. There are variants on the core narrative structure, but the essentials remain the same. For example, some
members reframe experience using the concept of shame or "toxic
shame." A member named Donna, for instance, explained that, as the
result of her history work, she had concluded that shame was the root
cause of her alcoholism.

> The way shame has manifested itself in my life is an awareness
> [of] the way I acted out not being wanted. It was a tremendous
> awareness for me when I realized I acted out my shame in many,
> many different ways in my adult life, and then I could go back
> and see where those feelings came from and why I did what I did
> as an adult. I came from a very dysfunctional family. My father
> died when I was two, and I was the last of eight children, and my
> mother was forty-two years old. I used to kid a lot about her not

> wanting me, and then I got in touch with the shame of not being wanted. I acted out that feeling of not being wanted through alcohol. Whenever I was feeling that I was not being wanted, I had to use other substances so that I couldn't feel. I came from another Twelve-Step program, and one of the biggest shame spirals that I felt as an adult was when I drank after eighteen years of sobriety. This was one of the most difficult things that I ever had to go through, and I realized—through CoDependents Anonymous— that the reason that I couldn't get sober again was because of my shame. I did not deserve to be sober. I was not wanted. I had no place in the universe. When I got to the place where I could see the shame behind this, the necessity to drink . . . left me.

Based on what Donna has said here, it is not clear how she was shamed as a child. Her reference to "kidding [about] not being wanted" has been transformed into the "reality" of not being wanted—a necessary condition for her later ability to "[get] in touch with the shame of not being wanted." Despite the ambiguities, however, what *is* clear is the role of the codependency narrative, and of history work, in how she has emplotted her life story. "Through CoDependents Anonymous," Donna has learned that she "did what [she] did as an adult," because, whether her mother did in fact tell her she was unwanted or not, Donna did not feel wanted. As a process addict, she "acted out" her shame about this "in many, many different ways," including alcoholism. Using the discourse to reconstruct and characterize her own actions, she sees now that she could not be sober because of her shame.

It is abundantly clear that CoDA members understand their membership to be contingent upon being able to produce the appropriate autobiographical credentials. The codependency narrative both requires their reconstruction of biography and provides them with the tools to accomplish it. This understanding underlies Sue's reference to codependency as "a handbook." In CoDA, she reported, she and her husband are

> learning that we have buttons that get pushed by each other and by other people if we let those buttons get pushed. . . . [I]f I get into having . . . discomfort, that definitely is a signal that there is a shame attack going on. . . . So what I've learned to do . . . is when I feel those signals coming on, *I get out my codependent's handbook and I look at the patterns and I look at the characteristics*

and I ask myself which one fits, what's going on with me right now? (emphasis added)

It is hard to imagine a clearer statement of the extent to which CoDA members realize that they must become adept at using the symbolic and narrative structure of codependency in order to formulate and tell their stories. Sue, as with Donna, has found "shame" in the codependent's handbook, and uses that concept to organize her understanding of experience and the story she now tells of her life.

The realization that being codependent requires telling a codependent's life story is encoded in and expressed by the very concept of history work; the idea of "getting our histories straight" suffuses CoDA meetings. At times, as might be expected, these biographical requirements engender stories containing curious connections and demanding a high level of credulity. May's story—which also works around the concept of shame—is a case in point.

> I'm shame-based. I don't want you to know who I am because that hurts. My shame originates with my family of origin. *I didn't know it until just joining CoDA.* I knew from another Twelve-Step program that I knew how to live with addicted people, but I didn't know why I responded the way I did all my life, and I knew it was more than just the addicted people in my life, that *it had to start from my family of origin, so I started searching back to that. And I came up with emotional incest,* a lot of verbal abuse, not so much directed at me as at my mother and other people in the family. A lot of complex, underneath type of derogatory remarks. I also felt that my nationality was questioned. I was a minority in a small farming community—I'm Norwegian, by the way, full-blooded Norwegian—and somebody once said to me as a child, "oh, you're a Swede turned inside out." I believed that. I didn't know the impression it had on me until CoDA. And being a girl, the last in a family of four, my mother and father were directly from Norway, and they spoke Norwegian when I was small. I didn't understand that. They argued a lot when I was small. I took that on as my responsibility, and I learned to be a people-pleaser; I learned how to smile when I was hurting inside and to laugh a lot. I learned how

to be a nice person. Today, I know that they were coping skills
to get along in life. (emphasis added)

Not "until [joining] CoDA" did May recognize the enduring significance
of her childhood experiences. Once in CoDA, May "knew" that her problems "had to" start with her family of origin. "So," as she says, "I started
searching back to that," and eventually she "came up with emotional
incest."

The point is not to impugn May, but to underscore the significance of
her remarks and of the codependency narrative's influence over the story
she now tells of her life: nothing she says suggests incest or explains what
"emotional incest" is. Furthermore, even the "verbal abuse" to which she
refers—if her anecdote about the ethnic insult is what she means by this
abuse—took place outside of her family. But whatever May might or
might not mean by her comments, she clearly understands that if she is to
be codependent, she is expected to get her history straight—to go back
into her past and "come up with" something, some incident of abuse, in
order to qualify as a *bona fide* member of the CoDA community.

The narrative requirements of membership also inform the following
brief observation. In the course of sharing the results of her own history
work, Pat announced to her CoDA group, "As some of you know, I know
I was abused as a child, I just don't remember it. But I've been working on
that in therapy—going back into the past and trying to bring the memories into clearer focus."

There is no irony in the members' uses of concepts such as "history
work," or their observations that they turn to the "codependent's handbook" in order to "come up with" the required biographical credentials.
Indeed, in all of the testimonials I heard over the course of my field observations at CoDA meetings, the most striking aspect of the members' stories—aside from their recurrent similarities—was their overarching
credulity. On only one occasion did a member's comments directly
address the degree to which CoDA and the narrative of codependency
structure rather than capture converts' life experiences. A man named
Dave, sharing at a CoDA meeting, announced that when he shares at
CoDA meetings, there have been times that

I've said things that, even while I'm saying them, I think to
myself—"Whoa, wait a minute. Did I just say that? Why? It's
not true. That never happened"—but I say them anyway.

Dave did not explore the implications of his remarks or develop them more fully. To do so would have violated the expectations of being codependent. As such, he concluded his testimony with the assertion that the disparity between his own life experiences and those his new reality requires of him is a by-product of the role itself:

> Part of it is that I'm not used to talking about my life to a group of people, and so I guess I get carried away, or something. I'm still learning how to share, and how to be comfortable doing that.

As Dave says, some of what he has said may reflect getting "carried away," but a far larger part of it is that the role of being codependent is determined by the narrative of codependency. The codependent life story provides adherents with a story to tell regardless of failed, nonexistent, or cloudy recollection, and being a CoDA member requires fitting one's life into that story. Thus, members interpret the absence of memories of abuse as a sign of denial, and an inability to remember the past as a certain indication that it is, as Mary said, "too scary or too painful to remember," rather than that the past may have simply been uneventful. The role of the codependent is defined by codependency's description of their problems as the signs of an addiction, and by its explanation that the addiction is caused by the abuses and abandonments of life in a repressive culture.

NARRATIVE, IDENTITY, AND CULTURAL CHANGE, REDUX

The recurrent underlying motif of codependents' stories is that the cultural changes of the past generation have had profound and often painful consequences for them, embodied especially in the instability of their most significant social relationships—families, friendships, neighborhoods, and communities. In CoDA, lonely and disillusioned people gather to commiserate with one another, listening to one another tell the stories of their struggles. Small wonder that CoDA members often refer to fellow members as their "family of affiliation," and identify their regular group as the "home meeting."

CoDA members themselves have learned to reframe their problems as symptoms of their own "disease" rather than as part of the larger dynamics of cultural and societal changes. As earlier testimonials have shown, the members' problems and how those problems are portrayed are often loosely coupled, at best. At times, this coupling is so loose that members temporarily slip out of the CoDA vernacular. At those moments, it is clear that immediate and pressing problems are central. Ron, for example, discussed the problems he has faced since his divorce. He had recently declared bankruptcy:

> But I don't want to talk about that so much. I've been having a hell of a time with my kids since the divorce—which also had something to do with my bankruptcy, too. But, I'm not getting a lot of time with my kids.

He explained that both of his sons are young teenagers, both have part-time jobs, and

> their jobs are at completely opposite ends of the city. So, I pick them up, take them to work, and go home. Pick them up again a few hours later. Shit. I don't call that top-notch time, do you?. . . When they aren't working, my youngest one wants me to be a "Disneyland Dad." You know, "Buy me this, buy me that." I love him with all my heart, and it's hard, because he just doesn't understand that I can't afford to do that. I'm broke, and even though I know better, I'm embarrassed about that.

He said that after he had dropped his boys off at their mother's a few nights earlier, he went home in low spirits.

> I walk into my pukey, quiet little apartment, and I turn on the television, and it's one of those 1940s, happy-ending, happy family movies, and I just lost it. Burst out crying—and I don't mean tears down the cheeks. I mean wailing like a baby. I'm sure my neighbors must've heard me, but I don't care. Anyway, I felt better after that cry. Still do. Things'll work out. It's just hard, is all. It *is* hard. I just thank God I've got you all to come babble at. Thanks.

Like Ron, CoDA members wrestle with such familiar problems as divorce, and the accompanying problems with money, child custody, loneliness, sadness, and disillusionment. Being codependent gives them somewhere to go, and someone with whom to share their burdens.

In and through the standard conventions for telling a plausible story, then, codependency provides—for those who "become" codependent—a way to make sense of the confounding, confusing, and frustrating nature of life in the wake of significant cultural and societal change. It is, at bottom, a simple narrative requiring no special aptitude or training to make it one's own. And the pay-off for becoming fluent at telling one's life story as the codependent narrative requires is the continued access to a group of people with similar problems, a shared orientation toward those problems, and a supportive and empathetic posture.

By offering a narrative of identity that went beyond liberation psychotherapy's solipsism, codependency engendered a social movement of substantial proportions. Unheard of before 1986, the narrative of codependency grew in its first four years to include 2,088 weekly CoDependents Anonymous meetings throughout the United States. This resounding success tells us a great deal not only about the continuing significance of narrative as a resource for the characterization of human action and the enduring importance of collective identity, but also, perhaps, about the impoverished communal vocabulary of the therapeutic culture.

NOTES

1. To speak of "significant" events and figures is to highlight the point that cultural history is invariably the product of selections from and interpretations of lived experience: someone, usually an elite (Rieff 1966), decides what will be selected and what will be excluded. On the general importance of selection processes in cultural history and analysis, see also Foucault 1972; Williams 1961; Wuthnow 1987.

2. Whatever else one makes of postmodern theory, its exponents have rightly called our attention to the narrative character of history in their discussions of "grand narratives" (and their demise: Gergen 1991; Lyotard 1984; for a different perspective on these points, see Kumar 1995). Although Lyotard receives recognition for the theme of "the death of grand narratives," the credit rightly goes to C. Wright Mills (1959), who framed his own analysis of the postmodern age in terms of the lost plausibility of such cultural narratives as freedom and reason.

3. It bears mentioning that even a rejection of one's cultural and societal context is to a significant degree shaped *by* culture, as well. As

MacIntyre puts it succinctly, "rebellion against my identity is always one possible way of expressing it" (1984: 221).

4. Revolutionary battles over social position and control over material resources are also battles over symbolic resources. The delegitimation of an established social and cultural order requires a stripping away of that order's claims—whether implicit or explicit—to a sacred status; so, too, the legitimation of a social and cultural order requires establishing its sacred status (Durkheim 1965: 244; see also Hunt 1984 and Mathiez 1904, which examine what Hunt calls the "transference of sacrality" from the *ancien régime* to the revolutionary order).

5. John Bradshaw outlines an extensive list of these process addictions, including perfectionism, striving for power and control, rage, arrogance, criticism, being judgmental, moralizing, caretaking, envy, people-pleasing, and being nice. Further, asserting that "any emotion can be addictive," Bradshaw identifies the addictive potential of sadness, rage, excitement, joy, and religious righteousness (1989: 103–104). "Religious addiction," he adds, "is a massive problem in our society" (104). Bradshaw also lists a wide variety of "activity addictions," including intellectualizing, working, buying, hoarding, reading, gambling, exercising, watching sports and TV, caring for pets, and engaging in sexual relations (105–106).

FIVE

Moving Toward the Light

Self, Other, and the Politics of Experience in New Age Narratives

MICHAEL F. BROWN

> Our behavior is a function of our experience. We act according
> to the way we see things. . . . If our experience is destroyed, we
> have lost our own selves.
>
> —Laing, *The Politics of Experience*

To read R. D. Laing's work today is to revisit an era—temporally close, temperamentally distant—when a renowned psychiatrist could conclude a book with fifteen pages of LSD-inspired word salad and still produce a bestseller.[1] Laing claimed that self-estrangement was ubiquitous in American society, and he blamed it on resistance to the truth of inner experience. In his quest for a prophetic language that would bridge therapy and religion by revealing how an authentic self can achieve healthy communion with others, the mercurial Laing mapped terrain still under exploration by the New Age movement today—more than three decades after the publication of Laing's *The Politics of Experience*.

Informed by a powerful current of millennialism, the New Age holds that humanity is entering a time of transition, at the end of which collective rediscovery of the divine will inspire a social and political renaissance unlike any other in human history. People wary of rigid categories are unlikely to apply one to themselves, and "New Age" is no exception. Some spurn the term; others use it only for ironic effect. But it has stuck nevertheless. Today "New Age" encompasses practices and philosophies as diverse as shamanism, neopaganism, aura reading, goddess worship, channeling, crystal healing, past-life regression therapy, and the performance of rituals inspired by American Indian traditions. Within its ample boundaries some scholars also locate certain new religions—the Church of Scientology, for instance—and quasi-religious groups that draw on the long-standing American obsession with self-improvement.

Since the New Age first came to public attention in the early 1970s, it has puzzled social scientists and cultural critics, who disagree about its scale, significance, and trajectory. Surveying recent publications, one finds some that confidently identify the New Age as a movement of massive proportions and others that dismiss it as an inconsequential audience cult. The popular media, perhaps taking their cue from this scholarly ambivalence, alternately portray the New Age as everywhere and as nowhere at all. The *New York Times* made the latter claim a decade ago in a front-page article assessing the results of a landmark survey of American religious affiliation: "And despite all the attention given to what devotees call the New Age, the number of adherents, 28,000 [in the entire U.S.] is practically insignificant" (Goldman 1991).[2] Only five years later, this supposedly trifling movement had taken up residence in the White House, where Hillary Clinton carried on imaginary conversations with Eleanor Roosevelt under the direction of the therapist Jean Houston. The magazine *Forbes*, a publication not generally known for interest in alternative spirituality, reported in the mid-1990s that New Age workshops, book sales, and related activities generate nearly $14 billion a year in personal spending (Ferguson and Lee 1996), a figure that, if accurate, offers compelling evidence that the movement has a significant public following.

If, as sociologists such as Brulle (1995: 316) argue, a movement's political power may be measured in part by how its rhetoric influences the "definition of what constitutes common-sense reality," then there is ample evidence that the New Age is more influential than many experts are willing to admit. The movement has made possible the emergence of new, explicitly spiritual forms of psychotherapy, a trend that will surely accelerate in the coming decades as affluent baby boomers grapple with mortality. The health-care industry has come to embrace alternative healing modalities—acupuncture, herbal medicines, natural childbirth, and the like—long championed by the New Age. Perhaps more surprising is the movement's impact on management consultants and motivational trainers whose clients include the nation's largest corporations (Bromley and Shupe 1990; Rupert 1992). The pervasiveness of New Age concepts in the world of training seminars came to wide public attention when it was revealed that the Federal Aviation Administration paid $1.4 million in fees to a disciple of the controversial channeler J. Z. Knight for stress management classes attended by FAA employees (Hosenball 1995). In this and other ways, the movement plays an important role in the relentless expansion of therapeutic idioms and perspectives in contemporary life (Nolan 1998; Rieff 1966).

However pervasive the New Age may be, its ideological diffuseness and anti-institutional thrust make it difficult to assess from a traditional social movements perspective. New Age followers typically express skepticism about conventional politics and show little interest in influencing media images of their goals. Social grievances or conflicts with the state seldom become a focus of movement activities.[3] Aside from rare instances when New Age spirituality has taken an authoritarian turn, the movement's collective projects tend to be short-lived, continuing only as long as participants find them mutually therapeutic. These features suggest that the New Age is best considered a "new social movement" (NSM) as defined by Johnston, Laraña, and Gusfield (1994). More than other NSMs, however, the New Age has a consumerist quality that has much to teach us about popular visions of social change in an era when capitalism and the project of the self have become so thoroughly intertwined that the act of making consumer choices is increasingly perceived as a logical and even sacred means of reshaping the social order.[4]

In common with other NSMs, the New Age benefits from the growing fragmentation of communications media. Infinite variations in belief can easily be accommodated by new Internet discussion groups or, to a more limited extent, by cable TV channels directed to niche audiences. This proliferation of media forums, many of which are accessible to groups possessing only modest financial resources, has exerted a powerful leveling effect, as audiences find it harder to distinguish mainstream information sources from those in the cultural borderlands. New Agers see this expansion of perspectives as a positive development, evidence that the monolithic truths of Western Christianity are being contested by more authentic voices.

Given the difficulties of tracking a movement that almost by definition shuns political action and conventional expressions of power, narrative offers a useful point of analytical purchase. Indeed, to an outside observer the New Age seems largely constituted *by* narratives: life histories, tales of spiritual adventure and "self-empowerment," moments of "personal sharing," and accounts of affliction and recovery. The movement's networks and collective gatherings are designed to provide opportunities for storytelling that serves as a unifying force in encounters

otherwise characterized by the centrifugality of individual needs and experiences. In these encounters, one witnesses a potent form of what Silverstein and Urban (1996: 2) call "entextualization," the use of texts to
"create a seemingly shareable, transmittable culture."

In the New Age case, the entextualization process is simultaneously
normative and oppositional. Narratives mobilize group sentiment, create a
web of shared meaning, and demonstrate to participants that their individual work contributes to a panhuman process of spiritual transformation. But narratives and other speech events are also used tactically in
ways that shed light on the movement's underlying misgivings about
stable organizations and their perceived pathologies. In this chapter I offer
an assessment of New Age stories and speech events that draws special
attention to how these contrasting principles are deployed in and through
narrative.[5]

My analysis is based on participant-observation fieldwork undertaken in various parts of the United States between 1990 and 1995. This
research primarily focused on the practice called channeling, a modern
version of spirit mediumship in which human "channels"—a term many
practitioners use in preference to the more familiar "channelers"—enter a
trance with the goal of opening themselves to spiritual beings, who then
communicate to an audience using the voice of their human ally. Because
people drawn to channeling events are also likely to participate in other
expressions of alternative spirituality, I found it necessary to familiarize
myself with related practices that ranged from prosperity consciousness to
fringe psychotherapy. Documenting such a sprawling movement presents
a daunting task for a single ethnographer. Fortunately, there is a growing
body of comparative literature against which my own research can be
evaluated. A review of these sources suggests the account that follows is
representative of New Age social practices, although it should be kept in
mind that some branches of the movement—neopagans, for example—
show greater organizational stability than do the groups documented
here.[6]

LIFE STORIES AS ORGANIZING NARRATIVES

As a movement focused on the transformation of individual lives and, by
a process of spiritual accumulation, all of humanity, it is hardly surprising
that life stories play a central role in New Age encounters. For practition-

ers of specific spiritual or healing techniques, a life-story narrative is a résumé that substitutes for university degrees and other professional credentials. Life histories are offered in background documents that advertise workshops or training sessions, and they may be presented orally by session leaders as part of an opening discussion. In explicitly therapeutic encounters, the life history of the client may be equally important. Indeed, interpretation of a client's life story may be the encounter's ostensible goal.

The life story of Mary Beth Allen, a woman who offers intuitive counseling to clients in Santa Fe, New Mexico, illustrates key features of New Age life stories.[7] Sitting in the shade of her small garden on a warm day in June, Mary Beth described herself as someone who was brought up in an achievement-focused middle-class Jewish household in New England. Her father was a Harvard-educated attorney, her mother a housewife. She is, she said, a "bridge person" who has made the transition from science to spirituality. Her formal education was an extended battle between the halves of the bicameral mind: the scientific half, which led her to complete most of a mathematics major in college, and the intuitive, expressive half, which pushed her in the direction of religion and the arts. A stint with the Peace Corps in Zaire exposed her to African religious practices and helped, as she put it, "to open up my mind." "By the end of my time in Zaire," she said, "I believed in sorcery. It made sense in the African context. Whatever belief system you have makes sense if everyone is believing in it and working from it."

Returning to the United States, she experienced growing tension between the career expectations of her family and internal spiritual currents unleashed by her experiences in Africa. As she commented, "I went through this period when everything fell apart. I've gone through it several times, where everything kind of crumbles and I need a change." She sold her belongings and moved to Santa Fe, which she heard was a beautiful place. There she gravitated to people involved in various kinds of spiritual work, and she began to see a professional psychic who helped to "open doorways." She contrasted the immediacy of these new religious experiences with the more abstract spirituality of her family's Judaism. "Judaism is about being a good person. But to me God was always far away, rather patriarchal. That didn't draw me in." Meditation and a related technique called "visualization," in contrast, gave Mary Beth "a more expanded vision of who and what I was. I felt more peaceful." Eventually her teachers convinced her that she had the gift of psychic insight: "I was told by different psychics that I had a gift. People who live in that realm looked at me and saw something that I was just coming into awareness of. I wound up going out in the world with it very slowly, bit by bit, feeling my way."

These experiments in trying on the role of a spiritual advisor gave Mary Beth new confidence in herself and a real sense of satisfaction. She saw her experience as a process of changing the "thought-forms" that pattern emotions. Most of us, she believes, are "trapped in our heads" and therefore unable to access higher truths that lie in the body:

> We are encouraged to rise up into the head a lot. That was my background. There is so much pain in this culture, so much pain—addictiveness, dysfunctional families . . . We need some way to deal with the violence inside ourselves. We need to find a loving place towards those parts of our self that are in fear. That's the way to make better choices.

She began to see her counseling goal as helping others find an appropriate path to self-understanding and self-love:

> When I work with people, I'm into personal answers. So I say, "There are many ways to worship God. Which one is your way?" That is my focus, not "Oh, you should become a Buddhist." I ask, "What is it that works for you and that really brings you to a fuller and richer life?"

She insisted that her openness leaves room for discrimination, the ability to separate spiritual wheat from chaff:

> I'm skeptical and leery. When I hear about movements like Ramtha [a being who speaks through J. Z. Knight, a celebrity channeler now based in Washington State], I'm sure that although there was some good stuff in there, for a lot of people it was just entertainment, like going to see the latest movie or something. In a way it makes me irritable. . . . I have heard bad stories about psychics who say you should do something this way or that way. They are so full of ego, but it's just crap.

Mary Beth felt that her life has finally arrived at a stage in which she is nearly liberated from the internal messages fostered by family upbringing and by society as a whole, which prevent her and others from understanding who they really are. Her personal history is part of a global process of transformation:

> There is definitely something happening now that is qualitatively and quantitatively different from anything we've faced before as a species. Things have come to a boiling point. We've leaped into global awareness. It's only been the last four hundred years. That's a miniscule amount of time. [New Age spirituality] is something transcendent and extremely powerful that can be used in everyday life, and it's now part of this culture that came out of the Industrial Revolution. It's like a new frontier. It's tremendous. I do believe that I'm part of some flux of awareness or consciousness. I'm just one little bit of it.

This life history underscores several themes common to New Age narratives. One is that contemporary American culture privileges reason over "inner knowing." Mary Beth's personal growth came when she succeeded in freeing herself from the false values of her upbringing and replacing them with a perspective that validated her spiritual gifts and sense of self-worth. This process of self-discovery never ends, for one's needs and understandings evolve throughout the life process. A second and related theme is the arbitrariness of belief, evident in her comments about thought-forms and their mutability. Beliefs and ideas that do not promote individual happiness should be discarded and replaced by ones that work better, a view that might be labeled "cognitive utilitarianism." This in turn helps to explain Mary Beth's insistence that she can be skeptical of spiritual practices that privilege the assertions of one person, usually a charismatic guru or teacher, over the actual experiences of another, typically an emotionally vulnerable client. A third motif concerns the important role that the spiritual efforts of isolated individuals play in contributing to a larger historical process, which will eventually give rise to spiritual rebirth on a global scale.

These themes map discursive fields within which social actors negotiate the collective dimension of New Age practice. By discursive fields I mean something akin to Goffman's "primary frameworks," structures of meaning that define "the sum total of forces and agents that these interpretive designs acknowledge to be loose in the world" (1974: 27). In the New Age case, two discursive fields are especially salient: Self/Other, which encompasses the tension between self-knowledge and group process, and Belief/Experience, which concerns the unstable relationship between discrimination and faith.

SELF AND OTHER: GROUP FEELING AND ITS LIMITS

A key expression of New Age practice is the workshop or "intensive" that brings together a spiritual counselor and an interested audience in an encounter that may last anywhere from a few hours to several weeks. To service the profusion of spirituality workshops across the nation, there has arisen a loose network of conference centers that provide meeting space and, in some cases, more elaborate facilities such as dormitories, meditation rooms, organic gardens, and cafeterias. Conference center catalogs inevitably include photographs of workshop participants basking in good fellowship: dancing, laughing at a speaker's humor, holding hands in a circle, or just sitting together in some attractive (usually rural) setting. In reality, the intimacy depicted in catalogs may be difficult to achieve in gatherings that bring together a group of strangers in an impersonal place. Mainline religious denominations solve this problem by following a liturgy, more or less invariant, that unites visitors in a familiar ritual process. People drawn to New Age events, however, typically value spontaneity and self-expression rather than liturgical order, which represents exactly the kind of formality that they endeavor to avoid. To the extent possible, New Age events should be interactive. Those who organize gatherings of this nature therefore face the challenge of successfully conveying their message, whatever it may be, while simultaneously creating a sense of community and allowing clients to have their say.

When dealing with small audiences, a common opening gambit of presenters is to invite participants to introduce themselves and perhaps offer a few comments about their background and interests. This bridges the distance between expert and audience while helping strangers feel comfortable with one another. Introductions also signal the interests and personal styles of attendees, information that a skilled presenter may use to tailor his or her workshop along appropriate lines. For large audiences, however, individual introductions generally prove impractical. A common alternative strategy is to propose an exercise in visualization, a guided meditation in which the group is led on a relaxing inner journey that binds them together through shared experience.

The following text is part of a guided meditation recorded during a 1991 workshop that took place in a small town in upstate New York. The speaker, a middle-aged woman named Sally, channels several spirit entities who provide her with information that she describes as life-transforming. The setting is a New Age bookstore that rents space for workshops during the evening hours.

> Just let your body relax and feel the individual muscles as they begin to release the tension. The body is a marvelous thing. It holds itself together by means of whirling energy patterns moving unpredictably, singing us to sleep as it clicks and whirs in its balance. So let your body completely relax, beginning with your toes, the outermost portions of your toes. There's a wonderful light around you. It's moving outward from your body, and it carries with it all of the tensions of the day. . . . The energy you release flows down to the water and out to the ocean. And eventually it evaporates and goes up to the sun and is purified. And so by the very act of breathing and of relaxing, you are an integral part of the universe. Your body adds to the body of our earth and is part of the song. Let your body completely find its right place in the universe. And find yourself in a room in which there is a scent that reminds you of the best thing you ever made. In this room there is a scent of you; it's the best flower, it's the best sky, it's the best childhood memory, and most of all it carries with it the balm of healing. It brings forth beautiful, beautiful visions of who you are, in your best and your highest self.

The complete meditation, which lasted approximately fifteen minutes, took Sally's audience into a magical land populated by helpful animal companions, babbling streams, and mysteriously glowing gemstones. Most guided meditations close by leading participants back to where they began, but the flow of Sally's exercise was interrupted by an incoming call on the bookstore's telephone—an unforeseen distraction that sparked audience laughter and unexpectedly helped to break the ice.

As a speech event, Sally's narrative has a performative intent: it seeks to constitute as well as to describe (Austin 1975). She aims to relax the audience, a goal furthered by the quiet, even tone of her voice and the soothing images of natural settings invoked by her narrative. The performance also knits participants into a group. For the fifteen minutes of the visualization sequence, the audience cedes its autonomy to Sally and allows her to shape an experience that, however superficially, unites them in a collective process.[8] A skillfully presented meditation induces a gentle euphoria that evokes sighs of satisfaction and even tears of joy from participants. Afterwards, they are likely to comment that the "room was really filled with energy" or that "something incredible happened in there."

Note that unlike recitation of a canonical text such as the Lord's Prayer, Sally's narrative does not ask anyone to endorse a specific message or set of beliefs. The few statements of fact (e.g., "The body is a marvelous thing. It holds itself together by means of whirling energy patterns") are sufficiently banal or metaphorical that few could disagree with them. Instead, members of the audience are asked to experience their *own* bodily process or to explore their *own* personal memories at the appropriate moments within the framework of the narrative. The group process of the exercise, in other words, is counterbalanced by ample provision for individual experience, which might be acknowledged by inviting participants to share their impressions of the exercise with the rest of the group. The resulting narratives are likely to include spontaneous personal confessions ("I'm an incest survivor," "I suddenly had an image of my mother as she was dying") that intensify the prevailing sense of shared intimacy. A proficient session leader will move deftly between these stories and themes central to his or her area of spiritual expertise. Leaders with less developed interpersonal skills sometimes allow the gathering to be dominated by members of the audience who doggedly insist on talking about their own personal concerns. Because New Age values provide few avenues for questioning the experience of others, it is a tricky business to steer discussion back to the session's main agenda, but successful session leaders soon master the art of keeping a workshop on track. Even in the best-run gathering, however, audience opinions about how the process is going are never far from the surface as speakers move nervously between comments about the event and metadiscourse about its meaning and direction. In this sense, their narratives embody what Anthony Giddens (1991: 32) calls the "reflexive project" of modernity—a constant self-monitoring of experience.

In gatherings of short duration—say, two hours or less—participants have little opportunity to challenge the presenter's leadership, although they may intervene obliquely by offering polite statements such as, "I was looking forward to some time for questions," or, "Some of us were hoping that you'd talk about X." Seminars that last for several days are more likely to see direct intervention by participants who are, for one reason or another, dissatisfied with the way things are going. The frankest expression of reflexivity is found in private, post hoc exchanges about workshops or seminars that participants found disappointing. After attending an expensive class led by a channel famous for his work with a prominent Hollywood actress, Donna Liston, a middle-class social worker from the New York suburbs, expressed her concern that "I didn't enjoy it when Mark just channeled all the time. I thought there was going to be more group participation. I wanted to be able to start learning how to do this myself." Donna acknowledged that the channeler was insightful and entertaining, but she was ultimately frustrated because he neglected to provide a forum in which she could expand her own spiritual understanding through personal experience.

Themes in Donna's critique are echoed in the account of Peter Goldman, a forty-year-old writer once deeply involved with the Church Universal and Triumphant, a Montana-based congregation led by the controversial channel Elizabeth Clare Prophet (see Lewis and Melton 1994). Unlike most New Age groups, Prophet's church is authoritarian and puritanical, which is why Peter labeled himself a "cult survivor." Peter described Prophet as "very powerful, very hypnotic, very charismatic." He reported that prior to her public channeling sessions, her assistants would lead the audience in a form of chanting called "decreeing," which he said produced a trance state that made Prophet's followers passive and emotionally malleable. Although Peter admitted that he found the experiences convincing at the time, he now rejects Prophet's teachings and the techniques that he saw used in her church, which he considers a form of brainwashing:

> I tend to base my evaluation on the bottom line. What does this do for people? Does it turn them into zombies or does it make them powerful? If something is liberating, it enables people to fulfill more of their potential in a context of freedom rather than in a context of servitude, which a lot of these organizations tend to foster. The power that they think they gained through their association with these groups or gurus or channelers is no power at all. It turns out to be an illusion. And I speak from my own experience.

In these excerpts from larger life-story narratives, Donna and Peter express doubt about spiritual leaders who fail to make allowances for the needs and interests of their followers. Both clearly want the emotional involvement that comes from working with a group, yet they also demand that this experience reaffirm their sense of themselves as unique individuals following a distinctive personal path.

BELIEF AND EXPERIENCE: CONTESTATIONS OF TRUTH

Stories of belief, doubt, and experience constitute another key discursive field for those involved in New Age practices. In contrast to popular portrayals of the movement as a haven for naive minds, discussions at New Age events often focus on the value of skepticism, on the grounds that firsthand experience should always trump belief based on simple faith.[9] The contextual nature of belief and skepticism was revealed in a workshop offered by Kevin Ryerson, a well-known trance channeler, to a paying crowd of forty at the Omega Institute for Holistic Studies, a major conference center located in Rhinebeck, New York. Ryerson opened the event by discussing his own experience of channeling, which includes serving as a medium for a host of historical figures. He believes in the scientific reality of the channeling phenomenon, he said, because the observations of his spirit-beings have been validated through empirical research:

> John [an entity channeled by Ryerson] once identified a site as a place that Hebrew rituals had been performed. Archaeologists denied that ancient Hebrews had built anything in this area. Yet two years later, the archaeological site was discovered. An archaeologist who had expressed doubt about John's information wrote to say that he had now become a believer.

Yet only moments after asserting the empirical truth of channeling's insights, Ryerson insisted that information about the activities of sinister extraterrestrial beings offered by other mediums cannot be taken literally; instead, it should be seen as metaphorical. The mediums who produce such information, he said, are "channeling through their fears."

Throughout the workshop, Ryerson distinguished between analytical thought and forms of understanding based on intuition and the emotions.

He explained that analytical thought is ultimately destructive because it leads to the runaway technologies that endanger the planet and fuel human alienation. "Constructive change can only come about through direct knowing," he emphasized. Audience reaction to these statements suggested that most were sympathetic to his invocation of the primacy of personal experience over other forms of understanding. I was therefore surprised when, during a breakfast conversation the following morning, three of my fellow participants recommended that I test the authenticity of Ryerson's channeled insight by asking his spirit entities for information that could only be known to me personally. Although my interlocutors declared themselves deeply committed to the expansion of intuitive, experiential understanding, they also readily embraced strategies of empirical validation when it suited their purposes.

This edgy tacking back and forth between different approaches to validation reflects underlying attitudes toward belief. In ways that mirror the critiques of positivism mounted by postmodernists, those drawn to New Age practices tend to think of beliefs as completely arbitrary, especially when organized into "belief systems," an expression that has come to connote the received orthodoxies of religion. A critique of belief systems as authoritarian and limiting is consistent with the observation (Heelas 1996: 155–159) that the New Age movement embraces the "de-traditionalization of self," a condition that Heelas associates with radical modernity. The de-traditionalized self thinks of social norms as constructed rather than as immutable and sacred, thus shifting the locus of moral authority to the individual. Personal growth becomes a process of shedding the artificial parochial accretions of social existence—"our cultural baggage," in the idiom of the movement—in favor of inner truths. Once traditions lose intrinsic moral worth, ideas can be freely detached from their cultural nexus. They become little more than floating signifiers, which explains why, to many observers, the ideology of the New Age resembles a vast smorgasbord from which people combine bits of tradition according to personal taste.

On what basis, then, can one distinguish between true and false beliefs? Sandy Randolph, a Santa Fe channeler who claims to bring forth information from a group of American Indian spirits called the Medicine Women, answered the question this way:

> I've learned, very much the hard way and through personal experience, that channeled information isn't all valid. I need to run it

through *me* and see what fits for *me*. Every time I channel for someone else now, the Medicine Women open with this little disclaimer. What they say is, "Take what's said to you, hold it in your heart. If it fits, it's yours. It's our gift to you. And if it doesn't fit, please let it go." And sometimes they'll add, "You could put it off to the muttering of some funny old ladies."

Sandy's statement is marked by striking contradictions. We can interpret the identity of her channeled source, a group of female American Indian healers, as an implicit appeal to the authenticity and wisdom that her clients find in indigenous peoples. Even as the identity of her spirit allies inspires trust, however, the entities' words encourage skepticism. We might dismiss their cautionary advice as a rhetorical strategy that disarms doubt. The question of whether the statement can be taken at face value is less important than the utilitarian calculus that it invokes: Are these ideas *useful?* Will they help me become what I want or acquire what I need?

Willingness to mix and match beliefs according to their perceived utility leads to situations such as that of women's identity groups conducting sweat-lodge ceremonies—even though the American Indian rituals that inspire such practices typically excluded women. When I pointed out this contradiction to interviewees, the reply was often something on the order of, "The belief that women are dangerous or polluting made sense for Indians, but it simply isn't useful anymore." An equally pragmatic approach to belief was offered by Peter Goldman, who embraces cognitive utilitarianism because of his earlier disappointment with the Church Universal and Triumphant. Here he explains his attraction to the work of Jach Pursel, who channels an entity named Lazaris:

I'm willing to believe that there's an energy called Lazaris that speaks through this guy Jach Pursel. I am willing to believe that based on what I've seen. I can neither prove nor disprove the solid, objective reality of what's going on there. If this fellow is just making it up, then he's one of the finest psychologists or teachers I've ever seen. When Lazaris leads a meditation, you can feel that power. You can feel the energy. You can even feel the love. Now maybe you can call that a subjective situation, and maybe I'm just making the whole thing up. Really, I'm willing to believe after checking it out carefully, reading the material, going to a few of the events, including a four-day intensive where he's talking a lot. What I hear Lazaris saying, and what I feel Lazaris saying, is of great benefit to me personally.

We can choose to believe anything we want. So why not choose to believe this is real if it's not hurting anybody, especially you, and if you could possibly benefit from it?

Similar logic informs the life-history narrative of Pamela Davis, a middle-aged woman who moved to New Mexico to pursue her interest in a range of spiritual practices, a journey that eventually led her to become a spiritual counselor to fee-paying clients. Pamela characterized herself as "very, very skeptical and very unsure of what this was all about when it first came to me—the [paranormal] phenomena stuff, the spaceships, and so on. I just stumbled in and I trusted my gut. I learned as I went, and I questioned." Learning and questioning, in other words, are consistent with choosing to believe only those ideas that can be confirmed through personal experience.

As a corollary to cognitive utilitarianism, New Agers hold that the imposition of one's beliefs on others should be avoided whenever possible. Jon Lockwood, an interior designer and channeler from northern New Mexico, warns his clients to avoid spiritual teachers who distract followers from the goal of listening to their own hearts. "This process is about connecting with all that is *inside,* not outside," he said. "We are in the process of re-identifying who we are and no longer using the external to identify ourselves." Pamela Davis developed this theme while describing her philosophy of dealing with clients. "I'm not going to put out any kind of dogma or any kind of structure that says, O.K., this is a little box, if you don't do it this way you're going to the fiery pit," she insisted. "No, I'm just going to offer the knowledge that I have, the philosophy. It can be accepted or rejected."

Critics of authoritarian gurus are often more forgiving in their assessment of the gurus' followers. While recounting her life story, Ellen Devens, a Massachusetts woman whom I interviewed in 1993, mentioned that she regretted having "given away" her free will to Scientology during her involvement with the church. Still, she suggested that participants in authoritarian groups may need the experience of yielding up personal sovereignty so that they can come to appreciate its value. Referring to the Branch Davidians and their charismatic prophet, David Koresh, Ellen insisted, "Even in Waco individuals were exploring the loss of free will. If individuals get involved with cults, I feel that most of them are sincerely doing what they feel they need to do. So who am I to judge?"

When considering stories such as those of Peter Goldman, Pamela Davis, and Ellen Devens, even a sympathetic listener may suddenly feel thrust into epistemological free-fall. Like many others whose stories I recorded, they articulate a species of relativism so absolute that each of us comes to occupy a nearly autonomous universe. Social scientists would be hard pressed to find a clearer expression of the multiplication of life-worlds that we now see as a hallmark of modernity. As Giddens (1991: 195–196) notes, most of us navigate this pluralized world on autopilot, insulated from the anxieties of radical doubt by the habituating structures of work and family. People drawn to New Age practices, in contrast, enthusiastically seek modernity's multiple possibilities, confident that above the infinite diversity of the self there lies transcendent unity.

At the same time, we should keep in mind that radical relativism and the autonomy of experience are ideals. They define this discursive field much as the axes of a graph set the limits of key variables. Speakers invoke the ideals as touchstones for their personal philosophy, but in the flow of everyday social interaction they also find ways to accommodate the beliefs of others in the pursuit of common goals. In a narrative context, this is accomplished through the use of abstract language that leaves considerable room for personal interpretation. Consider, for example, the following exchange during Kevin Ryerson's workshop at the Omega Institute. The main speaker is one of Ryerson's spirit entities, a 3,000-year-old Nubian priest named Atun-Re; audience responses are noted in brackets:

> Ah, I am being Atun-Re and I've come to speak with you. So how are you doing? ["Fine."] That is good. Well, you're feeling fine now, but after I'm done with you, we'll see. [General laughter.] Do you understand? ["Yes!"] . . . Now you are looking at this issue of intuition and futurism, is that not so? ["Yes."] Well, you know it has been said that in order to have a healthy future one must make peace with oneself. Do you understand? ["Yes."] It is, if you will, inside of you the balanced individual that is able to then move forward along the middle that is the successful path. Do you understand? ["Yes."] Isn't that fascinating? ["Yes."] Now you must come to know more fundamentally your true nature. Do you follow? ["Yes."] And your true nature is that you really are more beings of spirit than you are transitorily

through the body. The body is like the so-called cocoon—Do you understand?—that goes through the stages of transformation that allows you to command the full range of your spirit in the various transitory opportunities that allow you to present yourself. The full range of masks that you wear from youth to old age constitutes the fulfillment of a journey. . . . Do you understand? ["Yes."]

Given the aphoristic and metaphorical nature of Atun-Re's pronouncements, it was easy for listeners to bestow their assent even if, as I learned in subsequent interviews, a few doubted the authenticity of the channeled voice. Speech at most channeling events is likewise organized around evocative but vague words—"energy," "manifestation," "ascension," "oneness," and so on—that let listeners fill in the blanks according to their personal predilections. For their part, audience members are willing to adopt a laissez-faire attitude toward the assertions of spiritual teachers and fellow workshop participants as long as the general atmosphere remains nonjudgmental. This live-and-let-live approach to belief changes only when groups coalesce into more durable congregations based on a formal theology and a shared approach to spiritual practice.

FROM SINGULAR TO PLURAL AND BACK AGAIN

Although the New Age offers other discursive fields worthy of analysis, the two considered here stand as prominent landmarks on the movement's social map. The Self/Other field, which fosters wariness about subordinating individual process to collective needs, and the Belief/Experience field, which privileges experience over faith, together conspire against collective action.[10] When groups do coalesce for some joint purpose, their leadership tends to be indirect and their membership variable. Equally fluid is the content of New Age therapies and spiritual teachings. Although the movement's central goal of expanding individual consciousness has remained constant over the past three decades, specific techniques of self-expansion shift with the winds of fashion. Variability of content allows for the constant incorporation of new members while offering long-time participants opportunities to tailor their activities to fit constantly evolving personal needs.

The internal tensions characteristic of the Self/Other and Belief/Experience fields help to explain the relative rarity with which the movement has produced intentional communities similar to those that proliferated during earlier chapters of American religious experimentation. Although spiritually oriented communities such as the Findhorn in Scotland, Sirius in Massachusetts, and Sparrow Hawk in Oklahoma enjoy a hallowed place in movement ideology, they attract only a small percentage of those drawn to New Age activities. Ellen Cahill, a channeler from western Massachusetts, recalled her experience as a resident of one of these communities:

> [The members of the community] seemed like neat people, but after living there I decided I'd rather stick to my own path. There's always some kind of *stuff* to deal with in spiritual communities. It's hard to develop your own identity. There's usually some kind of leader, and you end up with a system that everyone's supposed to follow. . . . I came to realize that everyone has a different way of experiencing spirituality and that it's a very personal connection. Everyone goes at their own rate and opens up to different elements of it at their own time. After eight years of that, I finally gave up the path because I wanted to connect to my own source of spirit.

The salient issue in Ellen's statement is the alleged inability of stable groups to promote the personal growth that she actively seeks. Without inner change, group activities become another forum for the power games of a few dominant personalities.

It might seem from these narratives that New Age spirituality is so inherently atomistic that it scarcely qualifies as a social movement. Yet at the brink of anarchy its proponents step back from the individual and return to the social. This tendency to swerve rapidly from the individual to the collective is evident in the comments of Ted Berenson, a Santa Fe psychotherapist and channeler who offers well-attended workshops across the country:

> Whenever you get a church, you get hierarchy. We saw this happen with the Berkeley Psychic Institute [in the 1970s]. They turned it into the Church of Divine Man, and all of a sudden there were bishops and the Very Right Reverend this and that, and it was a hierarchy. It started to get political and you could see the writing on the wall. When people get into a church kind

of organization, they just can't help themselves. They get into the hierarchy business. To us that's not a sense of community. One of the reasons we increased our evening workshops here is because people really want a sense of community, when they can socialize and have a sense of camaraderie.

Ted Berenson's ambivalence about community brings the paired themes of group feeling and individual growth back to where we began: the need to have one's personal efforts ratified, even if only occasionally, by contact with other like-minded seekers. This attraction to the social is driven, in part, by practical considerations. Groups furnish interpersonal support and opportunities to learn new things, hear new stories. The catharsis offered by collective exploration of spirituality also affirms participants' faith that inner work produces better ways of being together. They can experience on a small scale what they expect will eventually take place at a global level. Their search for good fellowship, however, is tempered by assertions of autonomy and the primacy of personal experience, which participants surrender only with great reluctance.

To understand why people find such a fragmentary movement satisfying, the New Age must be seen against the larger backdrop of American religion. Wade Clark Roof (1993) and others have observed that the United States has become a nation of "religious shoppers" who are more inclined than their parents to change religious identification and to affiliate with groups that meet their personal needs. This instability has largely benefited nondenominational Christian congregations, mostly evangelical and conservative, but it also helps to fill halls at personal growth centers across the country. The life histories of the people who participate in the New Age movement often include a period of membership in an established congregation. The hierarchy and theological rigidity of a church eventually prove limiting for individuals who feel the need to explore more widely and to achieve a sense of spiritual mastery. This is especially true for women. Unlike mainstream Christianity and Judaism, which continue to be dominated by men, the New Age movement is open to female leadership and woman-centered theologies. What both men and women get from the movement, then, is the opportunity to craft a sense of their own spiritual strengths and understandings. Having achieved this understanding, many are willing to drift back to established denominations as their life circumstances change and they feel the need for more stable forms of religious community.

Let me close with a narrative performance that illustrates in microcosm the movement's remarkable ability to fashion contradictory ideas into an overarching vision that still privileges individual experience. The setting was an annual convention sponsored by a magazine devoted to the creative synthesis of Buddhist philosophy, alternative healing methods, and techniques of personal growth. Three thousand conventioneers, mostly affluent and well-educated, gathered in a hotel ballroom in the suburbs of Washington, D.C., for a lecture by one of the movement's stars, a woman known for her best-selling books on spirituality and health. Although the biography on the flyleaf of her books inevitably attaches "Ph.D." to her name and notes her long association with a distinguished medical school, on this occasion her talk used science as a foil for ruminations on the body's ability to access its own wisdom and to heal itself without the patriarchal intervention of Western medicine. Moving comfortably about the stage and emphasizing her points with visual images drawn from molecular biology, Hindu epics, and Greek mythology, she wove the lecture around a series of stories: her upbringing as a "recovering Jewish-American Princess" (which served as a launching-pad for jokes about the therapeutic possibilities of shopping), experiences with various alternative healers, and a recent brush with breast cancer—the latter cured by a combination of Jungian techniques and the timely intervention of a famous female surgeon. At the end of the talk, the audience leapt to its feet in thunderous applause.

The lecture's blend of science and myth, feminism and millenarianism, accommodation and resistance, high-tech and no-tech, personal anecdotes and sweeping generalizations, and above all, its message that each of us must craft a personal vision according to the dictates of experience, obviously struck a responsive chord in listeners, who are busily creating their own narratives. Having taken to heart R. D. Laing's claim that "the condition of alienation, of being asleep, of being unconscious, of being out of one's mind, is the condition of the normal man" (12), they are doing everything in their power to find the stories that will restore them to consciousness and cure the self-estrangement that today passes for normality. In so doing, they believe, they will improve the world as well as themselves. Laing, who was felled by a heart attack in 1989 during a game of tennis in St. Tropez, did not live long enough to see the full flowering of his ideas. As a classically trained intellectual, he might have deplored the commercial and, in some cases, superficial turn that the quest for self has taken since the appearance of *The Politics of Experience*. Then again, as one of the movement's philosopher kings, perhaps he would have enjoyed presiding over all this extravagant storytelling.

ACKNOWLEDGMENTS

I am grateful for helpful comments by Joseph Davis and David Bromley, neither of whom is responsible for any of the chapter's deficiencies. My fieldwork was made possible through the generous support of the School of American Research, the Wenner-Gren Foundation for Anthropological Research, and Williams College.

NOTES

1. Laing's life and work are documented in Burston 1996.

2. Experts who downplay the scale of the New Age movement include Finke and Stark 1992 and Kosmin and Lachman 1993.

3. Accounts critical of the movement, such as Kaminer 1999, Rossman 1979, and Schur 1976, portray it as irrational, self-indulgent, and fundamentally antipolitical. Such critiques tend to ignore offshoots of the New Age, such as goddess-focused ecofeminism, that welcome the expression of political and social grievances (Luhrmann 1993). Admittedly, however, these exceptions represent only a small percentage of those who participate in a movement that generally resists involvement in conventional politics.

4. "Market activities, and possibly voting," Robert Wuthnow (1987: 81) observes, "actually constitute the major forms of public participation. . . . The market, therefore, provides an important means of discharging moral responsibilities to the society in which we live."

5. Hank Johnston (1995) offers an ambitious formal approach for the analysis of social movement narrative, whose influence on this chapter I am happy to acknowledge. Although sympathetic to Johnston's search for rigor, I am skeptical that the flow of social life studied by ethnographers sorts itself into the bounded discursive units that Johnston apparently seeks. Johnston's declaration that "the fundamental task in the microanalysis of discourse and text is the specification of all sources of meaning" (220) is at once a truism and a search for the impossible. In this chapter I follow a looser approach to frame analysis based

on the assumption that readers are interested in the general question of how my subjects create, contest, and modify their social world through talk. The discreteness of the texts presented here is entirely artificial, and at present I see no practical alternative to that inherent artificiality.

6. Details of my research are presented in Brown 1997 and 1999. Other works on the New Age with a strong empirical foundation include Albanese 1990, Heelas 1996, Hess 1993, Lewis and Melton 1992, and York 1995.

7. For privacy reasons, I use pseudonyms for channels and, in some cases, for their spirits, whose identity is often closely tied to their human vehicles. The only exceptions are channels who qualify as public figures, including Kevin Ryerson, J. Z. Knight, and Elizabeth Clare Prophet. The narratives presented in this chapter have been edited for conciseness and continuity.

8. These observations are directly inspired by the late Roy A. Rappaport's work on the performative aspects of liturgical orders. "Liturgical orders are public," Rappaport (1979: 194) writes, "and participation in them constitutes a public acceptance of a public order, regardless of the private state of belief. Acceptance is, thus, a fundamental social act, and it forms a basis for public orders."

9. David J. Hess has analyzed how Shirley MacLaine uses skepticism for rhetorical effect in her best-selling book *Out on a Limb*. According to Hess (1993: 52), MacLaine projects a "New Age self" that "synthesizes a skeptical, scientific voice of an earlier phase of her life with a believing, spiritual voice of past lives and ancient knowledge."

10. In his presidential address to the Association for the Sociology of Religion, David G. Bromley (1997) proposes an analytical scheme that maps American social forms according to their position on two major ideological axes: covenantal/contractual and priestly/prophetic. Bromley's model is entirely compatible with the discursive fields (self/other and belief/experience) outlined in this chapter but takes them far beyond the narrow scope of my analysis. He places the New Age at the contractual and prophetic end of his analytical axes, a zone that in recent decades has expanded its influence in American social and political life (108, 127–129).

SIX

Fundamentalism

When History Goes Awry

JOSHUA J. YATES AND JAMES DAVISON HUNTER

Religious fundamentalism is a complex and diverse phenomenon. Fundamentalist movements are a highly contingent, historically specific set of local, regional, and national movements operating toward any number of discrete ends: some expressly political, some cultural, some theological, and most, various combinations of all three. As a global concept, "fundamentalism" has limitations, and attempts to ascribe a substantive degree of analytical unity to the term across the complexities of world-religious expression require caution. For every generalization, one could no doubt find an exception. Acknowledging this fact, however, does not imply that the term is conceptually fallow. Structuring the aspirations of fundamentalist movements grounded within specific cultures and religious traditions is a "symmetry of intention," which is nothing less than the reestablishment of social (and often political) order on a religious basis. This symmetry, we argue, is rooted in the shared narrative of modernity.

In this chapter, we seek to demonstrate the utility and importance of a narrative approach for making conceptual sense of religious fundamentalism as a global phenomenon. The first part considers conventional approaches to fundamentalist movements and argues that a narrative account greatly augments and strengthens standard treatments of the subject by introducing the discursive form that gives fundamentalism its evocative power. The second section takes a first step in applying a narrative approach to the study of fundamentalism by examining and comparing the

123

narratives of four fundamentalist movements—Protestant-Christian, Jewish, Islamic, and Hindu. The chapter concludes by arguing that despite the historically contingent and culturally distinct nature of various fundamentalist movements, a world-historical narrative—an overarching story of modernity and how it must be addressed—underlies each.

CONVENTIONAL APPROACHES TO FUNDAMENTALIST MOVEMENTS

Over the past decade an extensive literature on fundamentalism has emerged that not only gives testimony to the term's variability, but also acknowledges some degree of general applicability. As Martin Marty and R. Scott Appleby, coeditors of a comprehensive, multivolume study of fundamentalism, have pointed out, "despite the substantive differences among [various fundamentalist movements] . . . in terms of doctrine, cosmology, social composition, size, organization, and scope of influence, they share certain general traits" (1994: 1). For Marty, Appleby, and their contributors, these general traits include tremendous religious passion, resistance to the prevailing cultural and moral system, and a return to traditional religious ways of life. According to another noted fundamentalist scholar, fundamentalists "are above all religiously motivated individuals, drawn together into ideologically structured groups, for the purpose of promoting a vision of divine restoration" (Lawrence 1989: 1). With somewhat more specificity, Nielsen has characterized fundamentalism movements as "typically . . . ideologically reactive with a Manichaean-like sense of good and evil and [stressing] inerrancy, messianism, and millennialism" (1993: 8). In each of these views, fundamentalists are seen to be primarily concerned with protecting their distinct faith traditions, practices, and identities (the "fundamentals") against prevailing sociocultural practices that are perceived to be threatening them.

Political-Ideological and Resource Mobilization Approaches

Where scholarly analysis has taken fundamentalism seriously as an object of inquiry in its own right, it has largely concentrated on the sociopolitical goals of various religious movements as well as on the ability of these groups to recruit and direct their followers toward the achievement of movement goals. The focal point of such analyses is the struggle on the part of religious fundamentalist groups to secure social and institutional power. Within the contemporary American context, for instance, the fundamentalist label has been used to describe the mobilized and politically potent constituencies of the Moral Majority of the 1970s and early 1980s, and the Christian Coalition of the 1990s (Layman 1997).

A more global example of the political emphasis appears in analyses of the 1994 Cairo International Conference on Population and Development. Against the liberalizing intentions of feminist and other progressive delegates with respect to reproductive rights, participants representing historically antagonistic and dissimilar religious expressions, such as Muslims and Roman Catholics, formed a united front. In the final estimation of certain feminist theorists, the resistance put up by this coalition of fundamentalists at the Cairo conference represented little more than a traditionalist struggle to reclaim a lost social and political hegemony (see Bere and Ravindran 1996; Fredman 1996). In this way, scholars tend to apply the "fundamentalist" designation loosely to a variety of religiopolitical ideologies that are characterized as conservative or reactionary. But by casting fundamentalist movements in these terms, such theorists fail to take seriously the deeper fundamentalist critique of modern society. For fundamentalists, more than traditional power structures are at stake. Modernity itself is what brings fundamentalists to the awful conclusion that the fate of their society, their faith communities, and even the eternal order are in jeopardy.

Social movement scholars have also tended to concentrate on social and political agendas. Operating from a resource mobilization perspective, their analyses center on fundamentalisms' instrumental or organizational bases. The object of study is the ability of various movements and movement leaders to access and leverage constituents, finances, facilities, and institutions, as well as beliefs and "common sense" in order to achieve their respective religiopolitical goals (Ash 1972; Cameron 1974; Tilly 1978; Wuthnow and Lawson 1994). This emphasis is most useful in identifying some of the more explicit—and therefore measurable—aspects of fundamentalist activity and behavior. It is strongest on what makes religious fundamentalism, like other social movements, generically successful in terms of their ability to articulate desired social change, to identify and mobilize support, and to enact their respective transformative programs.

However, both political and resource mobilization approaches tend to miss what makes fundamentalist movements unique.[1] They ignore the symbolic-ideational dimensions that fuel the righteous indignation and resolute commitment to resistance, as well as the social and political activism of these movements. These approaches lack any compelling account of what "structures" religiopolitical ideology—myth, ritual, scriptural authority, and the sacred. To the extent that such aspects are considered, they are often dismissed as mere rhetorical schemes. The fundamentalist worldview itself is treated as epiphenomenal.

Symbolic-Ideational Approaches

Moving away from a primary emphasis on the political and organizational nature of fundamentalist movements, another group of researchers focuses on what makes fundamentalist movements distinct, both from other social movements and from other forms of authoritarian politics. In this approach, the uniqueness of fundamentalist movements is in the centrality of the religious mythos by which fundamentalists interpret contemporary social and political issues (see Halliday 1995). "Mythos" refers to that grouping of governing myths, stories, rituals, and beliefs that together form a symbolic system of thought or worldview (Nielsen 1993). For fundamentalists, mythos is objectified in holy texts, and forms a deep symbolic reserve on which movement leaders and laymen alike can draw to inform and justify their varying religiopolitical programs. In this sense, scripture is a crucial defining element of the monotheistic fundamentalist movements. "Remove scripture," contends Lawrence, "and you no longer have fundamentalism but some other, nonreligious social movement" (1989: 15).

Among social movement theorists, ideational and symbolic elements are usually considered from a "framing" perspective (see Snow et al. 1986; Snow and Benford 1988). "Frames" are "schemata of interpretation" that give meaning to events, organize experience, and provide guides for action. Mythos and scripture, in this approach, *frame* fundamentalist beliefs and actions, as well as the ways these beliefs and actions are rationalized and legitimated. Mythos and scripture provide the basis for locating the movement's identified problem within a specific moral order, for deciding what is to be done, and, importantly, for calling the faithful to action (Snow and Benford 1988). The resonance of these "diagnostic," "prognostic," and "motivational" frames, for both potential recruits and members, in turn, depends on the ability of fundamentalist movements to draw not only on the underlying mythos but on a broader cultural heritage of norms, symbols, and traditions. "Frames," Williams observes, "must connect the movement's purposes and programs with established cultural frames" (Williams 1994: 804). Otherwise, a movement's purposes and programs will likely be unintelligible.

Symbolic-ideational approaches provide a more comprehensive treatment of religious fundamentalist movements than do those approaches exclusively concentrating on movements' political-ideological agendas and resource mobilization capabilities. Yet even most symbolic-ideational approaches do not tell the full story. While understanding how religious mythos and scriptural idealism distinguish fundamentalist movements from other social movements and from one another is essential, it does not explain *how* these key sources of meaning motivate and mobilize adherents. Frames locate and name problems, identify their dimensions, and proffer solutions, but they do not in themselves explain *why* certain people find themselves compelled to draw on fundamentalist interpretations rather than on other sources of meaning for their identity and purpose. As Williams notes, "The mere existence of grievances is not enough. Many people will agree with any given movement frame; the more difficult task is to prompt significant numbers of those people to activism" (1994: 791). As important as mythos, scripturalism, and framing activities are, then, they lack a way of examining the particular form that brings these symbolic-ideational elements together in a manner that resonates with people and moves them to action.

Narrative Approaches

In general, there are at least two levels of narrative by which to approach the study of religious fundamentalisms as social movements. First, there is the level characterized by what Benford (chapter 3) refers to as "participant narratives." These are the stories about movement-related experiences told by fundamentalists themselves. The sharing of these personal stories grounds each individual member's identity in the collective identity of the movement and locates it within the movement's larger stories, which Benford refers to as "movement narratives." Fundamentalist movement narratives, drawing on selected religious legends and myths, locate and label antagonistic cultural and historical trends, while conferring honor on movement actors resisting such trends by proclaiming them guardians of truth and fidelity. Through movement narratives, each fundamentalist movement itself tells a collective story, a socially and historically grounded story of the faithful remnant standing for righteousness in a society gone astray.

It is at this second, or movement, level that narrative bridges the social and emotional distance between framing (the conscious, propositional rhetoric of movement activists) and the striking of a collective nerve among particular people (often particular groups of people). Fundamentalist narratives are exceedingly evocative and compelling because they "package" the religious mythos, scriptural idealism, and frames together in such a way as to place their hearers within a story, which they in turn must either endorse or reject. If they endorse the story, filled as it is with cosmic significance, subscribers are also endorsing their special place within that story, and accepting its attendant moral duties and religious obligations. If hearers reject the story, they reject their role in the Divine Plan and risk the coming judgment.

Beyond the participant and movement narratives identified by Benford, we add a third—the world-historical narrative. World-historical narratives are stories of far-reaching significance that situate movements not simply in local contexts, but in a global context as well. In examining the discrete movement narratives of specific fundamentalisms, we discern a common narrative of modernity and what it represents for the Divine plan and the duty of the believer. Indeed, as we will see, the most significant aspect of this world-historical narrative may not be what it tells us about religion or politics, but what it tells us about qualities intrinsic to the modern age.

The payoff of a narrative approach over other theoretical approaches and forms of movement discourse is that narrative forms a link between movement rhetoric and the moral and emotional sensibilities of potential and active members. It also illuminates the way in which fundamentalist movements are embedded within local *and* global contexts. Narrative opens the way for a theory of fundamentalism which advances our understanding of its worldwide contours as many social movements, each in some way at odds with the progression of modernity. Before turning to an empirical consideration of specific movement stories and the fundamentalist world-historical narrative, a few conceptual clarifications are in order.

Fundamentalism and Orthodoxy: The Essential Difference

The great pretense of all monotheistic fundamentalists is their conviction that what they espouse and what they seek to promote is a basic, unaltered orthodoxy. This, we would argue, is not at all the case. Fundamentalism differs from religious orthodoxy in a number of ways. Its expectations are generally eschatologically focused, even apocalyptic, as believers anticipate the fulfillment of scriptural prophecies. Fundamentalism is generally more literalist than orthodoxy in its reliance on and interpretation of holy texts. And, perhaps most distinctively, fundamentalism permits less ambiguity. The fundamentalist usually sees the world in clear, black-and-white terms of good and evil, of the faithful and the faithless. The orthodox are not as confident; mystery enjoys greater possibility.

Orthodoxy as a cultural system, moreover, represents what could be called a "consensus through time"—more specifically, a consensus based on the ancient rules and precepts derived from divine revelation over the course of human history. Its authority and its legitimacy derive from an unfaltering continuity with truth as originally revealed—truth in its primitive and purest expression (Hunter 1987). It is fair to say that fundamentalism is something else: fundamentalism is orthodoxy in confrontation with modernity. Indeed, one cannot accurately speak of premodern fundamentalism, although there have been numerous revivalist and zealot movements throughout history; rather, what is necessary for fundamentalism is a revolt against modernity—or more accurately, the disruptions caused by modernizing processes and the spread of various Western Enlightenment ideologies.[2]

From a sociological perspective, all religious traditions confronting the modern world order—its rationality, its pluralism, its public/private dualism, its subjectivism, and so on—are faced with three basic options: withdrawal, accommodation, or resistance. Fundamentalism derives its identity principally from a posture of resistance to the modern world order, even if this posture entails some accommodation (perhaps unwittingly). At root, then, there is no fundamentalism without modernity.

FUNDAMENTALIST WORLD-HISTORICAL NARRATIVE: MAKING HISTORY RIGHT AGAIN

Having briefly proposed the benefits of a narrative approach to the study of religious fundamentalist movements, we now turn to a consideration of the method's application. It should be noted at the outset that the four case studies that follow are offered less as a thoroughgoing treatment of fundamentalist movement narratives and more as an initial attempt to illustrate the conceptual power of a narrative approach. Indeed, each deserves much fuller treatment in its own right, as well as in comparison with others. Nevertheless, emerging from even this brief glance at the elemental form of these particular fundamentalist movement narratives is a parallel story of history.[3] Shaped by the defensive interplay of orthodoxy with modernity, this world-historical narrative unfolds in three steps. It begins with the deep and worrisome belief that history has gone awry, demonstrates that what "went wrong" with history is modernity in its various guises, and leads to the inescapable conclusion that the calling of the fundamentalist is to make history "right" again. What unites fundamentalisms worldwide derives from this basic plot.

Protestant Fundamentalism

[W]e begin to see our country, our republic, crumbling; we see a moving away from God and away from the principles responsible for her greatness. We feel, therefore, that it is high time for the people of God to awaken from their sleep. We thus feel a primary obligation, in these last days before Jesus comes, to call this nation back to God. (quoted in Pingry 1980: 6)

Thus proclaimed the Reverend Jerry Falwell at an "I Love America" rally in 1980. A decade later, his diagnosis was even more grim when he preached a sermon entitled "America Declares War with God" (quoted in Harding 1994: 73). Both the speech and sermon conjure alarming images of a back-slidden and degenerate America contrasted with a God-fearing and righteous past. Narratively, Falwell's analysis places both contemporary events and his listeners within a cosmic framework of meaning and responsibility. If immediate action is not taken, so the story implies, then not only will America lose its greatness, but will also be in mortal danger of divine judgment and retribution.

From the early New England colonial period to the late nineteenth century, there was tremendous optimism that God was doing a wondrous work in this world through the heirs of the Reformation, particularly those who settled on American shores. America would be a "Christian commonwealth," a "righteous empire," a "redeemer nation." The blessings of revivalistic awakenings, as well as the hardship of famine and war—first with the French and later with the British for independence, and even the Civil War—were all viewed as part of a providentialist design. God had called and blessed the American people to be light to the world: if God's people remained true to their faith, His favor would continue to rest on this new nation.

However, for a number of interrelated reasons, America had gotten off its divinely appointed track. What had gone wrong was an insidious assortment of "ideas" and systems of thought generally subsumed under the term *modernism*. In the forms of high criticism, evolution, the social gospel, ecumenism, and the like, modernism threatened not only the integrity of the true faith, as conservative Protestants saw it, but also the very hope of the cause of Christianity in America. It was up to the faithful followers of the gospel to set things right again.

In the early decades of the twentieth century, many conservative Protestants began a campaign to return to the true path through numerous crusades, public speeches, and publications. Their hope was to correct the direction in which society was heading and thereby repair the damage done by modernism. Here the issue of evolution is paradigmatic. From the infamous Scopes Trial in 1924 to the more recent controversies between evolutionism and creation science in public education, the contentious battle of origins has been the central staging ground for the fundamentalist-modernist conflict. Articulating the fundamentalist view during the Scopes trial, William Jennings Bryan announced that "all the ills from which America suffers can be traced to the teaching of evolution" (quoted in Lawrence 1989: 183).

Early on, the "keepers" of orthodoxy against modernism became known by the title of a set of popular essays entitled, "The Fundamentals." These essays outlined the so-called fundamentals of the Christian faith, such as the virgin birth, the resurrection, the second coming of Jesus Christ, and perhaps most important, the inerrancy of scripture. The term *fundamentalist* was first put into popular circulation by Curtis Lee Laws, editor of the northern Baptist newspaper, *The Watchman Examiner*, when he wrote that a "fundamentalist is a person willing to do battle royal for the fundamentals of the faith" (quoted in Ammerman 1991: 2). That this "call to arms" for the faith resonated with a significant portion of American Christians is evidenced by the emergence of dozens of Bible colleges and institutes, the founding of numerous fundamentalist periodicals, the establishment of the World Christian's Fundamentalist Association (1919), the conflicts within denominational seminaries, and so on. These concerned Christians took up the banner of fundamentalism to fight against the perversions of modernism in the religious life of the country. What is particularly significant in this initial mobilization of fundamentalists, however, is their decision not to engage in social and political activism but to separate themselves from the mainstream. Ironically, their tremendously productive zeal in the early decades of the twentieth century yielded not the reclamation of a fundamentalist-defined Christian America but fundamentalists' progressive ghettoization.

By the 1970s and 1980s, a half-century of isolation had convinced fundamentalists that as long as they remained isolated, modernism's pernicious effects, now subsumed under the banner of secular humanism, would continue to eat away at the traditional foundations of American society. If American fundamentalists were to set history right, they needed to impact the shaping of values in the broader society. In shifting to an activist stance, they centered their struggle for influence and relevance on the way America would view its past and its future (Ammerman 1991).

In their efforts to reclaim the past, fundamentalists selectively invoked images of the Puritan "city on a hill" and Christian Republicanism—common to American public culture at the time of the founding—as the true heritage of American society. Jerry Falwell, who has been considered by some scholars as the figure most responsible for the mobilization of fundamentalists into a relatively cohesive and influential political coalition, offers such an interpretation when he speaks of America as

> a nation founded by our forefathers as a Christian nation and as a base for world evangelization. For two hundred years God has blessed this country beyond all others, simply because here, in our environment of freedom and liberty, America has, more than any other nation in history, been allowed to give the gospel out to a world for whom Jesus died. (quoted in Pingry 1980: 6)

In defending the need to "reclaim America for Christ," pastor and popular radio program host D. James Kennedy argues that Americans owe their freedoms to "the fact that America was originally 'claimed' for Christ" (1998: Foreword). But as compelling as such claims to America's providentially ordained past are, they do not in themselves move beyond the power of nostalgia. The real force and urgency animating the fundamentalist story lies elsewhere.

The decisive force behind American Protestant fundamentalist narratives is found in the eschatological theology of *premillenial dispensational-*

ism. Put simply, this theology is centered in the belief that in the last days of history, when the world and the church has succumbed to great evil and apostasy, God will "rapture" his faithful remnant and then usher in the time of the great tribulation and judgment, leading up to the second coming of Christ. In premillennial theology, fundamentalists resisting modernity become the "faithful remnant" standing in obedient opposition to a world devoid of true faith and godliness in the last days. In short, this theology puts American fundamentalists' current troubles—humanism, evolutionism, secularism, and such—into cosmic perspective, a perspective in which their God is in control and will ultimately be victorious.

More immediately, however, dispensationalism provides fundamentalists a ready vocabulary with which they can precisely and unequivocally name the heroes and the villains, the righteous and the wicked, at the heart of their struggle. The protagonists are the Bible-believing, born-again Christians, while the antagonists are primarily the liberal humanists and, somewhat more recently, globalists (one-world proponents), who at their best act as pitiful pawns of evil forces, and at their worst, as conspirators with demonic agendas (see Harding 1994: 63). Likewise, dispensationalism makes biblical archetypes available to great rhetorical advantage. For instance, as one fundamentalist sees it, humanism is nothing less then the "abomination of desolation"—a Biblical phrase referring to desecration of the sacred—prefiguring the coming desecration of the Jewish temple by the Anti-Christ prior to Armageddon (Bowen 1984: 22). Similarly, Jerry Falwell admonishes, "There are states in these United States that now have legalized homosexual marriages. . . . I really cannot imagine that Sodom and Gomorrah had gotten that low, yet somehow we have. And if God allows America to continue, He owes an apology to Sodom and Gomorrah" (quoted in Pingry 1980: 7). These characterizations draw the sharpest possible contrast between the faithful and the evildoers, and provide direction to competently navigate the disorienting qualities of the modern (secular) age.

Curiously, fundamentalists also invoke dispensationalism as a basis for social engagement and political protest. Recent efforts to reverse the legal status of abortion, to delegitimate progressive sexual and familial attitudes, to return the practice of prayer to public schools, to elect Christian politicians, and so on have typically all been placed within a pre-apocalyptic narrative: the great tribulation is approaching, yet the immorality and godlessness may still be reversed. Best-selling author Tim LaHaye argues that there is still hope for America, but only if Christians rise up against the secular humanists and "are willing to become much more assertive in defense of morality and decency than they have been during the past three decades" (1980: 217–218). Bowen (1984), a fundamentalist critic, echoes this sentiment more emphatically:

> We need to get rid of the rapture fever. The time of our Lord's return is His business. We can't make it happen. He may tarry for years to give us time to do His work. But this work will not be accomplished if we mistakenly believe that "to occupy" merely means to occupy a pew. Unless we take a stand against ungodly rulers we will be forced to live under their tyranny. (155)

Through a reading of this discourse, we gain a sense of the urgency of the message: for the Protestant fundamentalist, nothing less than the very survival of American society—not only as a nation, but as God's chosen beacon of light to the world—is at stake. "If the atheistic, amoral, one-world humanists succeed in enslaving our country," worries LaHaye, "that missionary outlet will eventually be terminated. . . . The eternal souls of millions of people depend on us to supply them with the good news" (222). "The time is now," concludes Bowen, "for all to decide whether they are on the Lord's side—or Satan's" (1).

Islamic Fundamentalism

In broad outline, Islamic fundamentalism bears a strong resemblance to Protestant fundamentalism, but is different in its details. One such detail needs explicit elucidation. Protestant fundamentalism, while certainly encompassing a range of relatively diverse organizations, individuals, theological orientations, and the like, has nevertheless been largely restricted to a single historical, cultural, and national context—the United States. Islamic fundamentalism, in contrast, is composed of submovements deriving from many different societies with distinct histories and cultures. It is arguably a far less cohesive or unitary movement than American Protestant fundamentalism, and consequently much more difficult to subsume under a single heading. Yet, as a narrative analysis reveals, a world-historical narrative structures its various expressions.

Like early Protestant America, early Islamic history was also marked by tremendous success. The first community of nomadic believers expanded numerically, grew in geopolitical dominance, and prospered in their cultural and religious accomplishments. In its first five centuries, Islam coalesced into a new and vibrant civilization. To the faithful, these early successes confirmed that Allah was working out his divine plan within history itself. Even after the devastating Mongol invasion in the thirteenth century and the collapse of the growing Muslim dynasty, a revitalization and expansion of Arab civilization in its medieval period allowed Muslims to reinterpret this crisis as occurring within the divine pattern of historical development. However, such a reinterpretation has not yet been possible for Muslims in the face of Islam's most recent crisis: its confrontation with the modern world order.

This confrontation came as early as the seventeenth and eighteenth centuries with the expansion of Western capitalist economies into the Middle East, Mongol India, and the Ottoman Empire. By the end of the eighteenth century, various Western powers had established direct economic, political, and military control over much of that region. European hegemony meant, among other things, the introduction of radical political and administrative reform and the subjugation of Islamic culture and ideals to Western traditions of rationalism, secularism, and pluralism. In this way, Muslims increasingly found their societies penetrated by what the great American scholar of Islam, Marshall Hodgson, calls the "Great Western Transmutation" (1979). The once imperial civilization of Islam had lost control over its collective destiny; for emerging fundamentalist movements, history had gone awry.

After colonial rule came to an end, many postcolonial governments were transitioned to a Westernized Muslim administration that continued to embrace modern European modes of thought and rule and promised increased economic and social prosperity. For fundamentalists, however, this accommodation of modern Western values—through nationalist, pan-Arabist, and socialist experiments, as well as the secularizing of law, the courts, and public education, the appropriation of Western goods and advertising, and the adaptation of Western dress and ideas of gender equality—only meant moral and political decay (Lawrence 1989).

Westernized leadership in Muslim societies has brought about a "crisis" for many Islamic fundamentalists. Sayyid Qutb, leader of the Muslim Brotherhood, described the present moment this way: "Man is at the crossroads and that is the choice: Islam or *jahiliyya*. Modern style *jahiliyya* in the industrialized societies of Europe and America is essentially similar to old time *jahiliyya* in pagan and nomadic Arabia" (quoted in Sivan 1985: 24). By invoking *jahiliyya,* Qutb is using well-known imagery to contextualize the present. He is harkening back to the familiar story of the pre-Islamic period of Arabian tribalism and ignorance with respect to Allah. Modern *jahiliyya,* according to Qutb, is the secularizing ideology of nationalism that places patriotism to the state over common religious confession—thus destroying the continuity of the *umma,* or corporate solidarity of all Muslims—and which reduces *shari'a* (the "fundamentals" of Islamic conduct) to a Westernized, permissive ethic in Muslim trappings. Qutb concludes, "This is the most dangerous *jahiliyya* which has ever menaced our faith" (Sivan 1985: 25).

Another fundamentalist leader, Jalal Al-I Ahmad, writing from a Shi'ite perspective, similarly characterizes the unique destructive force of modernity as an unstoppable monstrous "machine." He writes, "We have been unable to preserve our own historical character in the face of the machine and its fateful onslaught" (1984: 31). At a societal level, modernity, or "Westoxification," is more destructive than "dynamite." "What border or domain," Ahmad quips, "can stand up to the influence of Pepsi Cola . . . ?" (75).

The Islamic fundamentalist's solution to the insidiousness of modernity, however conflated with the West, is to return to strict adherence to Islam in every sphere of life. A series of influential books by the fundamentalist activist Yusuf al-Qurdawi states the fundamentalist solution clearly: "The Islamic solution means that Islam is both the orienting maxim and the guide for the community in all areas of life, material as well as intellectual. The Islamic solution means that the entirety of life is molded into a fundamentally Islamic form and character" (quoted in Tibi 1988: 27). Like the earliest (protofundamentalist) reactions against the internal "deterioration" of Islam in the eighteenth and nineteenth centuries, twentieth-century fundamentalist movements all share the common passion to recover the classical experience of Islam, "a history without deviation," and the original meaning of the Islamic message, "a faith without distortion." The fundamentalist solution demands nothing less than the establishment of a totally Islamic social and political order.

The first step toward the new Islamic order is internal reform. Qurdawi writes, "In order to build this Islamic form of government or state we must . . . cleanse it of all foreign bodies and secret germs that have perverted it" (quoted in Tibi 1988: 28). The "foreign bodies" are Muslim intellectuals and political leaders, educated in Western institutions and embracing secular attitudes and values. Jalal Al-I Ahmad, sounding not unlike his Protestant counterparts decrying secular humanists, characterizes the "compromisers" this way:

> The occidentic is a man totally without belief or conviction, to such an extent that he not only believes in nothing, but also does not actively disbelieve in anything. . . . He cares neither whether society is transformed or not nor whether religion or irreligion prevails. He is not even irreligious. He is indifferent. He even goes to the mosque at times, just as he goes to the club or the movies. But everywhere he is only a spectator. (quoted in Nielsen 1993: 97)

Under the rule of these "Westernized elites," secular ideologies fail to provide a stable source of identity and meaning. In an attempt to recover their identity in Islam, fundamentalists first must rid themselves of these "compromised" elites.

Many Sunni Muslims interpreted the defeat of the Westernized secular Arab governments in the Six-Day War as a punishment of Allah for abandoning the true path to embrace the promises of secular progress. Society under these governments came to be seen as completely godless and irredeemable (see Voll 1991). As a result, militant fundamentalist groups such as *al-Jihad* concluded that their primary task was to forcibly overthrow the government of *jahiliyya*. Hence, after their successful assassination of President Anwar Sadat of Egypt, *al-Jihad* leader Muhamad Abd al-Salam Faray could hope that "once Pharaoh was killed, the faithful Egyptians would rise in holy war against the unbelieving state" (Voll 1991: 383). Here, Pharaoh serves as an archetype of the idolatrous tyrant usurping the rightful authority of the *umma* and denying *shari'a*.

Within Shi'ism, fundamentalist reform and resistance has marked a shift from the community's traditional quietist stance, or *taqiyya* (see Baram 1994). In Iraq, for instance, the *Da'wa*—The Call to Islam—has selectively combined the martyrdom of the third Shi'ite Imam (Husayn) with the *Mahdi*, or messianic promise of the return of the Twelfth Imam,[4] as its model and motivation for social and political engagement. They believe that whereas Muhammad was the "First Caller," who "replaced the First Jahiliyya with Islam," they must now call the faithful to action against the present *jahiliyya* (quoted in Baram 1994: 533). In contrast to the quietist tradition, the *Da'wa* believes that the idea of waiting quietly and peaceably for the *Mahdi* is neither instructed by the Koran, nor in accordance with *Shari'a*. Indeed, such passivity or "negative waiting" at this point in history is considered downright foolish; if anything, the current *jahiliyya* is seen as proof that the return of the Savior is imminent. Accordingly, one fundamentalist writer suggests that "the banners of the Promised Savior's journey . . . are already fluttering in the distant horizon" (quoted in Baram 1994: 561).

Beyond internal reform, the establishment of a new Islamic order also requires active resistance to the external influences of pagan societies. Nowhere has the shift from passive to active faith been more explicit than in contemporary Iran. By weaving together selective moments of Persian history into a militant theocratic and messianic movement narrative, the *ulama,* or traditional religious scholars, created the religious legitimization for a revolutionary resistance in what was the most modernizing society in the Middle East. In such a context, the Ayatollah Khomeini condemned all foreign powers, specifically Western powers, as necessarily Satanic. "Such Satanic power," he proclaimed, "can engender nothing but corruption on earth, the supreme evil which must be pitilessly fought and rooted out. To achieve that end, we have no recourse other than to overthrow all governments that do not rest on pure Islamic principles" (1980: 5). Those who do not surrender to Islam, according to the Ayatollah Khomeini, will be "put to the sword and dispatched to hell, where they shall roast forever" (quoted in Nielsen 1993: 89). From such incendiary speech, it is clear that for the Islamic fundamentalist, as for the Protestant, the stakes are of the gravest consequence—nothing less than the divine plan for history is in jeopardy.

Jewish Fundamentalism

In Judaism, fundamentalism takes form within religious Zionism. Its clearest expression is Gush Emunim, or the "Bloc of the Faithful." Although movements such as the Satmar Hasidism, the Agdath Israel, and the Neturei Karta bear strong resemblance in certain respects, Gush Emunim is emblematic (see Biale 1985; Lustick 1987; Seliktar 1983). But here a slight adjustment must be made to our argument. For the Gush

Emunim, it is not that history has gone wrong, but that history *could* go wrong.

The dominance of secular Judaism in Israel is a cause for great concern, but the forces of secularism have not—or at least not yet—subverted the divine will. Concerted action now can help ensure the fulfillment of God's will for His chosen people. To the Gush Emunim, as for Protestant and Islamic fundamentalists, history has a sacred quality, as God's means of communicating with His people. This historical communication is revealed through the dual significance of the end of the Jewish Diaspora and the reclamation of the land of Israel as a Jewish state. Around these two events a religious-Zionist narrative has emerged, focused on the messianic redemption and culmination of history. As the Gush Emunim's Manifesto states:

> Our aim is to bring about a large movement of reawakening among the Jewish people for the fulfillment of the Zionist vision in its full scope. . . . The sources of the vision are the Jewish tradition and roots, and its ultimate objective is the full redemption of the Jewish people and the entire world. (quoted in Sprinzak 1993: 117)

The religiously infused geopolitical ideology of the Gush Emunim is founded on the messianic spiritualism of Zvi Yehuda Kook, son of Rabbi Avarham Kook, the first chief rabbi of Palestine. Building on his father's messianic mysticism, the younger Kook infused a rising generation of Israelis with a theology rooted in the "whole land of Israel." Within this religious-Zionist narrative, the establishment of Israel in 1948 and its military victories in the Six-Day War of 1967 were signs of a providential process. Commenting on the official creation of modern Israel and the consequent end of Exile, Rabbi Kook proclaimed that "the state of Israel was created and established by the Council of Nations by order of the Sovereign Lord of the universe so that the clear commandment in the Torah 'that they shall inherit and settle the Land' would be fulfilled" (quoted in Nielsen 1993: 80). To Rabbi Kook and the core leadership of the Gush Emunim, these events signified the realization of the messianic promise.

To their view, present-day Israelis have a *mitva* (or *miztvot*)—a sacred duty—to repossess and settle the land, for the land itself contains an imminent holiness. Hence, the Gush Emunim's uncompromising practice of *hitnahlut*—the resettling of the land, particularly the most politically controversial areas such as the West Bank and the Gaza Strip—is properly understood not so much as a political statement, but as an eschatological proclamation. Withdrawal would contravene God's will and represent a step backward in the messianic process of redemption. Repossessing the land, Rabbi Yehuda Kook exhorts, "is the *miztvot* that, by means of our rule, can accomplish the act of Redemption" (Nielsen 1993: 81). For this reason, the men and women of Gush Emunim have made it their lifework to ensure that the occupied territories are incorporated permanently into the state of Israel, thus hastening the fulfillment of "Jewish destiny."

The activist-believers of the Gush Emunim "are motivated by a sense of participation in a great historical enterprise, or even a metaphysical one" (Aran 1991: 299). They are the modern-day Israelites, the Chosen People of Y-*hweh*. The basis for their sacred identity is rooted in the Hebrew scriptures, which refer to the Jews as "the people that dwells alone, and that will not be counted among the nations" (*Numbers* 23:9). As such, they are not under obligation to human law, but only to the Law of God. Rabbi Shlomo Aviner, disciple of Rabbi Kook the younger, writes, "Ours is not an autonomous scale of values, the product of human reason, but rather a heteronomous, or more correctly, a 'theonomous' scale rooted in the will of the Divine architect of the universe and its moral law" (quoted in Lustick 1993: 112). From this framework, Rabbi Aviner justifies the present-day activities of the Gush Emunim by comparing their seizure of occupied land to that of the ancient Hebrews. He writes, "From the standpoint of humanist morality we were wrong in taking [the land] from the Canaanites. There is only one catch. The command of God ordered *us* to be the people of the land of Israel" (quoted in Lustick 1993: 112; emphasis added). As this quote suggests, in explaining their mission, many of the religious leaders of the movement, when referring to the occupied territories, invoke their biblical names as well as recast their current enemies as the biblical enemies of the ancient Hebrews. In this way, the West Bank becomes Judea and Samaria and the Palestinians become the Canaanites.

Much the same notion of sacred identity applies to political life. To Gush Emunim, the creation of the territorial state of Israel, a restoration of the Promised Land takes priority over the politics of secular governments. As Rabbi Moshe Levinger—arguably the most important spiritual leader of the Gush Emunim today—contends, the modern secular state "can no more vote away Zionism, *aliyah* settlement, than it can vote that people should stop breathing or speaking." On the contrary, he argues, "the fate of Eretz Yisrael [the land of Israel] and a free and whole Jewish life in it are not subject to a minority vote" (quoted in Weisburd 1989: 35).

The threat of modernity in this narrative is subtle, but no less real; it goes to the very heart of religious, ethnic, and national identity for the Jews. Since the Enlightenment, world Jewry has faced, in various ways, its most difficult internal challenge—the challenge of secularism.[5] World Jewry has been divided into Jews maintaining a strong commitment to religious tradition and community and nonobservant secular Jews maintaining a commitment only to their cultural and ethnic heritage. For many Jewish fundamentalists, secularism is simply the latest version of Hellenism—the ways and attitudes of the gentile world—and is held responsible for delaying the redemptive trajectory of history. Indeed, for fundamentalists, the Yom Kippur War and the Camp David Accords represent proof that the secularism of a significant section of Israeli society and of the government are cause for more immediate concern than the constant aggression of the Arabs and Palestinians. The near-failure in the Yom Kippur War and the territorial concessions made by the secularists in the name of an ill-founded peace are jeopardizing the Jewish messianic destiny.

Distinct from other forms of fundamentalism—even Jewish fundamentalism—the Gush Emunim understands modern secularism to be a necessary step (albeit a transitory step) in the redemptive process of history rather than a complete deviation from the Divine Will in history. Following the teaching of the Rabbis Kook, the Gush Emunim believes that modern secular Judaism, along with Orthodox Judaism, will eventually give way to a new synthesis of "religious-national revolutionary Judaism" after completing their divinely appointed roles (Aran 1991: 276). Hence, in the wake of the Six-Day War, the Gush Emunim concluded that Israel's triumph signaled that the redemptive plan of Y-*hweh* was being realized. In this way, the Gush Emunim movement embraces both a short-range pessimism regarding the dominance of secular Judaism in Israel and a long-range optimism about the ultimate redemption of the land and people of Israel.

Hindu Fundamentalism

Turning to our last case study, a few qualifications are necessary. First, in contrast to Christianity, Islam, and Judaism, Hinduism is much less a unified, single religion.[6] Also, quite unlike the Semitic religions, which are all based in a monotheistic belief system and assume a more or less linear, teleological view of history, Hinduism is rooted in a polytheistic theology and posits a cyclical, infinitely repetitive cosmology. Additionally, Hinduism's epistemological assumptions are markedly different from those of its monotheistic counterparts. For fundamentalist movements within Protestantism, Islam, and Judaism there is a single, overriding cosmic Truth that is based outside of time and history and is knowable only as it is revealed through authoritative holy texts for which they believe themselves divinely appointed guardians. For Hindus, in contrast, there is no ultimate canon, creed, defined dogma, or even institutional structure; truth takes many forms, operates at many levels, and is not outside history (Embree 1994: 618). Consequently, while narrative remains an important discursive form for Hindu fundamentalists, the stories told neither possess the linearity nor the teleology of Christian, Islamic, or Jewish eschatological-messianic narratives. Nevertheless, Hindu fundamentalism also shares the same basic world-historical narrative of the faithful in confrontation with modernity.

Late nineteenth-century Hindu revivalists claimed that, after nearly a millennium of Muslim domination and almost two centuries of British colonialism, Hindu society had forgotten its majestic and resplendent past, once a vibrant and thriving Hindu civilization. The cause for both the foreign domination by the "Muslim and British villains" and the loss of cultural memory was a direct consequence of the failure of Indians to observe *dharma,* a Hindu code of conduct encompassing all aspects of life.[7] Moreover, because the "good society" can exist only when it is rooted on correct principles of *dharma,* India could not regenerate itself; antiquity could not be recovered until the rules of *dharma* were again properly observed. This conviction has been the central religious justification for most Hindu nationalist and independence movements of the twentieth century, and its most powerful proponent has been the Rashtriya Swayamsevak Sangh (RSS), or the "National Pure Service Society," the clearest expression of Hindu fundamentalism (see Malkani 1980; Mishra 1980).

Similar to the Gush Emunim, where sacredness is found in the "whole" land of Israel, the RSS finds sacredness in the "wholeness" of the

Hindu people. Indeed, some RSS publications have argued that the only real comparison with their understanding of *Hindutva* (Hindu nationhood) is Zionism. RSS intellectual Balasaheb makes this very comparison:

> Today we have been free for a quarter century. But what is our performance? They say we have had partition and refugees and four wars and droughts. Israel also had all that. It started with a partition. The bulk of its nationals were refugees. It has all through faced actual war and threat of war. Much of the country is desert. And yet, that small country is very strong. This is because it has a strong society. Our problem here also is man. We have to wake him up, organize him, strengthen him. That is the rationale of Hindu Sangathan. (quoted in Malkani 1980: 89)

Hindu unity is the aim and mantra of the RSS and the strength of its overwhelming attraction.

The RSS is acutely aware that modernity brings with it forces that wreak havoc with cultural identity, suffocate *dharma,* and divide Hindu people. RSS intellectual and leader B. D. Thengadi observes that, under influences of Western civilization, the traditional values of Hindus tend to become "subdued." He writes: "Signs of disintegration appear in the family, village, and communal life" (quoted in Mishra 1980: 135). Dina Nath Mishra, author and RSS sympathizer, uses stronger language: "The ersatz, sloganistic secularism has done great harm to the nation" (1980: 136).

Hindu fundamentalism does not see itself in confrontation with modernity per se, but with modernity in a particular secularizing sense; namely, with the kind of modern secularity that leads sections of the Indian intelligentsia (influenced by Western education and culture) to foreswear the centrality and uniqueness of the Hindu nation.[8] "Secularism" for Hindus does not mean the same thing as for the Semitic religions—as the wholesale rejection of transcendental realities. As Indians are quick to point out, Hindu culture, embedded in a polytheistic theology, has long been one of tolerance and openness. Differences in religious belief and practice are an intrinsic part of Hindu culture. Nielsen (1993: 106) observes, for example, that Hinduism allows for *bhakti marga* (salvation by faith), *karma marga* (salvation by works), and *jnana marga* (salvation by philosophical insight). What makes one a Hindu for the RSS is not so much religious orthodoxy (here defined as right belief rooted in an authoritative text) or orthopraxy, but whether one is a native of the Land of Mother India.

The problem with "secularism," in the Indian sense, is that it insists on neutrality with respect to all religions in matters of public policy. What the RSS objects to is how a "secular state" distorts the fundamental reality of Hindu culture by adopting the policy that Hinduism is merely one religion among others, including among foreign religions such as Christianity and Islam. The net effect of such "secular" policy, in its view, is the progressive denuding of *dharma*. Modernity is a problem to the extent that it results in the de-Hinduization of the Indian people and culture. To those perpetrating the values responsible for this cultural annulment, whether Indian or non-Indian, the RSS offers only one choice. As RSS leader M. S. Golwalkar warns:

> The non-Hindu people in Hindustan must adopt the Hindu culture and religion, must learn to respect and hold in reverence Hindu religion, and must entertain no ideas but those of glorification of the Hindu race and culture . . . claiming no privileges . . . not even citizen's rights. (quoted in Nielsen 1993: 111)

At the heart of RSS collective action is an acute sense of loss, a lament for a forgotten Hindu civilization and *Hindutva,* or cultural unity. This sentiment is captured in some of the more nostalgic writing of M. S. Golwalkar:

> The origins of our people, the date from which we have been living here as a civilized entity, is unknown to the scholars of history. . . . We existed when there was no necessity for any name. We were the good, the enlightened people. We were the people who knew about the laws of nature and the laws of the Spirit. We built a great civilization, a great culture, and a unique social order. We had brought into life almost everything that was beneficial to man. (quoted in Embree 1994: 630)

Thus, the famous RSS intellectual, Shri Guruji, could argue about the desecration of dividing "our national history into a Hindu period, a Muslim period, and a British period; history cannot be named after rulers; a proper history has to be a history of the people. And so our entire history is Hindu history" (quoted in Malkani 1980: 43). To the RSS, Hindu history recalls a time when India was a great civilization, when *dharma* held the people in harmony. Since its confrontation with Islam, the colonial British, and more recently, with the divisive proclivities of India's own secularized elite, Indian society has been filled with the dissonance of a nation divided against itself. Speaking to this problem of *asangathan* (disunity) in an address in 1973, Balasaheb proclaimed that, "Today, the Hindu is weak and divided. Once he becomes strong and united the whole country will become strong and united" (quoted in Malkani 1980: 89). But in order for this to occur, the corrosive and divisive influence of non-Hindu values must be stopped.

The RSS has dedicated itself to eradicating non-Hindu values within India. Inspired by the warriorlike ethos idealized in quasi-sacred texts like the *Bhagavad Gita,* the RSS has reintroduced the ancient practice of *Karmayoga,* a discipline which attempts to combine *dharma* and *moksha*—a life of action and religious devotion. In addition, through the creation of a vast national network of *shakhas* (local RSS chapters) and a host of related political, cultural, and humanitarian organizations, RSS organizers have dedicated their lives to spreading the message of *Hindutva* to the entire Hindu people. Their fervent prayer combines the memory of past glory with the hope of a future unified people: "Forever I bow to Thee, O Loving Motherland! O Motherland of us Hindus. . . . May our victorious organized power of action, by Thy Grace, fully protect our *dharma* and lead this nation of ours to the highest pinnacle of glory" (quoted in Malkani 1980: 199).

CONCLUSION

From this brief excursion into specific movement narratives from a variety of the world's major religions, it should be evident that despite fundamentalist movements' obvious differences—whether theological, cultural, or historical—they all share a common story of how history has gone awry. While each fundamentalist community has its own particular account of modernity's perversion—or potential perversion—of history, all have engaged in a quest to restore history to its sacral path or to keep it on such a course, and all use their movement narratives to inspire and motivate their faithful to pursue specific aspects of this quest. In short, the foregoing review does suggest that there may be an empirical and conceptual basis for a general theory of fundamentalism when examined through the lens of narrative.

Social movement scholars have not attempted any systematic narrative approach to the study of religious fundamentalism. The standard works center on the (sometimes militant) political agendas of fundamentalist movements and on their mobilization of institutional and social resources. These works typically neglect—and therefore minimize—the symbolic-ideational dimensions that are the real source of fundamentalist collective action and resolve. Sufficient effort has not yet been made to move to a deeper appreciation of these dimensions. Studying fundamentalist narratives, we have argued, is an important place to start.

To the standard treatments, a narrative approach adds significant empirical and theoretical advantages. Narrative bridges the social and emotional distance between movement rhetoric and calls to action, on the one hand, and the degree of actual resonance such rhetoric elicits, on the other. Hence, an analysis of fundamentalist movement narratives reveals their evocative power, rooted as they are in frameworks of cosmological significance and meaning. At the same time, the world-historical narrative of fundamentalism clarifies the central role of the confrontation with modernity in these movements, which together represent a counterpoint to the disorienting forces of secularism, pluralism, and rationalism—the rival narrative of modernity—in the name of religious faithfulness. This world-historical narrative constitutes the central point of unity across movements and highlights their difference from other religious expressions, including religious orthodoxy.

But the fundamentalist world-historical narrative is no theological abstraction. It animates the orthopraxy inherent in many fundamentalist movements; specifies a theonomic basis for religious and political authority over against modern Western dualism; and acts as the hermeneutic justification for selective, if literal, scriptural idealism, at once undeniable and absolute. In these ways, the fundamentalist world-historical narrative of modernity also provides a window through which one can see the pressures and strains modernity creates for ordinary people and for the religious communities in which they abide.

While we have but touched here on these points, narrative analysis of fundamentalist movements opens up an avenue for further research into this significant worldwide phenomenon.

NOTES

1. Rhys H. Williams (1994: 824) suggests that fundamentalisms demonstrate the archetype of social movements. "They are ideologically

driven forces for social change," he writes, "often fluid, and draw many varied issues, social groups, and historical periods under their rhetorical umbrellas. At the same time, fundamentalist movements are committed to embodying timeless truths, institutionalizing 'proper' ways of living, and instrumental and secular action combined with their expressive forms. The potential internal tensions within fundamentalist movements as they attempt to manage ideological fidelity and organizational survival offer a clear picture of the roles of ideology, organization, and power in movement dynamics."

2. Arguments over the meaning, periodization, and overall usefulness of the concept of "modernity" are well-known, and we accept many of the criticisms of what is often referred to as modernization theory, especially with respect to the simplistic characterization of modernization as a unified, orderly, progressive transformation of the world into a single world order which is overwhelmingly secular, democratic, individualistic, and rationalized—and therefore better. However, we also maintain that modernity (or modernities) is a useful, even fruitful way of bringing conceptual order to the indisputably dramatic transformations (again, please note the use of the plural), which at different times and places have been at work throughout the world over the past five centuries. Some of the more well-known characteristics of the modernizing process include increasing degrees of cultural pluralism, institutional differentiation, the disarticulation of status, and the compartmentalization of everyday life.

3. By elemental form, we refer to those components which are considered basic to narrative structure in general—for example, emplotment, contextualization, and characterization. For a fuller treatment of these elements we refer readers to chapter 1 of this volume.

4. While not possessing the integrative power of *premillennialism,* the doctrine of the *Mahdi* is a defining element of certain strands of Shi'ism. Perhaps the most well-known are the "Twelvers," or *Ithna Asharis.* They believe that the Twelfth Imam—the last Imam in direct line with Muhammad and who disappeared in 874—will eventually return at the end of the world to vindicate his loyal followers, restore the community to its rightful place, and usher in a perfect Islamic society (see Esposito 1991: 46–47).

5. As Bruce Lawrence points out, the conventional treatment of Jewish history (quite understandably) focuses on the role of European anti-Semitism leading to the Holocaust, Palestinian resistance to the Zionist movement, and the aggression of Israel's neighbors. However, there is a fourth challenge: Enlightenment secularism, which has been as potent, if

less obvious, than these others. It has its roots in the internal divisions between groups like the *Hasidim* (Orthodox Jews) and the *Maskilim* ("Enlightened Jews") in Eastern Europe in the late nineteenth century (see Lawrence 1989: 124–127).

6. According to some, Hinduism is best understood as the parent of a family of faiths: Janism, Buddhism, and Sikhism all have their origins in Hinduism (see Embree 1994: 629; Nielsen 1993: 105).

7. While there is no equivalent to *dharma* in English, it can generally be understood as a code of good conduct, pattern of noble living, and/or religious rules and observance.

8. Not to be confused with Indian government; to the RSS, religion, culture, and nation are one and the same (see Embree 1994).

SEVEN

Drug Court Stories

Transforming American Jurisprudence

JAMES L. NOLAN JR.

R ecent social movement scholarship has usefully shifted attention to the important cultural variables that drive and give meaning to social movements—a focus that was given limited attention for many years. In this chapter, I analyze an important movement within the American criminal justice system that gives empirical support to the legitimacy of this new focus. While the drug court movement might invite a *prima facie* analysis based on the conventional structural categories, a comprehensive investigation of the movement makes evident the limitations of such a focus.

Drawing on ethnographic observation of twenty-one drug courts throughout the United States, attendance at three national drug court conferences, participation in two mentoring court training sessions, interviews with twenty-four drug court judges and dozens of other drug court officials, observation—over a several-month period—of the planning of a local drug court, and additional supporting data from more than forty drug courts around the country,[1] I show in this chapter how the rapid expansion of and widespread enthusiasm with the drug court phenomenon only makes sense when certain cultural forces are considered in the larger equation. And central to the impact of these cultural forces is the defining and energizing influence of narrative discourse.

THE DRUG COURT MOVEMENT

Before considering the significance of the different structural and cultural factors driving this social movement, I first provide a brief overview of the defining features of the drug court. The first drug court was established in Dade County, Florida in 1989. Janet Reno, the state's attorney for Dade County at the time, was among those who spearheaded the effort. Since then, more than six hundred similar courts have been started or are in the planning stages. The rapid expansion of the drug court model has led participants and observers alike to label the phenomenon a "movement," even a "revolution" in criminal justice—the proposed causes for which we will consider in the next section.

The drug court offers drug offenders the option of court-monitored treatment as an alternative to the normal adjudication process. Defendants participate in various treatment modalities including acupuncture, individual and group counseling sessions, and self-help groups like Alcoholics Anonymous (AA) or Narcotics Anonymous (NA). Offenders also submit to periodic urinalysis testing and regularly (every one to four weeks) report back to the judge, who checks on their treatment progress. The program is usually expected to last one year, but often lasts much longer. Most drug courts offer defendants, as an incentive for participating in the drug court, the dismissal of their criminal charge or the expungement of their drug arrest on successful completion of the program. Other courts actually mandate drug court, often as a condition of probation.

The drug court fundamentally alters the traditional adjudication process. For example, the relationship between the judge and the defendant (or "client," as they are often referred to in the drug court) is radically different from a normal criminal court. The judge engages the client directly, asks personal questions, and encourages the client in the treatment process. Judges operate more like proactive therapists than dispassionate judicial officers in the way they interact with clients. The attorney's role is also substantially altered in the drug court. Not only is the relationship between public defender and prosecutor no longer adversarial, but lawyers generally play a less prominent role. As one drug court judge explains, "lawyers literally and figuratively take a step back" (Tauber 1993: 8). In many drug courts the lawyers do not even show up for the regular drug court sessions, and when they do, it is often difficult to determine just who the attorneys are in the courtroom drama. At a mentoring court training session in

Rochester, New York, for example, one first-time observer of the drug court suggested that the district attorney reminded him of a "potted plant" because of the limited role he performed.

The drug court has received considerable support at both the grassroots and national levels. The Department of Justice opened a Drug Courts Program Office in 1995, through which planning, implementation, and enhancement grants for existing or emerging drug courts have since been awarded. Funding for these grants has increased steadily since the Office was established. In fiscal year 1995, the office granted $12 million to drug courts. This increased to $15 million in 1996, to $30 million in both 1997 and 1998, and then to $40 million in 1999. An additional $20 million has been given to drug courts from other federal agencies. Only a percentage of courts rely on federal grants; many started with no federal or even state support. To pay for drug courts, some courts require a fee from participating clients, others have solicited private money, while others have raised the cost of drunk driving schools. Some have raised local sales taxes, and still others have simply reallocated existing resources. Even bankrupt Orange County, California was able to start a drug court without any initial state or federal government support. Over the past decade, more than $45 million has been spent on drug courts from nonfederal sources. Thus, interest in the drug court is pronounced both at the national and grassroots levels. As Tim Murray, former director of the Drug Courts Program Office put it, "It's probably the only movement in the judicial system that has bubbled up from the grassroots to the Federal government" (Drug Strategies 1997: 21).

That the drug court phenomenon is a movement within the criminal justice system makes it somewhat anomalous according to conventional social scientific conceptions of social movements. Typically, social movements are conceived as collective social behavior seeking to effect change from outside the political process. In the case of the drug court movement, contrastingly, the major advocates of social change are the political (or more specifically, the judicial) actors themselves. Court officials, internal to the judicial process, often seek to gain support from the public (those external to the judicial process), rather than the other way around. Those gathering at the annual national conventions, for example, are almost exclusively insiders to the drug court process—judges, district attorneys, public defenders, acupuncturists, and treatment providers. When they gather, they actually strategize about the ways they can get outsiders to accept and support the drug court program. Conference panels have focused, for example, on such topics as "Strategies for Attracting Community Resources," "Accessing Community Resources," and "Getting Local Government and the Community to 'Buy In' to a Drug Court Program."[2] But the drug court movement is very much a social movement—even according to conventional conceptualizations—in that the various actors have joined together with the expressed purpose of fundamentally altering the American judicial system, making it less traditional and more therapeutic in orientation.

The change that judges and other drug court officials seek to effect is anything but modest. As one judge told a group of judges gathering at a drug court conference in Washington, D.C., "What we are doing here is no less than a complete revolution in jurisprudence. . . . We are the judges that get to color outside the lines." This departure from the "traditional jurisprudential role" is replaced by an uncompromising commitment to the "new way of therapeutic jurisprudence." Or as another judge put it at a drug court conference in Portland, "What we are doing is we are reinventing justice." This new form of justice is spreading not only with the expansion of the drug court, but in the application of the drug court model to other criminal behaviors, such as to petty theft, prostitution, DUI/DWI, and domestic violence cases.[3]

Separate domestic violence, juvenile, and community courts based on the drug court model have already been established. Moreover, judges are beginning to introduce drug court strategies even into regular court dockets, as illustrated by the focus of such conference panels as "Using Drug Court Skills without a Drug Court." In this particular session, judges discussed the innovative ways they have implemented drug court methods in regular court sessions. Advocates celebrate the "potential for tremendous growth as this model is adapted for other types of criminal cases" (Drug Strategies 1997: 30).

EXPLAINING THE DRUG COURT

But why the widespread enthusiasm for this radically new form of criminal adjudication? The conventional structural variables of "economic pressures," the "expansion of political opportunities," "resource mobilization," and the like, provide partial explanations for the popularity of this innovative form of criminal adjudication. Advocates of the drug court often speak of the structural pressures that they believe gave birth to the movement. For example, the growing number of drug offenses, the high recidivism rates among drug offenders, overcrowded jails, the expense of incarceration (as opposed to the cheaper costs of treatment), and heavy criminal court caseloads, are all justifications given by drug court officials for the necessity of drug courts. These were the kind of explanations offered in Miami and in other jurisdictions where drug courts have been established since. As it is often argued, the criminal justice system was faced with a situation where something new had to be tried. "What we were doing before simply was not working" is the common justificatory dictum offered by drug court officials. The drug court promises to relieve overcrowded jails of nonviolent offenders, reduce the heavy case loads of criminal court dockets, and lower the expense of incarcerating offenders with the alternatively cheaper cost of court-monitored treatment. From this perspective, the structural realities of the contemporary criminal justice landscape invited the establishment of a new method for adjudicating drug offenders.

And the ability of certain political actors to highlight these pressures and make available necessary economic resources played a role in advancing the movement. For example, federal funding was sustained for fiscal year 1995—after an initial scare that the money might be cut—because of the lobbying efforts of drug court judges and the establishment of the National Association of Drug Court Professionals (NADCP), the headquarters of which is strategically located in the Washington, D.C. area. Drug court advocates have also rallied support and resources through annual national conferences, the establishment of a national resource center (the Drug Court Clearinghouse and Technical Assistance Project, located at American University), and the institutionalization of mentoring courts for the purpose of helping emerging drug courts establish their programs.

While these are important variables which certainly explain part of the emergence and expansion of the drug court, they do not explain all of it. The structural developments may provide certain opportunities. But as the drug court movement demonstrates, it is cultural factors—ideas, beliefs, worldviews, the collective consciousness—that drive and give direction to social movements. Such a relationship between structural and cultural variables is in keeping with Doug McAdam's general assessment of social movements. "Expanding political opportunities," according to McAdam, "do not, in any simple sense, produce a social movement . . . they only offer insurgents a certain objective 'structural potential' for collective political action" (1994: 39). Or, as Neil Smelser put it much earlier, certain institutional conditions establish a "structural conduciveness" for social change (1962: 15). As such, the pressures of increasing case loads, high recidivism rates, mandatory minimum sentences for felony drug charges, and so on, provide the "structural potential" or "structural conduciveness" for particular innovations in the criminal justice system. But it is certain cultural sensibilities that give meaning and guidance to the direction these innovative efforts take. If this is the case, then what cultural tendencies have justified and energized the advancement of the drug court movement?

As I have argued elsewhere, the therapeutic culture has significantly impacted a number of major institutions in the late twentieth-century American state, including the criminal justice system.[4] Not surprisingly, then, the therapeutic ethos offers itself as a likely candidate to give philosophical energy to a movement that is taking place within the criminal justice system. Furthermore, narrative discourse or the telling of stories is the dominant vehicle through which therapeutic sensibilities are carried in this social movement. Put another way, storytelling is a fitting rhetorical medium through which to communicate the defining qualities of the therapeutic ethos, characterized as it is by an elevated concern with the self, by a conspicuously emotivist form of discourse and self-understanding, and by a proclivity to invoke the language of victimhood and to view behaviors in pathological terms.

For example, individual narrative, rather than the less personalized discourse possible within the parameters of the traditional metanarratives, makes sense in a cultural situation where the self has become, as Daniel Bell puts it, "the touchstone of cultural judgment" (1978: xxi). Personal narrative, in other words, best expresses the concerns, ideas, beliefs, perceptions, and rights of the unencumbered self. Moreover, the language of victimhood is almost uniformly characterized by the individual stories of oppression, injury, or abuse told by the victimized self. Legal scholars, for example, see individual stories as what constitutes the very essence of "victim impact statements" and argue that these "stories of [the] victimized . . . should have a greater place in the law" (Gewirtz 1996: 143).

But storytelling is perhaps best suited to the therapeutic orientation in the way in which it favors the communication of emotions. Classical understandings of legal and political rhetoric regarded as more important the persuasive saliency of logic, syllogistic reasoning, and rational argument over emotions in the legal setting. According to Aristotle, the use of syllogistic reasoning or rhetorical enthymemes—what he regarded as most central to legal or forensic rhetoric—could actually thwart the speaker's ability to arouse emotion.[5] Thus, he understood an essential incompatibility between logic and emotions. The introduction of storytelling into legal processes, however, offers a style of discourse more conducive to the communication of emotions. There is, one might say, an elective affinity between the two. As Gerald Lopez puts it: "Stories and storytelling de-emphasize the logical and resurrect the emotive and intuitive" (Farber and Sherry 1996: 43). Therefore, not only is narrative an important vehicle through which cultural tendencies incite and advance social movements (Fine 1995), but it is a communication style that is particularly well-suited to carrying cultural ideals informed by the ethic of emotivism and other therapeutic tendencies.

Curiously, at the same time that sociologists have discovered the significance of storytelling in social movements, a growing number of legal scholars have become interested in the place of narrative discourse in legal processes (Brooks and Gewirtz 1996; Scheppele 1989; Massaro 1989). The drug court movement brings these two scholarly enterprises together; it is at once an important and rapidly expanding social movement in the justice system, and is a legal development where narrative discourse plays a very critical role. In the conclusion of this chapter, I will touch on some of the issues raised among legal scholars about the place of narrative in the law, and relate these to the substance of storytelling in the drug court movement. It is to a fuller discussion of the latter that I now turn.

STORYTELLING IN THE DRUG COURT MOVEMENT

Narrative is central to the drug court in many ways. The drug court drama itself is very much a performance in the Goffmanian (see Goffman 1959) sense, where participants are conscious of a defined backstage and frontstage, where movement advocates actually speak of the local drug court drama as "theater," and where personal narrative is perhaps the archetypal form of discourse. Narrative discourse, in fact, is evident at several levels. In the counseling sessions, in the regular trips to the courtroom, and in the graduation ceremonies, clients regularly give testimony about the effect that drugs have had on their lives and the impact of drug court in helping them to overcome their addictions. Likewise, the counselors—many of whom are recovering addicts themselves—share personal

testimonies about their own recoveries as they help their clients to overcome drug addictions. Even some of the judges have been aided through
treatment in their own efforts to overcome addiction to alcohol or ciga-
rettes, and talk publicly about the positive effect treatment has had on
their own lives. Therefore, at the level of the local drug court drama, narrative is a core feature of the adjudicative process. As Judge Jeffrey Tauber
put it in instructions to a group of new drug court judges, "You are the
storyteller. Through the people who appear before you and their interaction with you, your staff, and the audience, the story (and promise) of
your program is told" (Tauber 1993: 8).

This local-level narrative is not unrelated to the larger drug court
movement. Often the stories told at the local level are retold in order to
justify the movement and convince others of its efficacy. As such, these
local-level stories have national, even international, import. The second
form of discourse in the drug court movement, then, is what could be
called national- or movement-level narrative; that is, storytelling that is
concerned with the public advocacy of the drug court for political and
public relations purposes. As at the local level, storytelling is a dominant
form of discourse. As we will see, however, the distinction between local
and national is useful mainly for conceptual purposes. The stories in the
former often become the justificatory narratives retold in the latter.

According to Gary Fine, movement stories are of three general types:
(1) affronts to the movement actor, or "horror stories," which are often
recounted to justify one's participation in the movement; (2) collective
experiences within the movement, or "war stories," which are often told
for the purpose of encouraging the troops to persevere in the battle; and
(3) stories that reaffirm the value of the movement, or "happy endings"
(Fine 1995: 135–136). Fine's typology provides a useful heuristic for
making sense of the drug court movement. The three types of stories, as
told within the movement, assume different themes, plots, central actors,
and common story lines. The protagonist in "horror stories" and "happy
endings," for example, is typically the drug offender. As told in the
former, the drug offender is harmed by lack of access to a drug court program, while in the latter he or she benefits from involvement in a local
drug court.

"War stories," on the other hand, more often feature the crusading
drug court practitioner who steadfastly faces and overcomes various
obstacles in advancing the drug court movement. All three types of stories

are characterized by a certain emphasis on emotions, a quality that is perhaps most pronounced in happy endings. Again, this represents an important departure from classical understandings of legal rhetoric. Though pathos, from the classical perspective, was always present in different types of oratory, it was seen as less central to political and legal oratory than was "ethos"—the credibility of the speaker—and "logos"—the logical viability of the argument. Contemporary legal and political oratory inverts the classical emphasis and gives much greater import to pathos (Nolan 1996, 1998: 235–279). The telling of stories in the drug court movement is no exception to this contemporary trend.

Indeed, the identification, assessment, and communication of emotions are central to the change process that is endemic to the drug court program. In as much as the drug court is committed to treating drug offenders, engagement with the defendant's inner life is a central focus. The judge is not simply concerned with making a judgment about whether or not a "defendant" committed some illegal behavior, but he or she is actively involved in the process of helping the "client" or "patient" recover, heal, and overcome an addictive lifestyle. Given this orientation, the judges and treatment providers necessarily explore the inner emotive regions of the defendant in order to effect this change, and clients, through reference to feelings and other defining features of the therapeutic sensibility, tell stories of their recoveries. As we will see, the drug court world encourages a particular kind of story, with common themes and a typical story line. In other words, the successful client is encouraged to tell his or her story in a particular kind of way, and may suffer consequences for failing to do so.

The notion of "emplotment," as such, is most detectable in happy endings. That the right story is so critical in this instance suggests that happy endings are probably the most important kind of story told in the drug court movement. Indeed, happy endings often represent the reference point for the other two types of stories. That is, the success stories of clients (who tell the right story) are often incorporated into the war stories of crusading drug court practitioners and represent the ideal against which horror stories are contrasted. Both war stories and horror stories, in other words, point to the correctly conveyed happy endings. This will become clear as we begin with a consideration of horror stories, the type of story against which happy endings represent a stark and welcomed contrast.

Horror Stories

Horror stories, according to Fine, are told by movement actors in reference to a time when things were bad; to a time or situation that prompted a change in their own perspective or at least signified to them—and implicitly to others—the need for change. Drug court horror stories clearly fit within this genre of narrative, as they regularly are offered by advocates to illustrate the deplorable condition of the criminal justice system and the desperate need for reform. Often drug court judges told me of their disgust with the way they did things before becoming drug court judges, the frustration they experienced with seeing the same people arrested and rearrested, and the structurally imposed inability they felt to help defendants address their "core problem," for example, drug addiction. In contrast, the drug courts, as the stories are told, provide opportunities whereby judges can be more directly involved in the lives of their clients, helping them to conquer drug dependency, pass a high school GED (Graduation Equivalency Degree) test, get a job, and become contributing, taxpaying citizens. Almost uniformly, judges describe their involvement in drug court as the highlight of their careers. The horror stories are told to underscore the viability of this new approach in contrast to the old.

Consider two examples. The first is a story I heard told on two occasions by Guy Wheeler, the director of the treatment facility at the Broward County (Fort Lauderdale) drug court. The first time I heard the story was in an interview with Wheeler during my visit to his facility. Wheeler was speaking of the benefits of the drug court—in particular, the fact that defendants who succeed in the program have their drug arrest expunged from their record. "Here is the biggest issue of the movement, why I like the drug court movement: it drops charges. That is the biggest reason why I like it." Wheeler's enthusiasm about this feature of the drug court had to do with his belief that a criminal record made it difficult for offenders to get employment, a point he illustrates with a story about his own uncle.

> You can't get a job. It is very difficult to get one. I'm not saying you can't. But, it is extremely difficult. So, guess what? You are going to have crime back in the neighborhoods. I can attest to this. I had an uncle, who joined the army, served, did everything he was supposed to do. He sold some drugs. Boom. Got popped.

He could never get a job. I was saying, "You're lazy. You're no good. You don't want to get a job." He says, "Okay, you take me out there to find a job." I took him everywhere to get a job. Everywhere he would go—very bright man, very articulate man—they turned him down. He couldn't get a job. Guess what, they killed him in the street. Black on black crime . . . Somebody killed him. Blew his brains out.

This "horror story" is told to provide a compelling example for the necessity of the drug court. Without the possibility of a clean record, individuals who commit drug-related crimes will simply continue in criminal activity. The drug court provides an opportunity for offenders to deal with their drug problem and avoid future criminal activity. Wheeler went on to link the potency of his personal story with the significance of the drug court movement.

So, these kids come in here, and they say, "I want a job. Where can I get a job?" Their families don't own businesses. . . . So, the biggest reason why I like the movement is that it gets charges dropped. We say, "They don't want to work, they just don't want to work." And you need to ask the question, who is going to hire them? They can't get hired until somebody becomes an advocate for them.

According to Wheeler, this advocacy includes education, treatment, and the other features of the drug court. In fact, the particular drug court of which he is a part helps place drug court clients in employment positions. The drug court, as such, is the vehicle through which this needed advocacy is realized.

Eleven months after our interview, Wheeler told the story again, this time to an audience of over six hundred at a drug court conference in Portland, Oregon. The story came at the end of his lecture and was told even more dramatically than in our previous interview.

It is extremely difficult for these clients to get jobs. You see, I know about this personally. I had an uncle. His name was Uncle David, and I loved my Uncle David. My Uncle David fought in the Vietnam War and he had a drug charge. And Uncle David couldn't get a job. And I kept saying, "Uncle David, you're lazy. Get off your butt. Go get a job. Go get a job." He kept saying, "I can't get a job. I've got a drug charge." I said, "No, Uncle David,

I'll go out and help you find a job." Everybody turned my uncle down. Five years later my uncle was trying to hustle. . . . Someone blew his brains out on 6th Street and 9th Avenue in Fort Lauderdale, Florida. You see, I lost my uncle. If we had had a drug court treatment program a long time ago, things may have turned out differently for my uncle. Maybe he could be here. He was brighter, he was smarter than me. And he could stand here right now. So, I say to you in all honesty, America we need programs of this nature. Because if we don't, guess what? We will reap what we sow.

In the conference presentation Wheeler more directly connected the story about his uncle with the need for the drug courts, and used the example to encourage people to continue with or start a drug court in their own region.

Another horror story was conveyed to me in an interview with Judge William Schma, a drug court judge from Kalamazoo, Michigan. The purpose of his story was to illustrate the harmfulness of a system that does not have the adjudicative features of the drug court. In addition to his drug court duties, Judge Schma also has a regular court docket, where he uses drug-court-like methods in the way he treats defendants.

One example of this is his "First Monday Club," where he tells certain defendants (who presumably are on probation) to come to his court every Monday at 4:00 P.M. During these sessions he engages the clients in a therapeutic encounter, that is, he discusses with the clients how they are doing personally and how they are progressing in their recovery process. As Judge Schma explained, "It's kind of a way of doing some drug court stuff without a drug court," a practice, as noted earlier, other judges are employing. With the First Monday Club he is still able to put some "therapeutic things . . . into the system." At the time of our interview he had eight clients in this program.

One story he told involved a former participant in the First Monday Club named Tim. According to Judge Schma, Tim was a drug addict, but entered the criminal justice system for "pushing bad paper" (writing bad checks). Judge Schma put him on probation and for six months he attended First Monday Club, during which time he allegedly stayed off drugs. Because of his success, Judge Schma eventually released him from court oversight. Once back on the street, according to Schma, Tim stayed clean for awhile, but was encouraged back into drug use by the influence of a police informant. This is how Schma tells the story.

> Well, what happened to this guy when he got back on the streets? He stayed clean, he had a job, he didn't commit crimes, he didn't use. The cops get an informant to work on this guy because he had such a long history in the drug world. The cops get an informant to work on this guy to start dealing drugs with the informant. And the next thing you know he's using and dealing drugs, and he's busted again and this time some other judge put him in prison for four years. Now that's fucking dumb. That is unbelievable. . . . He told me this at the sentencing. I had heard that this is what had happened, but I had him tell me the story.

The horror story that Judge Schma conveys, then, illustrates the problems with the pre-drug court way of doing things, and the contrasting efficacy of the drug court method. The standard judicial practice is problematic. The story conveys the need for a transformation, suggesting that without change, more people like Tim will be harmed by the system. Judge Schma makes this very link as he continues the story.

> Now if I had kept that guy in the drug court . . . I could have hung onto him. I would have known he wasn't going to his meetings. You know, you get so you can just tell by the way they behave what's going on. His slipping back into drugs wouldn't have happened. And I could have done that for him for less than two thousand bucks a year. And now we are paying a hundred thousand dollars [to keep him in prison for four years]. That is just stupid, under anybody's terms, anybody's definition! That's not a happy story, but it's a real story about why we need to be doing what we're doing.

Like Guy Wheeler, Judge Schma understands the potency of this story, and consciously uses it to convince skeptics about the benefits of the drug court. With pungent indignation, Schma promises to use the story of how Tim was "dragged back into the gutter" to promote drug courts. "I'm going to use this example. I'm going to throw it out to every politician I get a chance to talk to, because it is absolutely insane."

War Stories

If "horror stories" such as these are offered to help convert unbelievers to the movement, the second type of social movement narrative aims to embolden the already converted. "War stories" are put forth in order to encourage the faithful to stay the course, to press forward, and to resist opposition, however formidable it may be. As Gary Fine explains of this second class of stories, "Like soldiers after a battle, members may be exhilarated by the accounts of comrades-in-arms" (1995: 136). This type of story is particularly evident at the various conferences and training seminars I attended. At these events, judges and other officials from more developed drug courts give lectures or speak on panels with the explicit aim of instructing newer courts on how to operate a drug court.

Stories told at these events identify likely obstacles drug court personnel will face, and give advice on how to overcome them. War stories, according to Fine, may recount either triumphs or temporary setbacks, but irrespective are told to strengthen the resolve of the troops. I will consider examples of both (triumphs and setbacks) with stories told by drug court movement activists. The first was told at the 1996 drug court conference in Washington, D.C., by Wendy Lindley, a judge from Laguna Niguel, California. Like Judge Schma, Lindley was attempting to implement the therapeutic methods of the drug court into a regular criminal court docket.

Like many of the drug court judges, Lindley was frustrated with the conventional adjudicative method. She spoke of her frustration with "just recycling these people" through the system, and decided something new must be tried. So she started a therapeutically oriented court program with offenders who had "blood alcohol levels over 2.0" at the time of their arrest. She worked on a bench with thirteen other judges and told them about what she was doing. According to Judge Lindley, they were not receptive to her efforts. "They were so negative," Lindley explains. "They called me a social worker. And I said, 'Thank you.'" Judge Lindley reflected on the reasons for her coworkers' resistance in her comments during the panel discussion.

> Many, many judges have a very strong sense of feeling that you
> handle a case in a certain way. You process justice efficiently,
> and you move on, and you don't care what happens. And they
> have said that to me, "I don't care what happens when this

person leaves this courtroom. It's not my business. I'm a judge, not a social worker." So, to me, that whole issue obviously brings out quite a bit of emotion, and exposing them to it does not seem to make a difference. I invited a number of them to come watch. I had one judge come watch, and he still didn't do it, in spite of the fact that the stories these people told as they stood up and graduated brought me to tears. So, I don't know what the answer is to this resistance other than just continued judicial education, and hoping to change the way people think about what the job of the judge is in our contemporary society.

Notice that she turns her defeat into an opportunity to encourage herself and others to persevere in helping the unbelieving find the true judicial light. Judge Lindley not only found the individual narratives of the clients to be emotively persuasive, but she anticipated that these stories would convince her cohorts, and was surprised and disappointed when they did not.

Here again we see the intersection of local- and national-level narrative. Lindley was conveying to a national audience the difficulties she faced in implementing therapeutic justice at the local level. In the course of this account she referred to the individual emotionally laden stories of clients who graduated from her program, stories she believed had a persuasive quality to them. As such she was both employing a narrative form of discourse and was referring to the ostensible persuasiveness of individual local narratives, which themselves defined the form of adjudication she was defending.

I turn now to a second example of a war story, this by Claire McCaskill, a drug court prosecuting attorney in Kansas City, Missouri, and an officer of the National Association of Drug Court Professionals (NADCP). As with Guy Wheeler, I heard McCaskill's story both in an interview with her and in a lecture she gave at the 1995 national drug court conference in Portland, Oregon. In the latter, McCaskill was very deliberately encouraging the faithful in their efforts to advance the drug court movement against possible obstacles. Among the obstacles that she faced in her own work and in her involvement in the national movement was resistance from other district attorneys.

The prosecutors in this country are not going for this because they are politically chicken. They are afraid that to be for this concept will somehow give them labels as soft and squishy, that they are looking at defendants as victims, or God forbid, clients. So, how do you overcome that problem?

McCaskill offers a number of strategies for winning over the resistant—including the tactic of publicly emphasizing the tough and intrusive features of the drug court program—and in the end recalls the success her drug court had in converting recalcitrant district attorneys.

> And all of the prosecutors who have served that capacity in my office have enjoyed the experience and have come to me later, even though some of them went kicking and screaming, and came to me after the fact and said, "I'm glad I did that. It will help me in my work as an assistant prosecutor."

One of her favorite strategies for persuading reluctant prosecutors and other skeptics in the community, interestingly, is making public the stories of successful drug court clients. Once again the telling of stories is seen as essential to the continued advancement of the movement. And once again we have an example of local-level discourse taking on national movement significance:

> The graduations [of clients who have successfully completed the program] are a great media opportunity. Alumni are a wonderful media opportunity. Give your articulate alumni an opportunity to interact with the media, because they are great stuff. They grab the interest of people, because their histories are usually something that is far afield from the experience of most people who are watching. Most people have a hard time, thank goodness, relating to someone who started using hallucinating drugs at the age of eight. But, we know that those folks are in drug court. When they get better and they become contributing members of society, and they are articulate, we need to give them opportunities to talk to the community.

McCaskill proposes that successful drug court alumni be put on stage, that they be given an opportunity to tell their stories, with the anticipated end of generating community support for drug courts. These are the "happy ending" stories we will consider in the next section. In closing her remarks, McCaskill reached out to the movement activists or "comrades-in-arms" in attendance. "We do all feel like brothers and sisters. Welcome to the fold."

Happy Endings

The third and final type of story in social movements, according to the schemata advanced by Fine, are "happy endings"—the success stories of individuals who have clearly benefited from the actions and ideals of the movement. These stories, according to Fine, "provide a morale boost and directly reinforce movement involvement." Repeatedly, judges and other drug court officials with whom I spoke told stories of clients who had turned their lives around because of the drug court. Most media accounts of the drug court—the large majority of which have been positive—feature a particular client who has done well in the program, or who graduated and is off drugs, is working, and so on. In essence, this is the application of the strategy recommended by Claire McCaskill. The significant message conveyed in these stories is that the drug court is a cause worthy of support.

Consider several examples of these types of stories. The first story is told by a judge from one of the first drug courts in the country. Judge Robert Fogan tells the story of Melanie, a graduate of his drug court, who had formerly prostituted herself to support her crack cocaine addiction. According to Fogan,

> Melanie was on the street for years, selling herself to get drugs, hopelessly addicted. She is now in treatment. She was in our first graduating class. . . . She is a beautiful woman now. She is a manager at one of the local restaurants in town. She came from walking the streets into treatment. She was so badly addicted when she first got into the drug treatment program. She knew she was dirty, so she would just call it in. "Hey, Phil, I'm dirty. No sense, in me coming in and dropping [a urine sample] off. I'll tell you I'm dirty." So, she gets busted again for another possession charge out on the street. We brought her back into the program. . . . I put her into the intensive residential treatment program, kept her in treatment. She came out. She finally got it, and started moving along.

Melanie is also featured on a promotional videotape that this particular drug court shows to new participants and other interested parties. This is her account of her experience in the drug court.

> I was never clean for the first three weeks. Then I got arrested again—the day I was supposed to go into court. I was in jail the day I was supposed to go in front of the judge. And they let me out forty-five minutes before, and I had no shoes on, no nothing. I had to come into the courtroom with no shoes on. That is how I went to my arraignment. And that was pretty scary. I was pretty rough. I wish I could get the mug shot so you could see the before and after picture—two different people. Believe it! So when I came into court for the arraignment. . . . I had been up for probably two or three days at that time. So, I was in pretty rough shape. I usually went four or five days with no food, no water, nothing, just smoking. So, when I went into the court-room, I was not very alert or anything. I wanted to just go to sleep and just not worry about it. But Judge Fogan ordered me to detox.

Like a religious conversion story, Melanie recounts her previous condition, and the moment of crisis that marked the beginning of her turn around. She recalls how she resisted the court's insistence that she go into intensive treatment.

> I cried and screamed and hollered. . . . I was not going to go. Period. They said they didn't care. "You're going. That is the way it is. Either go there or go to jail." I did do a couple hits before I went to detox. I had my boyfriend come pick me up. I was pretty pissed off. My last high. He brought me a dime rock, and he took a hit off of that before he even saw me. "This is my last one, you idiot." So, anyhow, I did get that one last little hit before I went into detox. Because that is the way I was. I would have done it forever. That is the way of the drug addict. So, I went into detox.

Melanie tells of her experience in detox, in intensive treatment, and then in a halfway house, and expresses her gratitude that she is finally free from drug dependency. "I just thank God I am at where I am at today." So compelling is Melanie's story that the drug court uses it to garner public support for the program. As Judge Fogan explains, "She is one of our best spokespersons. She speaks at functions around town." In Melanie's case we see the very direct connection between the individual story and the larger movement. The story told at the local level is rebroadcast to a much wider audience. The purpose for doing this is literally to gain public support for the movement and encourage its further expansion. This kind of retelling of client's stories is typical.

Happy endings are also told at drug court conferences. In fact, one judge was so taken by a courtroom encounter with a client that he had the transcripts of the court session copied and distributed at one of the drug court conferences. At another conference a group of juvenile offenders were brought to restage a juvenile drug court drama. Each client participating in this exercise told his or her individual story. Another judge, Judge Frank Hoover of the Bakersfield drug court, brought a successful client to a conference to tell her success story. This particular story was aided by courtroom video clips of the client at different stages in the drug court program, as well as the interpretive expertise of a treatment provider. In their stories, as will become clear, the judge and treatment provider essentially established the frame within which the client would tell her story. This is how Judge Frank Hoover, of the Bakersfield drug court, introduced the story.

> The reason why I've come here, and I've brought some people with me, is to tell you a story. And I have to apologize in advance, I'm not a professional storyteller, and the story we tell comes out of drug court. And we are going to tell the story of a woman named Valerie, whom I first met in late 1996. But let me tell you the story in a different way . . . quite often depending on who tells the story and in what context the story is told people draw different conclusions from the story. So, I can only hope in telling the story three different ways to give you all the benefit of three different perspectives.

Judge Hoover offered his perspective first. He described Valerie's initial contact with the criminal justice system and the consequence of having to give up her son, Dominic, to foster care. He also described her impersonal encounters with a local hospital, the police department, the county jail, the district attorney's office, the public defender's office, and the court, all of which made up separate files on Valerie's situation and/or her criminal status. To demonstrate the impersonal nature of the system, Hoover dramatically placed a new file on the podium for every agency Valerie encountered. Pointing to the stack of files, Hoover argued,

> This is what Valerie looks like to many people in the criminal justice system. . . . This doesn't make any sense. All we do is make up files. Who is this person? And why in the world are we prepared to spend so much money on her every two or three months when something bizarre happens in her life? Maybe somebody ought to try to deal with her personally. Drug court does that.

Fortunately for Valerie, according to Hoover, she averted another potential horror story, by ending up in a place where she would be cared for personally, the Bakersfield drug court program. Hoover then introduced the second storyteller, Angelina, a treatment provider in the Bakersfield program. Angelina interpreted the courtroom video clips showing Valerie's progress throughout the drug court program. Angelina's commentary, not surprisingly, was sprinkled with the symbolic reference points of feelings and self-esteem that define the therapeutic perspective and characterize the discourse of pathos popular in the contemporary context. Interpreting the first clip, for example, Angelina opined, "Look at her [Valerie's] body language, it's screaming low self-esteem, no self-worth." In another clip, showing Valerie at a later stage in the recovery process, Angelina noted, "In this episode she is looking great, feeling confident. I really think that she's taking a turn in her treatment at this point. By this point she is personalizing it. It is now her treatment and she's become more involved."

Finally, Valerie herself was brought to the stage and asked by Judge Hoover to offer her perspective on the drug court program. She began by discussing her recollections of her very first appearance in the drug court, and much like her counselor, invoked the common themes of therapeutic discourse.

> Okay, the day of my intake I remember feeling dispirited, bankrupt. I remember tremendous feelings of guilt and shame for losing Dominic. Feelings of worthlessness, my self-esteem was gone out the door. I remember being scared, very frightened, not knowing what I was getting into at drug court. And I knew that I wanted help. I believed that I needed the guidance to be shown

where to go to get it. Because we [who] are in our disease feel we don't know which way we want to go for help. You just go to the next place to get high.

Judge Hoover then had the video clips shown a second time, and asked Valerie to offer commentary. After watching one clip Valerie recalled

I remember feeling just so helpless, so desperate. I mean, in case you didn't notice my voice was just cracking because I just wanted to cry out, and I felt like just nobody was listening to me, and my life was just no longer mine. And in all essence it was no longer mine. It was in the hand of the court and I'm thankful that it was.

After another video clip Valerie commented on her own progress in the recovery process.

Yeah, this is when I started doing better and I started trying. I started realizing that a little bit of effort was going a long way for me. I had a feeling of pride in me, growing inside of me, especially after getting praise from Judge Hoover for doing well. Just my self-esteem was growing, confidence was growing inside of me. After going to court and getting a pat on the back for doing well was like no other, no drug I could find out on the street, no high could ever replace that feeling.

Finally, again following the descriptive cues of those who proceeded her, Valerie discussed her feelings in one of the last video clips, in which she was visibly more healthy and alert than in her first court appearances. "Yeah, the next time after I'd started working my [twelve] steps, and I was getting really involved with my recovery and my program. It was a very emotional day for me, I can remember it so well now."

At the end of Valerie's presentation, Judge Hoover offered, "That's our story." As in the other examples above, telling the story had a purpose: to demonstrate the worth of drug court. As Judge Hoover himself explained,

Now I'd like to close by saying that there are Valeries all over this country . . . This is why you do drug court. You don't do drug court to process cases, and you don't do drug court to come up with some moral, civil penance for some misdeed that's being done to satisfy the politicians. What you do drug court for is for Valerie, for her baby Dominic, for her sisters and her brothers and her mother and her father and her friends and the judges and her future employers.

Moreover, according to Hoover, Valerie's happy ending is offered as an incentive to prospective drug courts to press forward with their programs. Like Valerie, if others

> can find the strength and the hope and pride to go to those places in their heart and find the dignity that's there for everyone, then they can have their lives back, and that's what these drug courts are all about. And that's why you should do them.

Valerie's success story is similar to many others. Avoiding the horror of an uncaring bureaucratic judicial system, the drug court aids the victim of drug addiction, helps to raise her self-esteem, and to live a normal and productive life. The emotively compelling stories are offered to justify the movement, to encourage others to join the ranks, and to persuade skeptics of the movement's salutary effects.

TELLING THE RIGHT STORY

It is important, in this regard, that clients tell the right story. It is clear that Valerie was following a particular script. She used the same language and appealed to the same therapeutic symbols—for example, references to self-esteem, ownership of treatment, assessment of feelings—as did her treatment counselor. The right story was told here, just as the right story must be told in the local drug court drama. That is, clients are expected to accept a particular worldview, a particular understanding of themselves, and they are expected to express this understanding according to therapeutically defined categories. Not telling the right story, moreover, is also interpreted in therapeutic terms. The person who fails to accept treatment with a certain attitude and the "right words" will be interpreted as being in denial—as not complying or not buying into treatment. Failure to tell the right story can have consequences for the client.

Consider an example from the Dade County court. With a large Hispanic population in Miami, a significant percentage of drug court clients, not surprisingly, are from Latin American countries, particularly Cuba.

According to two Dade County treatment counselors with whom I spoke, Hispanic clients often have difficulty, at least initially, accepting therapeutic interpretations of their behavior. They do not readily embrace the belief that they are addicts, that they have a disease, and are in need of treatment. It goes against their cultural sensibilities. As one counselor explained, for many Hispanics there "is kind of a stigma attached to having something wrong with you, to having a disease." The counselors, however, interpret this antipathy to treatment in therapeutic terms. As one counselor put it, "Their denial is bigger." As he sees it, the problem lies in a lack of education about the "facts" of drug addiction. "Education about addiction is very poor in Latin America."

Therefore, though addicted Hispanics initially may be "very resistant" to treatment, over time, and with enough education, "peer pressure," and exposure to therapeutic modalities, "They become more and more accepting of the fact that addiction is a problem that they have to deal with." As they are "more cultured to the American system, Hispanics can become more open" to treatment. Therefore, though it may at first be difficult for a client to say, " 'Hi, I'm so and so and I'm an addict,' after months and months of treatment, then that concept becomes a little easier." This is the ideal perspective to which the Dade County drug court counselors hope to bring their clients. "What we would like to do is have people get over their denial and say 'Hi, I'm Joe, I'm an addict. I'm in treatment to help myself.' "

That complying with treatment and telling the right story can help a client get through the program was made particularly evident in a visit to the Oakland drug court. The setting was a meeting with Judge Tauber and a probation officer prior to a drug court session. In this meeting the probation officer reviewed with the judge the different clients who would come before the judge that day. The probation officer—who in Oakland acts as a treatment provider—recommended to the judge the rewards or sanctions she believed each client deserved. The discussion of one male client was particularly noteworthy. This client, though he did not have clean urine tests, was viewed favorably, according to the probation officer, because "he is buying into treatment." He had assumed the right attitude, the right disposition toward treatment; he was telling the right story. And though there was no evidence that he had stopped using drugs, the probation officer recommended that he be graduated to the next level of treatment. His case illustrates how telling the right story can benefit a client and expedite his release from the court.

Consider another case where there was evidently no drug use. A client in the Portland, Oregon drug court reported that she was arrested for having a crack pipe in her car. She claimed that the pipe had been left in her car by a friend. She was pulled over by a police officer and the pipe was discovered. Because crack residue remained in the pipe, she was arrested for possession of narcotics. This was the defendant's first arrest, and though she claimed to have never used drugs, she enrolled in the drug court for the purpose of maintaining a clean criminal record, for in Portland successful completion of the drug court program results in the expungement of an arrest. This client's claim to have never used drugs was supported by the fact that she had not turned up a single dirty urine test since enrolling in drug court.

How, one might ask, could this client tell the right story according to therapeutic terms? Isn't the purpose of treatment to help someone overcome drug addiction? In this case there was no apparent drug problem. Though not a drug user, this client still employed therapeutic themes to describe her situation. She realized that though she was not an addict per se, she did have a "liking to drinking" and saw herself as living a lifestyle that was leading to drug use and, ultimately, addiction. Moreover, she had come to see herself as an "enabler" of her drug-using friends. As she explained, "I was enabling. I was bailing people out of jail with my college money. I was a people-pleaser." Through treatment she came to terms with these "negative" tendencies, so much so that now she "doesn't help anybody anymore." The client told her story to a small group of visiting drug court personnel. Afterward, two treatment providers, who were a part of the visiting group, discussed the client's story and her claim to have not used drugs. "At first I thought she was in denial," said one to the other. After the client's therapeutically inspired interpretation of her biography and the confirmation that she had indeed had no positive urine tests, they came to believe her story. Their initial response is nonetheless revealing.

One final example of the pressure put on clients to tell a story about themselves according to the treatment paradigm was offered by Jose Suarez. Suarez is the supervisor of the Criminal Justice Unit of the New York State Office of Alcoholism and Substance Abuse. He recounted to me an incident involving a struggle between a client and one of the counselors he supervised. The difficulty between the two stemmed from the client's unwillingness to identify himself as an addict. The client had become involved in a Pentecostal church and, in keeping with his religious worldview, saw his drug and alcohol problem not as a disease but as a matter of "demon possession." To the counselor this was unacceptable.

According to Suarez, "The counselor was pissed off." Though the client was admittedly not using drugs or alcohol, the counselor still saw the client as being "in denial" and as refusing to "accept the fact that he [was] an alcoholic and an addict." From Suarez's perspective, the client had come to terms with his drug use, "he just wasn't accepting the label of addiction that this institution was imposing on him." According to Suarez, the problem was with the counselor who had a "control issue" and could only see the client's behavior according to a particular paradigm. He could only see the client as "not complying, not buying into treatment, as still being in denial." The problem, in short, was that the client "was not saying what he [the counselor] wanted him to say." In other words, he was not telling the right story.

This scenario gets played out often in the drug court, according to Suarez. The court is in a position of "interpreting whether the person is sincere or not." Suarez acknowledges that "that is very subjective. What constitutes sincerity? What constitutes motivation?" In this situation, Suarez admonished the counselor for being too rigid and encouraged him to "go with the demon possession thing." Consider his instructions to the counselor: "Why are you making this person say what you want him to say? So the person won't admit he is an addict, but he is admitting that he is possessed. So what. So he is possessed. You go with that." According to Suarez, this situation was salvaged because of "good supervision," though he admits that in "a lot of places the supervision is really poor." If so, one is left to wonder how many similar clients are likewise encouraged to interpret their drug use in a certain way in order to please the counselor who in many instances controls the client's status in the program. One also suspects that, unlike Valerie, this client's story is not going to be showcased at a national drug court conference.

CONCLUSION

As mentioned previously, storytelling in the drug court movement has emerged at the same time that legal scholarship has begun to concern itself with the storytelling process in modern jurisprudence. This literature both celebrates and raises some concerns about the emphasis on narrative in legal proceedings. Some see the emotivist emphasis in legal storytelling as a welcomed adjustment to rational proceduralism. From this perspective, emotivist narrative represents a benign, if not more beneficial, supplement to logical reasoning (Delgado 1989; Dalton 1996; Gewirtz 1996). Advocates of legal storytelling "valorize narrative as more authentic, concrete, and embodied than traditional legal syllogism" (Brooks 1996: 16), and see narrative as a more persuasive form of legal argument. "Both critical legal scholars and storytellers find the emotive or nonrational aspects of language much more persuasive than rational argument" (Farber and Sherry 1996: 43). Catherine MacKinnon goes so far as to suggest that, in fact, storytelling is what has always been done—it has just been cloaked in the illusive guise of modern legal rationalism. Debunking the "metanarrative" of logical reasoning, MacKinnon asserts, "Dominant narratives are not called stories. They are called reality." Though even MacKinnon makes the "embarrassingly non-postmodern" concession that "lies are the ultimate risk of storytelling as method" (1996: 235).

Other legal scholars see this risk as a very dangerous one, and are much less inclined to celebrate the emergence of storytelling in the law. Alan Dershowitz, for example, believes that "when we import narrative form of storytelling into our legal system, we confuse fiction with fact and endanger the truth-finding function of the adjudicative process" (1996: 101). Anthony Kronman similarly believes that storytelling, though it may serve the purpose of "energiz[ing] right reason," is "always in a position of moral dependency." Stories, according to Kronman, "contribute no independent moral insight of their own" (1996: 56).

While it is beyond the scope of this chapter to directly enter into this debate, it is worth noting that the drug court movement is very relevant to it. That is, the drug courts represent the institutionalization of storytelling into the jurisprudential process—the institutionalization that advocates of legal storytelling endorse. But rather than simply asserting the analytical import of storytelling in legal processes, the drug court actually transforms the adjudicative process according to the narrative method. That is, the process of administering justice is actually altered in deference to the saliency of storytelling. Toni Massaro, in reflecting on the apparent incongruence between traditional legal processes and the therapeutically based orientation of empathetic storytelling, observes that to really conflate such divergent paradigms "empathy advocates must favor a radical restructuring of court procedures to make them more congenial" to the storytelling method (1989: 2108). This is precisely what the drug court does, and is a development that promoters of legal storytelling would no doubt celebrate.

The drug court, as such, represents a fairly decisive departure from ideal typical Weberian legal rationalism. The enthusiasm of the judges with whom I spoke seemed to be driven by just this notion. That is, they see themselves as attempting to reinvigorate or reenchant what they believe is an ineffective, dry, and cumbersome legal system with something that will give it more meaning, more color, and more legitimacy. Consider the reflections of Judge Judith Kaye, Chief Judge of the New York Court of Appeals: "Courts today face a public that by and large, is cynical and distrustful of all government, including the judicial system. Courts can no longer just assume they enjoy the public's trust. . . . We have to earn it" (1998: 3). Judge Kaye believes drug court is one program that can help to recapture the public's trust. Why? Not just because of statistically demonstrated success rates. In fact, Kaye acknowledges that "long term impacts are still being studied" (1998: 5). Rather she points to the emotional resonance of witnessing the testimonies of various drug court success stories. "Having attended several Drug Court graduation ceremonies," Kaye says, "I can tell you they are extremely moving events. Each graduate's personal achievement is recognized by applause and sometimes a few tears from family and court staff. 'I didn't just get arrested,' one recent graduate observed, 'I got saved'" (1998: 5).

To Judge Kaye, then, the stories successfully demonstrate the program's efficacy. So compelling are these individual testimonies of drug court successes that evaluations of individual drug court sites typically include these stories along with more statistical assessments of recidivism rates and the like (Goldkamp and Weiland 1993; Harrell and Cavanaugh 1996; Harrell and Smith 1996). A study by W. Terry Clinton of the Fort Lauderdale drug court went so far as to conclude, though he found no real difference in re-arrest rates between drug court and non-drug court participants, that "[t]here is absolutely no question that the drug court is having a very positive effect upon the lives of many people." Like Judge Kaye, Clinton arrives at this belief because at "the personal level, one is moved when hearing the individual success stories of persons who have turned their lives around as the result of the Drug Court" (Clinton 1993: 26).

In this case, then, the stories are viewed as more persuasive and credible than traditional empirical measurements. So common is this kind of defense for drug courts that at one conference, David Mactas, the Director of the Center for Substance Abuse Treatment (CSAT, an agency that funds drug courts), expressed his frustration with the lack of discussion among drug court officials about the empirical evidence that supports the efficacy of the treatment approach, evidence he believes is available. Mactas complained, "What you don't hear is scholarship, discovery, revelation, findings, research, data, outcomes. You hear, oh boy, I was at a graduation last week, and you should have been there. I hugged all those people. It feels great."

What Mactas may not fully appreciate, however, is that in today's culture great feelings, as such, may be a more convincing way to persuade individuals to support drug courts. And storytelling is a very helpful communication style within which to express them. Drug court judges and other movement advocates are certainly cognizant of the persuasive potency of pathos, and believe that enthusiasm for the movement is best captured in the "from the heart" stories of drug court graduates like Valerie. In other words, in a culture where "all points seem to revolve around the individual's subjective feelings" (Elshtain 1986: 23), emotionally charged stories are a highly effective and compelling form of persuasion. Movement activists employ them not only to garner support for drug courts but to engender greater trust and reestablish legitimacy in the judicial system.

As in past analyses of social movements, the important role of culture in understanding legal change has too often been ignored. In a welcomed corrective to this tendency, David Garland convincingly points out that "penal practices exist within a specific penal culture which is itself supported and made meaningful by wider cultural forms" (Garland 1990: 211). As the drug court movement demonstrates, legal processes, social movements, and social movements within legal structures are successfully advanced, and analytically made sense of, in direct relationship to dominant cultural currents. The success of drug courts then must be understood, in part, by the ability of movement advocates to tap into the defining qualities of the contemporary *zeitgeist*. Judge Kaye, for one, applauds drug courts for doing just this, for offering a form of "justice that is responsive to today's realities and public expectations" (1998:6). As the rhetoric employed within the drug court movement demonstrates, the emotionally resonate drug court stories are commensurate with the realities and public expectations of today's therapeutic culture. To ignore these stories would be to overlook a defining feature of, and a significant force within, the drug court movement.

NOTES

1. Data used in this article is drawn from my larger research project investigating the drug court movement. The names of drug court clients cited in the article are pseudonyms. Information given about others associated with the drug court—such as judges, attorneys, treatment providers—are actual names and titles.

2. From titles of panel sessions at the Portland (1995) and Washington, D.C. (1996) drug court conference programs.

3. For discussion of the expansion of drug courts to other types of crime, see Drug Strategies 1997: 30 and Goldkamp and Weiland 1993: 35.

4. The "therapeutic culture" is understood here as first put forth by Philip Rieff (1966) in his seminal work on the "triumph of the therapeutic." Since then, Christopher Lasch (1978), Robert Bellah et al. (1985), and others have discussed the pervasiveness of the therapeutic ethos in American culture. In *The Therapeutic State* (1998), I analyze the extent to which this tendency has institutionalized itself into the functions of the modern American state. The revised structure of the drug court model is only plausible given the cultural context within which it has emerged; the therapeutic culture makes therapeutic justice meaningful and acceptable.

5. As Aristotle writes in Book III of *The 'Art' of Rhetoric,* "And whenever you wish to arouse emotion, do not use an enthymeme, for it will either drive out the emotion or it will be useless" (1926: 455).

EIGHT

Compassion on Trial

*Movement Narrative in a Court Conflict over
Physician-Assisted Suicide*

JEFFERY D. TATUM

O ne of the salutary effects of the recent cultural shift in social movements research has been to focus new attention on the stories told
within movements by their members (Fine 1995; many of the chapters in
this volume). The study of such "internal narratives" yields insight into
many of the movement's features, including how group culture is developed, meanings are shared, participants are constituted, supportive emotions are called out, and social control is maintained. Relatively less
attention, however, has been paid to the way that movements construct
narratives for outside audiences. Among other things, stories are also used
to recruit new members, to mobilize resources, and when the movement is
struggling for state legitimation, to persuade those in authority, be they
legislators, voters, judges, or jurors. Analysis of such "external narratives"
can shed light on how movements struggle to depict themselves and their
agenda to outsiders. Studying storytelling in nonsupportive and hostile
arenas can also illuminate dynamics of political and cultural conflict and
the strategies of movements to impose their social vision. This chapter is
addressed to one significant case, the use of narratives in a contest for
state legitimation of physician-assisted suicide.[1]

In the last twenty years, the struggle to gain acceptance of physician-
assisted suicide has emerged as a significant social movement (Filene 1998;
Fox, Kamakahi, and Čapek 1999; Hoefler and Kamoie 1994). The public

179

narratives told by physician-assisted suicide proponents present several questions that can be asked generally of movements engaged in conflicts over the law: How does the movement use narrative in the judicial system, the public forum where so many struggles for legitimation are being fought? What is the relationship between the narratives told in court and the movements' collective action frames? If there are inconsistencies between court narratives and frames, what do these inconsistencies indicate? What advantages might studies of narrative provide in order to understand movement rhetorical strategies for winning over the unconvinced?

In order to explore these questions, I analyzed the transcript from the 1996 criminal trial of Jack Kevorkian, a Michigan physician, where Kevorkian stood accused of illegally assisting in the suicide of two persons.[2] In particular, I consider the opening and closing statements, and the direct and cross examinations of Kevorkian.[3] Because my aim is to gain a better understanding of how the assisted suicide movement uses narratives, I focus on the case presented by the defense which, throughout the trial, used carefully scripted stories to persuade the judge and twelve-person jury that physician-assisted suicide was legitimate in this instance.

I begin by briefly discussing the relationship between frames and narratives and the challenges presented by audiences external to the movement. I then consider the significance of the Kevorkian trial and outline the three principal narratives told by the defense at the trial. I conclude with an analysis of these narratives and what their construction and use might tell us about social movement persuasion.

FRAMES, NARRATIVES, AND THE CHALLENGES
OF AN EXTERNAL AUDIENCE

Events, such as the actions of a doctor in intentionally ending a patient's life, are subject to widely different interpretations. Variances in the framework used to interpret such events can have a significant impact on the meaning attributed to these events and the consequences that follow. Social movement scholars have used the concept of "frames" to denote such frameworks, the "schemata of interpretation" that individuals and collectivities use to render events or occurrences meaningful, and so organize experience and guide action (Snow et al. 1986: 464). In the study of movements, frame analysis is concerned with the manner in which events are collectively interpreted, the ways in which collective action frames are developed, diffused, and acted on, and the processes through which individuals' frames and movement frames are aligned.

Frame analysis does not assume a completely static structure of interpretations within a movement. On the contrary, frames are seen to expand, shift, and change as the social ecology giving rise to the movement and its perspectives changes. In framing theory, movements that fail to adapt their frames to a changing environment will ultimately wither away. At the same time, the concept of frames assumes a degree of internal coherence and consistency over at least the near term. Collective action frames are developed through group interaction (at least among the most active participants), serve to identify and label the problems or injustices the movement seeks to address, specify remedies, and provide a rationale for sacrifices for the cause. While not static, to be useful in guiding collective action, frames must maintain an internal coherence and cannot be transformed too often or too radically.

Many narratives told by movement participants mesh tightly with the movement's frames and express them. Activists tell stories, for instance, to illustrate the movement's assertions that a problem or injustice exists, that collective action can or has been successful in achieving desired change, that participation in the movement is urgent and necessary. Movements also use stories to inculcate new members into the group culture and foster common understandings. In these cases, studies of movement narratives illuminate the implicit components of movement frames (Fine 1995).

But the relationship between movement frames and narratives may also be more complicated. Collective action frames, being products of group interaction, cannot give voice to all the perspectives and pressures experienced within the movement. Narratives may more accurately mirror competing concerns and contradictory pressures, and may anticipate and even compel frame transformation. When addressed to outside audiences, uncontrollable factors, including the type of audience, the presence of opposing parties, or situation-specific rules of allowable discourse (as in a court of law), can pressure activists to tell stories that are not completely consistent with the movement's frames. In such cases, stories may afford a more subtle indicator than frames of the actual cultural workings of social movements. Moreover, even when broadly consistent with movement frames, stories told to outsiders may condense movement perspectives to very simple and widely accepted values that can persuade people to act for movement interests without requiring them to fully adopt the frames. This sort of condensation, as will be seen in the Kevorkian case, can occur for two reasons.

First, in seeking to persuade outsiders, movement activists must appeal to broad, commonly held sentiments. With external audiences, activists cannot make many of the assumptions that enable a smooth flow of discourse within the movement. They cannot assume the audience shares movement goals or detailed frame knowledge. Perhaps most important, they cannot assume that external audiences share the types of personal experience that trigger movement involvement. For example, many participants in the assisted suicide movement have experienced the death of an intimate or they work with terminally ill or dying persons. They have seen, firsthand, that the social practices surrounding death have been radically transformed by modern medical technology, often leaving patients with little capacity to control the circumstances of their treatment (Callahan 1993). Without that experience, external audience members may have little sense of the circumstances of death in the modern hospital setting (Fox, Kamakahi, and Ĉapek 1999). Consequently, they may lack the sense of urgency, common to movement participants, concerning issues of patient autonomy, the changing notions of compassion and suffering, and the nonpecuniary costs and benefits of medical progress (Aries 1981; Nuland 1995; Quill 1996). While participants and audience share a common public culture, the shared bases for movement-related discourse are much thinner. To build bridges to outsiders and to reduce the risk of giving offense, activists often eschew elaborate ideological justifications and subtle arguments, relying instead on appeals to values and perspectives broadly shared outside the movement.

Second, in seeking to persuade external audiences, movements often simplify their discourse so that it may be apprehended quickly (Hunter 1994). Activists cannot assume that outsiders will invest the time or attention necessary to understand complex movement arguments or ideologies. In fact, outsiders, even within a movement's constituency, are often unwilling to invest much intellectual energy in movement concerns; to be persuasive, activists often gloss over nuances in order to strike at the heart of the matters of concern.

Compelling stories address both the bridge-building and simplification tasks well. While frames tend to emphasize rational coherence and consistency within the movement perspective (Davis, chapter 1), stories are freer of these constraints. Narratives, and their implicit arguments, do not need to be rigorously logical or resolve inconsistencies. Their immediacy can stimulate strong emotions—defiance, outrage, or compassion—that call for a response quite apart from a wider or more systematic commitment to specific changes. They can bestow moral legitimation through pathos. And they can do these things in a way that is easily apprehended without specialized knowledge or prior learning. Given these advantages and others, narratives can be of considerable tactical usefulness in persuasion efforts aimed at movement outsiders.

To explore such tactical use of movement narratives, I turn to the trial of Jack Kevorkian.

PHYSICIAN-ASSISTED SUICIDE: THE CONTEXT OF THE TRIAL

Laws specifically banning assisted suicide have long been on the books in the United States. Over the past two centuries, all states that have addressed the issue prohibited it, with the recent exception of Oregon (Marzen et al. 1985).[4] Before the 1970s, American advocates of physician-assisted suicide enjoyed little success in creating a broad movement for increasing patient control over the time and manner of death. In the 1970s and 1980s, however, the movement rapidly gathered steam as an increasing number of mercy killing cases came to light and the topic became the subject of a broader public discussion. A small number of widely publicized cases brought public attention to the problem of giving patients greater control of medical treatment, including the right to refuse continued care in the face of terminal illness or catastrophic injury.[5] At the same time, a number of assisted-suicide advocacy groups emerged and rapidly grew in the United States, and end-of-life issues became a matter of common discourse and concern among the general population (Filene 1998: 223; Fox, Kamakahi, and Ĉapek 1999; Hoefler and Kamoie 1994: 21).

Since June 1990, when Kevorkian first facilitated the suicide of a patient, the debate over the legality of physician-assisted suicide has been rising to a crescendo in the United States. Between 1994 and mid-1997, bills offered in nineteen states to allow physician-assisted suicide were rejected, while another three states outlawed it. Although assisted suicide currently is outlawed in forty-nine states, advocates' increasing ability to put their case before legislatures and courts is strong evidence of the growth and momentum of the movement. In addition, a countermovement has arisen: several organizations already organized around other issues have begun to commit resources to resist legalization of assisted suicide

and euthanasia. The debate has become a national struggle over fundamental propositions of public culture, such as the possible reaches of personal autonomy (Kevorkian 1991), the role of medicine (Gomez 1991),
the nature of personal rights (Hoefler and Kamoie 1994), and the definition and role of compassion in medical ethics (Battin 1994).

In the midst of this conflict, Kevorkian's willingness to break the law
by openly providing assisted-suicide services has attracted immense attention. Kevorkian, a retired Michigan pathologist, is an outspoken proponent of physician-assisted suicide. While Kevorkian is not the only
physician in American history to be prosecuted for euthanasia or assisted
suicide, he has been far more systematic, confrontational, and public in
his work, and has been connected to more cases of assisted suicide than
any physician in United States history. As of April 1999, Kevorkian had,
by his estimate, participated in more than 130 deaths. Kevorkian's attorney often reported the deaths to the police and issued a press statement,
making Kevorkian one of the central public figures in the debate.

The subject of this study—the first jury trial of Kevorkian—was held
over the course of several weeks in February and March of 1996.
Although Kevorkian had answered charges in courts before, none had
involved the formality of a full jury trial based on a Michigan statute
directly prohibiting assisted suicide. The charges stemmed from the deaths
of Merian Frederick and Ali Khalili, Kevorkian's twentieth and twenty-
first cases.[6] The trial became an important media event, televised by
Court-TV and given extensive nationwide press coverage. Because of the
immense publicity, both sides of the right-to-die debate viewed the trial as
a small but highly significant skirmish in the effort to resymbolize assisted
suicide.

THE KEY TRIAL NARRATIVES

In order to win this particular case, the prosecution had to prove the elements of the Michigan assisted-suicide statute. The elements were (1)
knowledge—Kevorkian knew Frederick and Khalili intended to commit
suicide; (2) action—Kevorkian provided the means and participated in
the physical acts by which they committed suicide; and (3) intent—
Kevorkian intended to cause death, and did not act with the intent to
relieve pain and suffering (an exception in the statute). As part of that
proof, the prosecution argued that Kevorkian's intent stemmed not from

compassion, but out of a desire to gain a widespread acceptance of physician-assisted suicide.

In response, Kevorkian's defense used three principle narratives. As is common in the broader social movement (Fox, Kamakahi, and Ĉapek 1999), they told the stories of the life, suffering, and desires of the patients, Frederick and Khalili. In addition, they recounted a story of Kevorkian's character and motives.

The Story of Merian Frederick

In his opening statement, Kevorkian's attorney Geoffrey Fieger pointedly told the jury, "Let me talk to you about who is really on trial," and then told the story of Merian Frederick. Frederick was a Michigan woman, mother of seven grown children. She was very active in her community, volunteering her time in grassroots politics, even considering a run for Congress. She was very involved in the Unitarian church; she loved literature; she was intelligent and vibrant. She had, Fieger argued, lived her life to the fullest.

At the time of her death, Frederick was in the advanced stages of the muscular degenerative disease, Amyotrophic Lateral Sclerosis (ALS), also known as Lou Gehrig's disease. In his opening statement, Fieger carefully described the effects of the disease.

> The prosecutor described it to you, but he didn't tell you half the horror that she was faced with. Let me tell you about the disease from which she was suffering every day. She was suffering every single day a disease that was destroying her ability to live and a disease that not only caused profound agony but terror. ALS is an insidious disease. The way ALS works is it destroys nerve fibers. . . . ALS is insidious because the one thing it doesn't do is it never affects the mind so the person who is stricken down with ALS knows it and has the terror of knowing what is going to happen to them and will suffer it until the last moment.

Fieger emphasized how the disease destroys the ability to move and talk. Because the head is relatively heavy, it will begin to hang because of the lack of control over neck muscles.

But another thing it does is it destroys the nerve fibers that allow you to breathe and so you slowly suffocate. And the way that you finally go, after years and then months and then days and you know it, is you suffocate. You choke on your own spit in your final death throes and that is the destiny of Merian Frederick that was tearing her apart. The pain was unbelievable, and the knowledge and inability to breathe.

When she contacted Kevorkian, months before her death, Frederick had mild paralysis throughout her body and could still walk, but her neck was almost completely paralyzed. She could no longer swallow and was fed through a stomach tube, and she was beginning to have her saliva suctioned to avoid choking.

Fieger related Frederick's decision to contact Kevorkian and her subsequent efforts to obtain further medical care from other doctors. Her family doctor determined that her ALS was in the end stages, and that she needed continued hospice care, with a life expectancy of less than six months. Though Frederick could only write when she contacted Kevorkian, Fieger expressed her story through her voice:

> This woman is a woman who had lived life to the fullest and said, "I have suffered enough. I have suffered bravely. I suffered through 1989 and 1990 and 1991 and 1992 and at the end my suffering is too great. Do I have the right to look somebody in the eye and say, 'Please, now, the pain and the agony is too great. Help me cross that threshold which I am going to anyway; this tender vessel, this soft machine. I will go into the next world inevitably and surely from this disease. I wish to stop this suffering now.'"

After an initial discussion, she sent all of her medical records to Kevorkian, and they met for a series of interviews. Frederick brought her minister to the meetings. The minister took the stand and confirmed the meetings and Frederick's decision.

Kevorkian urged Frederick to seek other medical care, particularly for her neck, though she seemed to have few alternatives. In the words of Frederick's daughter:

> People—they turn their backs to me. They won't come to the home. I finally forced myself into an office to talk to an orthope-

dic surgeon—orthopedic—he's a doctor of orthopedic medicine. He was talking about drilling holes—he does spinal cord injuries where they supported the head and the way they do it is they drill holes into the skull to hold it permanently up. He was not willing to think about alternative solutions for something more comfortable that could be taken off and on. This was too unusual.

In the end, Frederick decided to end her suffering. She signed a form Kevorkian had prepared, affirming that she wanted to end her life with his assistance, and setting forth the proposed manner of death. Then Kevorkian, Frederick, her immediate family, and minister held a final meeting at Kevorkian's apartment, where Frederick indicated she was ready. Fieger questioned Kevorkian at trial about her intentions.

Q. Dr. Kevorkian, what were her desires at that time?
A. To proceed as fast as possible.
Q. Did you have an understanding why she wished to proceed?
A. Only my personal conclusion.
Q. Which was?
A. That she wanted to end her suffering as quickly as possible.
Q. Was she supported—we've listened to the testimony of Carol Poenisch and Ola Frederick, Rick Frederick and Reverend Phifer. Was she supported in her desire at that time by the people who were present?
A. Everybody in that room respected her autonomy. In that degree they supported her.

A carbon monoxide tube was connected to a mask secured over her face, with the tube bent and held crimped with a paper clip. Kevorkian directed that the carbon monoxide be started, and when Frederick pulled the clip off the gas began flowing. Although she had several minutes to pull off the mask, she did not, and passed away.

Strikingly, the defense used videotaped interviews to allow Frederick herself to "tell" some of her story. As part of his protocol, Kevorkian recorded a final interview with every person using his services, in the hours immediately before their death. Kevorkian testified that he took these videos in order to preserve information for medical research. Fieger played Frederick's final interview earlier in the trial, and again in the closing statements, in order to show the jury her medical condition. The videotapes had special promise as evidence because they allowed the jury to become visually acquainted with Frederick and to observe her condition hours before death. The jury could see Frederick's condition for themselves, take stock of her, and watch her communicate her choice of assisted suicide.

The Story of Ali Khalili

The defense spent less time relating Khalili's story, but filled in the same details regarding his illness, treatment options, and condition when he approached Kevorkian.

Khalili was a licensed medical doctor, professor, and specialist in rehabilitation medicine, and had devoted long years to care for his patients. He was married and had a family. Khalili suffered from bone cancer (reputedly one of the most painful forms of cancer) and was treated at the Mayo Clinic, one of the world's foremost cancer clinics. When he saw Kevorkian, Khalili was wearing a morphine pump and yet complained of torturous pain. Khalili told Kevorkian that he feared quadriplegia most of all, and had already suffered several breaks in his vertebrae as well as lesions to his cervical vertebrae, which foreshadowed future breaks in that area.

After recalling testimony that Khalili was a "world-renowned specialist in pain management" and that his greatest fear was the collapse of his spine, Fieger read portions of Khalili's last statements to Kevorkian.

> I may have cancerous lesions on my spine right now. I know it's going down. Now the pain is severe. The pain is worse every day, every day. I know what the hell is going on here. I know if a fracture takes place here this is a mess. This is a postoperative area. You'd have to be a superman to be able to—you're talking about a tumor that's fractured, it has been repaired, intermedial rods, radiated. The disease has been progressing and now there is further tumor. What to do? What to do? The cost is horrendous. And why, why put that money to me? For what? Let's spend that money on somebody else for some other cause. . . . It's a disease, it's a serious disease, it's a terminal disease, it's a painful disease. And not only the disease is a problem; its complications of the disease are sometimes as bad as the disease and there is no

option. I suffer. My suffering is awful, and there is no answer to my pain. . . . I want to live quite bad. But the last thing that I want is to live with the impaired quality of life. That's the last thing I want.

Like Frederick's story, the defense described all of Khalili's interactions with Kevorkian, the support Khalili had from his family in making his decision to end his life, and the final minutes of Khalili's life. Once again, the defense played the videotape of Khalili's final interview with Kevorkian, wherein Khalili justified his decision to end his life.

The Story of Jack Kevorkian

Several witnesses, including the families of the decedents and the decedents themselves, told Kevorkian's story. At the end of the trial, Kevorkian also took the stand in his own defense.

Kevorkian was portrayed as valorous and virtuous. He pursued a simple lifestyle, buying his clothes from the Salvation Army. The jury was told about his integrity (he called the police after every assisted suicide because that was the law, and he refused to take a fee for his work); his compassion (his intent was to relieve suffering and to help all suffering people, and he sometimes cried when they died); and his courage (he stood up to the bullying local prosecutor to promote needed changes in medicine and law). Care was taken to show that Kevorkian did not oppose religion but only opposed religious demagogues. Witnesses described how he encouraged his patients to meet with their spiritual advisers, and how he met with Frederick's pastor and allowed him to be present at her death.

Kevorkian told how the patients sought him out, repeatedly asked for his services, and met with him on several occasions before their deaths. Eyewitnesses related how Kevorkian met, screened, examined, and otherwise worked with his patients. The videotaped encounters allowed the jurors to watch the interaction between Kevorkian and his patients, and to witness his professionalism and bedside manner.

Kevorkian testified about his medical career, research, and motives for advocating legalized assisted suicide. The motive for his life's work, he avowed, was to relieve suffering. He also testified about his meetings with Frederick, her condition, the protocol he used with her, his purposes in helping her end her life, and their final meeting. Kevorkian also repeated Khalili's story. Each time, the story culminated with Fieger asking about intentions.

> Q. What do you intend, Dr. Kevorkian?
> A. That their suffering ended. That's the only relief I have, but it isn't enough to counteract the negative emotional responses I have.
> Q. What do you mean?
> A. It's not—its not nice to see a human life ended, but when the agony is ended it ameliorates the pain I feel.

In addition to good character, professionalism, and pure motives, the Kevorkian story told by the defense also included a narrative of unjust persecution. This narrative focused on the prosecution's motives, methods, and morality. The defense told how the police and prosecutor pressed charges against Kevorkian over the families' protests, and how they forced the families to testify, further exacerbating their grief. The police raided Kevorkian's house and seized his medical files and tapes. The prosecution charged only Kevorkian, although others were more active in the final set-up of the assisted-suicide procedures. The prosecution labeled Kevorkian a Nazi, and yet never talked to him personally about his intent in any of the cases. Fieger argued that the prosecution was not so much concerned about enforcing the law as it was in singling out Kevorkian and persecuting him. In his summation, Fieger concluded:

> Now of course we had a prosecution that said they're interested in enforcing the law, but they're not. They malign, they disparage, they—you heard everybody who knew Dr. Kevorkian tell you about him, and the only person, without any evidence, who says what a terrible person he is, is a man who has never even spoken to him [the prosecutor]. You heard everybody. Now how, in a free society? Sure they have the power. They're the bureaucrats. They have the power. They can do this. They can bring you before—they can attempt to ruin your life.
>
> Perhaps the most poignant thing I think that was stated in this trial at all was Carol Poenisch's testimony and Rick Frederick's and Ola Frederick's about the last night that Merian Frederick spent with her family. Remember? Everyone had come together from different parts of the country. Rick and Ola had

come from Texas, one son had come from North Carolina, Carol and her sisters were there. And they talked about joining a circle and they talked about hugging and they talked about the love that existed in that family, and that was the circle. That was the circle. Where in the world were these people in that circle—with all due respect to the fine job I know they're doing for their boss, how dare they? How dare they come into that sacred circle of love? It boggles my mind to think that was some kind—that sacred circle was some kind of—the way they described it, circle of death, circle of nonfeeling, circle of suicide? Please—please.

At the end of the trial, the jury acquitted Kevorkian of all charges. Kevorkian's acquittal is all the more interesting in light of the fact that Kevorkian made it clear that he provided assistance in the two deaths. He met with the decedents, provided technical expertise, made arrangements for the delivery of the carbon monoxide, directed them in how to use the equipment, and was present with them at the time of their deaths. He wrote at the time of their deaths and admitted again on the stand that he was the "action obitiatrist" who assisted in both suicides.

ANALYSIS

Narratives in the Courtroom

Unlike most settings, the discourse in trials is governed by detailed rules that control the content and delivery of what is presented by the witnesses, lawyers, and judges. The purpose of a criminal trial is twofold: to determine a narrative of what happened and with what consequences, and to determine if it should be punished.

The telling of this narrative is stylized and constrained in a jury trial in several unique ways. First, all testimony and argument must be presented according to the rules of evidence, which seek to formalize the conditions of storytelling and keep out types of storytelling and sources that are regarded as generally unreliable. The judge regulates these rules of evidence, determining how the story is told. Second, the stories are elicited from one witness at a time in response to hostile or friendly questions posed by the attorneys. No single person relates the tale in a continuous presentation; rather, the elements of a story are dispersed across competing and often contradictory witnesses sponsored by the opposing parties, and intermingled with many other stories, arguments, and interrogations over the course of the trial. This leaves the jury to piece together the final narrative from the fragmented accounts and decide the consequences. Third, once the trial begins the attorneys are not permitted to interact with the jurors except in a very formal, one-sided fashion. Jurors typically are barred from asking questions, even to clarify testimony and legal procedures. Finally, the attorneys, knowing very little about the background or views of the jurors, must construct arguments on the broadest appeal possible. The jury pool is screened to exclude persons with personal knowledge of the case, parties, or attorneys, or with a commitment to the issue at stake strong enough to inhibit their enforcement of the law, and the attorneys cannot obtain clear feedback from them to indicate the degree of their understanding or acceptance.

Despite these constraints, personal stories can be a highly effective tool in the courtroom. By suspending judgments and avoiding drawn-out implications—or by making it difficult for the listener to do so on the spot—stories allow for considerable ambiguity (which can be intentionally created) and even outright contradictions. Narratives do not demand clearly stated premises or principles, making refutation more difficult; an argument embedded within a story is more difficult to challenge without challenging the story itself, which may seem very real and with which the listener may intuitively identify (at some level).

To explore the uses and purposes of such narrative more fully, I analyze the narrative elements and then look at how these elements were employed for the immediate purpose of clearing Kevorkian and for the larger purpose of expounding movement principles.

Moral Character

Four main actors emerge from the defense narratives: Kevorkian the protagonist; the prosecutor and the process he represents as antagonist; and Frederick and Khalili, the potential victims and pivotal storytellers.

Not surprisingly, Kevorkian emerges as the hero of the defense narratives, the one who "saves" the potential victims by helping them achieve their desired resolution. With its stories, the defense went to great lengths to construct a clear and detailed account of Kevorkian's virtuous character. Though clearly related to his long unemployment, the defense turned

Kevorkian's impoverished lifestyle—his Spartan apartment, old van, and Salvation Army clothes—into the virtue of simplicity (see Weisberg 1996: 81). Not only did the stories portray him as a man of integrity, compassion, and courage, but they characterized his motivations and the quality of his work as rigorously professional: he did not exercise undue coercion over his patients, he followed a strict protocol (see below), he conducted extensive interviews and investigations into the physical conditions and histories of his patients. In this way, too, the stories of Kevorkian's character linked the juror's personal experience of medical care and professionalism to the events they were called to judge; Kevorkian's assistance was simply another instance of compassionately motivated medical treatment that Frederick and Khalili needed and desired. According to Kevorkian himself:

> My goal is a physician's duty, to ameliorate pain and suffering. You know, a physician's [duty] isn't just to extend life whereas eliminating suffering and pain is the road to extending life. . . . My aim isn't to end human life. . . . I encourage them to do all they can to ameliorate their condition if there is any option. Some take it; some refuse to take it. It's their choice. I can't force a patient to do something.

Moreover, in the defense's story, Kevorkian was a martyr, victimized by oppressive police practices and a relentless prosecutor that sought to disrupt his work of ending the needless suffering of the dying.

The prosecutor, by contrast, was characterized as the victimizer, the impersonal "bureaucrat," who "maligned" and "disparaged" the good Doctor and audaciously forced his way into "that sacred circle of love" around Frederick's family. According to the defense narratives, he was motivated by a blind spite for Kevorkian, whom he had never talked to, and wielded his considerable power without any regard for the needs or desires of the decedents.

In the defense narratives, Frederick and Khalili were the potential victims, and it was on their stories that the defense implicitly hung its case. To convict, on the one hand, the defense implied, would not only unjustly punish Kevorkian but it would victimize Frederick and Khalili. A conviction would necessarily taint their good names, besmirch the dignified death they had sought, and deny their courage and character and that of their close-knit family. Ending the trial with an acquittal, on the other hand, would put the jury on the side of the decedents and their families, preserving their reputations and honoring their difficult choices in the midst of great suffering.

Personal Identification

Not only were the characters of the narratives important, but also the way the narratives were told. Through the videotapes and the testimony of the family members and friends, the jury was given the opportunity to form an emotional, empathetic bond with Frederick and Khalili themselves. Any such bond would increase jury sympathy with their plight and open-ness to the resolution they sought. Watching the decedents firsthand, rather than simply hearing about them from others, also gave the defense narratives greater weight and credibility. Trust and rapport established with the decedents could spill over, so to speak, to the other storytellers.

Beyond fostering an empathetic identification, the defense also used the decedents' firsthand testimonies to implicitly invoke the jurors' self-interest. Through the decedents' stories, the jurors were asked to place themselves in the situation of the storyteller: the active person who, through no fault of their own, suffers a catastrophic accident or terminal illness. Such personal experience narratives have a "discursive immediacy and the power of the personal connection between narrator and audi-ence," which gives them great rhetorical force (Fine 1995: 137). The fear-ful elements in these stories—a slow, disfiguring death, unsympathetic doctors—took the issue before the jury from the realm of a general threat to society and personalized it as a threat that each one of them might face. Not only does this personalization produce greater sympathy and tight-ened personal identification, but it connects the jurors' sense of self-inter-est with the changes in law and medical practice—the legalization of physician-assisted suicide—that the defense argued were necessary to bring a dignified end to the suffering. What was at stake was not just about "them," but about "us."

Progress, Self-Determination, and Compassion

Three central themes emerged from the defense narratives: progress, ratio-nal self-determination, and most important, compassion.

Progress. The defense narratives of Frederick, Khalili, and Kevorkian each featured a segment concerning a proposed protocol that Kevorkian had published in a peer-reviewed medical journal, and which he attempted to follow in administering both assisted suicides. In the protocol, patients were to be screened out if they were not terminal, could still benefit significantly from palliative care, were temporarily depressed, or were coerced by family members or financial pressures. The emphasis on the protocol in each story accomplished two rhetorical tasks. First, the use of an official protocol strengthened the link between Kevorkian's work and the professional practice of medicine. Second, because Kevorkian's protocol for selecting and servicing assisted-suicide patients had been published in a peer-reviewed journal, it appeared to represent a new medically recognized form of treatment, a legitimate alternative more in keeping with the patients' desires. In the defense narratives, the use of the protocol was presented as an act of progress over customary medical treatments of the terminally ill, which were depicted as blindly keeping patients alive as long as possible, despite the suffering and degradations that result.

Rational Self-Determination. Building on the idea of progress, the defense sought to assure the jury that Frederick and Khalili's deaths were entirely voluntary and that these cases were a properly delimited exercise of the right to die. In its stories, the defense distinguished the deaths from suicide. Frederick and Khalili did not so much choose to die as they made rational decisions for dignity ("the last thing that I want is to live with the impaired quality of life"); peace ("she wanted to end her suffering as quickly as possible"); and family ("And why, why put that money to me?") in the face of catastrophic illness and impending death. This emphasis dovetailed with Kevorkian's claim that his assistance was not of suicide but of the eradication of suffering. The recounting of Kevorkian's professionalism and his use of a strict protocol also implied rationality and an authorized decision-making process. Finally, the defense narratives implied institutional support for the decisions of Frederick and Khalili, in the involvement of both their families and, in the case of Frederick, a church official.

Compassion. The most prevalent theme in the defense narratives was that physician-assisted suicide was a compassionate act, given the patients' suffering and prognosis. In telling the emotional stories of Frederick and Khalili, the defense took the case out of an abstract question of how to objectively apply a statute to fact and made a here-and-now argument that the statute on its face and as applied to the facts of these cases was immoral, because of the suffering it would prolong. Invoking compassion allowed the defense to question the moral legitimacy of any law that would bar assisted suicide. According to its stories, physician-assisted suicide is what medical conscience calls for in the face of such suffering—that it would be inhumane to ignore requests for permanent relief.

The Use of the Narratives

In order to understand how narratives can shed new light on movements, the purposes that the narratives served in this trial must first be understood. Like the broader movement, the defense could only improve its position if it could interpret itself, diffuse opposition, and build an empathetic bond with its target audience.

Kevorkian never denied that he participated in the deaths of Frederick and Khalili. Rather, the defense made three arguments. First, they denied that Kevorkian had the intent to kill—his intent was to remove suffering. Second, they argued that the final act that led to Frederick's death (the pulled paper clip) was Frederick's act, not Kevorkian's. And third, they argued that if the law were to bar assisted suicide in these two cases, then the law would be immoral, thereby implying that the jury ought to refuse to enforce it, regardless of whether Kevorkian's conduct violated the statute. This last argument, for the jury to ignore the court's instruction and acquit Kevorkian in order to defeat an immoral law, is one for "jury nullification" of the law, and was never made explicit, since the court would have barred it. Although the key thrusts of the defense strategy can be easily and logically laid out, the bulk of the defense was spent not on laying out logical argument, but on telling stories.

The tasks confronting Kevorkian's defense team can be likened to the tasks confronting any social movement seeking to produce policy change. In order to win state legitimacy, such a movement has to interpret itself to outsiders, making its case to those opposed as well as those neutral to it. To accomplish this task, a movement must, *inter alia,* acquire channels to spread its message; win support and assuage the misgivings of those who have not taken a stand; give adherents a sense of agency in addressing the problem; allay or discredit the arguments of the opposition; and frame movement tenets and goals so as to resonate with broad cultural understandings. Movement actors use narratives for these different tasks, all of which can be seen in this trial.

Ambiguity as Tactic

As noted above, stories allow for ambiguity and even contradictions. In more propositional and logical forms of discourse, as tends to characterize the articulation of collective action frames, indeterminacies over major points are difficult to maintain. Glosses are easier to spot and hearer demands for clarification can force a resolution of inconsistencies or their explicit recognition. This is not so in stories, where the teller is freer to create ambiguity and inconsistencies when they serve his or her rhetorical purpose. Such was the tactic of the defense in the way it characterized law and medicine in its narratives.

Ambiguity about the Law. The narratives embodied an ambiguity about the morality of the legal system. On the one hand, the defense portrayed the legal system as bad, as represented by the antagonist, the prosecutor. Fieger cast the trial itself as an effort on the part of the prosecution to make the jury smear the decedents' names and say that compassion, choice, and control over the manner of one's suffering is against the law in America. The narratives imply, but do not directly state, that the law prohibiting assisted suicide is immoral and stands in the way of human progress.

And yet, the judge was explicitly regarded as authoritative and implicitly as just and fair. The judicial system was not attacked, even though it was enforcing the law through arrest and trial. Similarly, the defense valued the role and power of the jurors, calling for the jury to serve as the community conscience, to "send a message" that new laws are needed—yet the unjust prosecutor and police force would be the very ones to enforce any new laws. The narratives valorized the court, which ironically worked closely with the antagonists and could send Kevorkian to prison. Who gave the police the permission to search his premises and seize evidence? The court did, but such inconsistencies were glossed over at the trial, and matters were left intentionally ambiguous. In this way, the defense could treat the prosecutor and his office as antagonists and victimizers without appearing to be challenging basic American notions of justice or the legitimacy of the trial proceedings.

Ambiguity about Medicine.   The defense narratives also embodied deep ambiguities about the practice of medicine. In the stories, the medical system was characterized as callous, bureaucratic, and possibly more interested in profits than patients. Other doctors, for example, refused to help Kevorkian with the protocol for Frederick, so that he could not follow all the steps, such as securing a psychiatric evaluation. Doctors refused to make house calls to Frederick, refused to offer or consider any alternative short of drilling holes in her skull to rig her head up to a frame, and could not (would not) save her from a horrible death. The doctors who came in to testify against Kevorkian, such as the medical examiner, were portrayed as paid guns in the prosecutor's camp, strangers to the families involved. Hospitals were depicted as leaving patients to suffer, stripping them not only of their assets and identity, but of their fundamental rights as American citizens to choose how they live and die.

At the same time, however, the jury was being asked to affirm a doctor who, without any accountability to higher authority, intentionally helped to end the lives of two patients. Kevorkian justified his actions by appealing to motivations from medicine: "My goal is a physician's duty." And his published protocol was used in the defense narratives to give his prior research a stamp of scientific and medical validity. The defense, moreover, in implicitly calling for the legalization of assisted suicide, also implied without reservation that doctors were the right professionals to carry it out. In short, the ambiguity about medicine in the narratives allowed the defense to simultaneously argue that doctors and the medical establishment conspired against the best interests of Frederick and Khalili, and that doctors and medicine are also progressive, scientific, compassionate, and capable of running an official system of assisted suicide that will respect the desires of future patients (including perhaps the jurors).

Narratives and Theoretical Reasoning

At the end of the trial, the jurors were to answer a simple question: whether Kevorkian violated the statute. But that statute involved a series of difficult questions: (1) What constitutes "participation" in the physical act by which Frederick and Khalili committed suicide?; (2) What constitutes an intent to cause death?; and (3) What distinguishes that intent from an intent to relieve pain and suffering? Can you intend an act, knowing that it will certainly have a secondary effect that is barred under law, and yet not intend this "double effect"? In the context of a criminal trial, the application of the law to the facts could give rise to even more fundamental questions concerning the power of the state to limit the individuals' power of self-determination, the contours and qualities of compassion, and the validity of traditional moral taboos against suicide and assisted suicide. These deeper questions depend on assumptions, such as the character of individualism and community, which are rarely articulated by most people, and not always rooted in their minds in any explicit philosophical or theoretical system.

When pressed to justify personal stances on the source of rights, the proper balance of individualism and communitarianism, or the problems of pain and suffering in a technological society, few people can articulate theoretically sophisticated answers; much of their position is pretheoretical (Bellah et al. 1985). As defined by Berger and Luckmann, pretheoretical knowledge is "what everyone knows" and is set forth in proverbs, maxims, values, and beliefs that govern the everyday living of most people. Few people take the time to organize such knowledge into a cohesive theoretical system. "Theoretical knowledge," they argue, "is only a small and by no means the most important part of what passes for knowledge in a society. . . . The primary knowledge about the institutional order is knowledge on the pre-theoretical level" (Berger and Luckmann 1966: 65).

As demonstrated in this trial, narrative operates effectively precisely because it is primarily interchange at the pretheoretical level. As discussed, narratives constituted the bulk of the defense strategy of persuading the jurors of the validity of assisted suicide in this case. By contrast, very little testimony was used to construct any theoretical defense of the practice. On the face of it, this is surprising, since the jury was being asked to pass a theoretical judgment on the question of whether the intent exercised in this case is an acceptable type of intent under the law. But arguments made by the defense on a theoretical level would have required jurors to reach a decision in terms of explicit legal and moral principles, with the concomitant task of figuring out for themselves what principles they accepted or thought appropriate and how to apply them. By making arguments through personal experience narratives, the defense bypassed these knotty and cognitively challenging issues. By setting up a narrow and highly personal protagonist-antagonist conflict, for instance, the narratives drew attention to the immediate personalities and away from the legal statute and its interpretation. Invoking an emotional identification with the decedents and sympathy for their plight, the narratives made abstract legal and ethical principles seem out of place and those who raised them as insensitive and uncaring. Drawing on and embedding protean American cultural themes of progress, self-determination, and compassion, the narratives bestowed moral legitimacy on assisted suicide without reference to such abstract principles or the articulation of elaborated rationales.

Finally, the defense narratives invited, even empowered, the jury to write the final chapter to all three stories. None of the stories had reached their conclusion: the names of Frederick and Khalili could be smeared by a finding that their final acts were criminal in nature, and the hero, Dr. Kevorkian, could be put in prison. It was up to the jury to secure the final happy ending. The stories called less for applying the law to the facts than for the jury to simply make everything right; the jury members were not impartial judges, but narrative participants who could both prevent the victimization of the decedents and end the senseless persecution of the man who helped them end their suffering.

CONCLUSION

As one of the key cultural gatekeepers of American society, the courts are an important forum for pursuing movement goals (Hunter 1991: 250–251, 270–271). While court decisions may not result in immediate policy changes, they are almost always an important symbolic resource in the struggle for public acceptance. In court, movements face the task of persuading outsiders (here, the jurors) to deliver a favorable verdict. Their only link to these bystanders may be widespread cultural understandings and broadly accepted values such as, in the Kevorkian case, self-determination, compassion, and progress. However, as the trial studied here makes clear, that may be all that is necessary. In winning the support of outsiders, the defense did not have to convince the jurors to accept elaborated movement frames, much less an ideology of total autonomy. Nor did they have to deal with all the complexities of the right to die or the subtleties of movement arguments. Rather, they simply told stories that unfolded so as to make any other outcome than the desired one appear to be a violation of the values the jurors, like other Americans, hold dear. This tactic is certainly not unique to this case.

Social movement analysis that seeks to make coherent and consistent sense of movement perspectives may fail to capture the tactics and content of movement persuasion in important ways. In the heat of cultural conflict, a movement's use of narratives and rhetoric may be less shaped and constrained by its frames than by values and perspectives found in the common culture. Thus, narrative study may provide insight into the complexities, contradictions, and inconsistencies found within movements, thereby providing a richer, more complex sense of the symbolic/expressive flow that movements contain. Further, frame analysis may overcomplexify the rhetoric of a movement, in that the movement's primary tools may be not be cognitive, but rather emotional or visceral. Regardless of the reality of the stories or their actual representativeness, they may have an immediate, gut-wrenching impact that does not fit neatly into a theoretical, ethical, or ideological system. Yet such stories will be indicative of the less ordered elements at play in the social movement.

ACKNOWLEDGMENT

The purchase of the trial transcript was made possible through the generous support of the Institute for Advanced Studies in Culture at the University of Virginia.

NOTES

1. As is common in cultural conflict, the terms of the debate have become politicized (Luker 1984: 2). The practice of a physician providing materials or expertise so that a person may act to end his own life is generally referred to as "physician-assisted suicide." Kevorkian has referred to the practice as "medicide" (which he translated to mean medically assisted suicide) or, later on, as "patholysis" (eradication of suffering) (Kevorkian 1991). But because the practice is commonly referred to as "physician-assisted suicide," I will use that term. This practice is to be distinguished from instances when the physician performs the final acts, and the person who dies does not, which is a practice some call "euthanasia." The appropriateness of the term "suicide" was an issue in the trial studied here.

Activists also dispute what to call the decedents who have used Kevorkian's assistance to end their lives. To call them "patients" seems to assume the very questions at stake: whether assisted suicide is a legitimate part of the panoply of services that a physician may offer, and whether or not this is a physician-patient relationship. To call them "victims" errs in the opposite direction. "Customers" does not fit either, because Kevorkian refused payment for the services. One possible choice may be "clients," because these persons were consumers of professional services. But because both the prosecution and defense at trial referred to the decedents as *patients,* I will use that term in this paper.

2. People of the State of Michigan v. Dr. Jack Kevorkian, Defendant, No. 93-129832-FH and 94-130248-FH (Oakland County Circuit Court, Michigan, February–March 1996). The opening statements, direct and cross examination of Kevorkian, and closing statements amounted to 642 pages of transcript, as transcribed by the court reporter.

3. In addition, I reviewed materials posted on the Internet by the Hemlock Society, the Euthanasia Research and Guidance Organization (referred to as ERGO)—both advocates of physician-assisted suicide—and the National Right to Life Committee, the American Life League, the International Anti-Euthanasia Task Force, and Not Dead Yet, which oppose physician-assisted suicide. I also received direct mail packets from The Hemlock Society USA and The National Right to Life Committee, which are two of the principle organizations involved in the physician-assisted suicide conflict in the United States.

4. English common law prohibited assisted suicide as accessory to the crime of suicide. Such was the practice in most of the colonies. The first American statute prohibiting assisted suicide in any context was passed by New York in 1828 (Marzen et al. 1985).

5. See, for example, Washington v. Glucksberg, 117 S. Ct. 2258, 138 L. Ed. 2d 772, 1997 US LEXIS 4039 (1997).

6. By the time the trial was held, Kevorkian acknowledged participating in a total of twenty-five suicides.

NINE

Movement Advocates as Battered Women's Storytellers

From Varied Experiences, One Message

BESS ROTHENBERG

L enore Walker opens her influential book, *The Battered Woman,* with the long and explicit "story of Anne." The story is one of unrelenting physical abuse and personal degradation:

> There was a long period of time when he didn't hurt me . . . [but] the more he drank the more violent he got. . . . He wouldn't let me associate with any of my friends that he didn't like. He would threaten to hurt me if I did. . . . He used the threat of hurting me physically more and more to get me to stay. . . . He had taken a gun to me before and told me that if I didn't straighten up, this was going to be it. . . . He treated me like [a child] by not letting me have my name on the checking account, which had my money in it, and giving me a two-dollar-a-week allowance. . . . Sex with my husband was more like rape. . . . He did some really weird things to me. Like in the middle of the night, he held me down and cut off all my pubic hair. . . . Pride got in my way, and I hadn't wanted my parents to know what was going on. (1979: 1–9)

By beginning her book with Anne's story, Walker relies on narrative to produce shock, sympathy, and outrage at the ways in which women like Anne are mistreated. For Walker, as for many other movement activists who tell the stories of battered women, harrowing accounts mobilize strong emotions and a sense of injustice while personifying and expressing the claims of the movement. By selecting the "right" accounts, advocates harness the evocative power of narrative and show how the lived experiences of individual women align with their definition of the domestic violence problem. In this chapter, I analyze this use of narrative and argue that through the strategic retelling of victims' stories, battered women's advocates conform the complicated and heterogeneous experiences of many different women into the single and consistent public voice of the movement.

In the mid-1970s, a relatively loose coalition of feminists, academics, mental health professionals, and social workers first mobilized to define domestic violence as an urgent social problem. This initial coalition and the attention it generated from policy makers, the media, and the public launched the "battered women's movement." Employing an analysis drawn in part from the antirape movement that had begun just a few years earlier (Rose 1977; Schechter 1982), battered women's advocates argued that domestic violence, like rape, should be understood as a product of the gendered power relations in a patriarchal society. The initial movement activism also followed the pattern of the antirape campaign. On the local level, movement advocates established battered women's shelters and made hotlines and counseling available to abused women. They formed coalitions at the local, state, and national level to educate the public about domestic violence and to push for reforms in public policy. They also criticized inadequate and harmful police practices and pressed the criminal justice system to establish policies that would make it easier for women to leave abusive partners.

Over the past twenty-five years, many of the initial goals of the movement have found institutionalization through legislation, lobbying, organizations, and shelters. Advocates have established battered women's shelters in every major U.S. city and in many small towns. Police have instituted policies such as mandatory arrests on domestic violence calls and required sensitivity training in order to better protect and improve interactions with abused women. Every level of government has also responded to the problem with legislation designed to improve the conditions of battered women seeking help, including, most notably, the federal Violence Against Women Act of 1994. The media have devoted increasing attention to battering as a social problem and provided activists with a means for making their claims heard. In assessing the movement's achievements, Tierney concludes that, already by the early 1980s, advocates had succeeded in making the "plight of battered women, once socially invisible," a subject of public discussion (1982: 215).

With these accomplishments behind them, the battered women's movement, as a movement, has left its initial mobilization phase and has moved on to a stage of institutionalization. Although domestic violence is still a social problem requiring advocate and public support, the movement itself has left its early phase of activism. The understanding of battering we have today, however, follows the original framing of the early activists. This framing of domestic violence as a social problem has depended on women's stories as a means of making the issue both realistic and urgent.

Initial movement activists relied heavily on the personal stories of abused women in order to make their case and to help put a human face on a once publicly invisible phenomenon. Lenore Walker, a psychologist and prominent movement activist, explains the importance of telling such narratives: "I believe it will only be through listening to what battered women say that we will be able to understand what happens to a battered woman, how she is victimized, and how we can help a society change so that this horrible crime can no longer be perpetrated upon women" (1979: xiii). Activists have thus come to serve as the intermediaries between victims and the larger public. Advocates both solicit and listen to victims' narratives in private forums, such as in shelters, counseling or therapy sessions, or in personal communications, before selecting certain stories for public retelling. This selection process has always been guided by the goal of winning public sympathy and support for domestic violence victims and advocating specific remedies. Because of this, stories are chosen or interpreted to communicate one image of the victim, the "battered woman." As I will show, this storytelling process by the movement works to delimit the complex and diverse experiences of domestic violence to a single ideal-typical model that both confirms and reproduces movement frames.

In the following pages, I address the major recurring themes that have come to structure movement storytelling. My data are drawn from a review of prominent works by domestic violence advocates written in the 1970s and 1980s. After outlining the prominent narrative themes, I then consider features of domestic violence that are not represented in the writings of battered women's advocates or the stories they tell. The empirical studies on domestic violence conducted at the time the movement emerged present a much more heterogeneous view of this phenomena than the one communicated by battered women's advocates. As I argue, by choosing, editing, interpreting, or omitting stories, advocates have emphasized certain aspects of domestic violence but not others. In this manner, the movement has achieved a unified and coherent voice that speaks out against violence against women and continues to structure the framing of the domestic violence movement today. I conclude with some observations about the use of narrative in social movements as a tool for reproducing categories and presenting simplified pictures of complex realities.

THE PROTOTYPICAL NARRATIVE THEMES

In its effort to change public perceptions and social policy, the battered women's movement frames domestic violence and its victims according to several key claims. The first-person stories of victimization used by movement advocates, in turn, symbolize those claims and provide the human element that both concretizes and personalizes the social problem. Like Lenore Walker and other early movement writers, Del Martin introduces the first chapter of her book, *Battered Wives,* with an extended and prototypical story. Virtually everything the movement means by "battered woman" is contained in the story; I quote it, therefore, at some length.

> I am in my thirties and so is my husband. . . . My husband is a college graduate and a professional in his field. We are both attractive and, for the most part, respected and well-liked. We have four children and live in a middle-class home with all the comforts we could possibly want. . . .
>
> For most of my married life I have been periodically beaten by my husband. What do I mean by "beaten"? I mean that parts of my body have been hit violently and repeatedly, and that painful bruises, swelling, bleeding wounds, unconsciousness, and combinations of these things have resulted. . . . I have had glasses thrown at me. I have been kicked in the abdomen when I was visibly pregnant. I have been kicked off the bed and hit while lying on the floor—again, while I was pregnant. I have been whipped, kicked and thrown, picked up again and thrown down again. I have been punched and kicked in the head, chest, face,

and abdomen more times than I can count. I have been slapped for saying something about politics, for having a different view about religion, for swearing, for crying, for wanting to have intercourse. . . .

Now, the first response to this story, which I myself think of, will be "Why didn't you seek help?" I did. Early in our marriage I went to a clergyman who, after a few visits, told me that my husband meant no real harm, that he was just confused and felt insecure. I was encouraged to be more tolerant and understanding. . . . Things continued. Next time I turned to a doctor. I was given little pills to relax me and told to take things a little easier. I was just too nervous. I turned to a friend, and when her husband found out, he accused me of making things up or exaggerating the situation. She was told to stay away from me. . . . I turned to a professional family guidance agency. . . . At the agency I found I had to defend myself against the suspicion that I wanted to be hit, that I invited the beatings. . . . I called the police one time. They not only did not respond to the call, they called several hours later to ask if things had "settled down." I could have been dead by then!

I have nowhere to go if it happens again. No one wants to take in a woman with four children. . . . Everyone I have gone to for help has somehow wanted to blame me and vindicate my husband. . . . I may be his excuse but I have never been his reason. . . . No one has to "provoke" a wife-beater. He will strike out when he's ready and for whatever reason he has at the moment. . . . I have suffered physical and emotional battering and spiritual rape because the structure of my world says I cannot do anything about a man who wants to beat me. (1981: 1–3)

In presenting and commenting on this story, Martin suggests that, as in this case, the victim of domestic violence is a *woman* who is savagely beaten by a male abuser for no reason. By definition, the "battered woman" category has little place for men as victims of domestic abuse. Indeed, the larger category of domestic violence has, over time, come to be understood as women (and sometimes children) abused by men, thus excluding other forms of familial or intimate violence. From its inception, the battered women's movement has relied heavily on a feminist framework to ground their claims in the belief that domestic violence is rooted in patriarchy. Walker explains: "My feminist analysis of all violence is that sexism is the real underbelly of human suffering" (1979: xi). Following this initial framing, men were rarely acknowledged as domestic violence victims and continue today to be mostly overlooked.

Martin also relies on the above passage to argue that domestic violence victims are trapped, for a variety of reasons, into staying with their abusive partner against their will. In suggesting that she is in some way to blame for the abuse, potential help sources further victimize the battered woman. Martin maintains that those who could come to her aid often ignore victims who request assistance or attempt to leave. With this story, Martin also conveys the movement claim that the domestic violence victim is an "everywoman," indistinguishable from nonvictims and as likely to be from the upper as from the lower social classes. Together, these general arguments frame the category of the battered woman for the movement. In the following sections, I briefly discuss each of these claims and the stories that advocates select to symbolize them.

Severely Beaten and Abused

From the outset, movement activists typified domestic violence victims as women who are severely beaten and abused by their husbands or male partners. The framing of domestic violence, as Loseke observes, has been "about violence that is severe, frequent, unstoppable, and multiply-consequential" (1992: 39). Accordingly, in selecting victim stories, advocates have presented cases in which women describe vicious, potentially fatal, beatings at the hands of their partners. NiCarthy, for example, cites a story of the physical damage inflicted on Chris by her husband:

> At a family picnic Chris threw some food away and Wes slapped her to the ground and repeatedly kicked her in the head with his steel-toed boots. . . . Three weeks later Chris began to have headaches and grand mal seizures. The kicking had resulted in temporal lobe damage on both sides of her head. (1987: 114)

Due to this brutal beating, Chris was diagnosed with epilepsy and has had to live with seizures ever since. This narrative drives home advocates' claim that domestic abuse can have far-reaching and frightening consequences.

Activists have also selected stories of other forms of serious abuse. Walker, for example, emphasizes the cruelty that victims endure by drawing on graphic descriptions of sexual abuse in which women are forced to have intercourse with animals, objects, and other men. In one particularly disturbing tale, she quotes Lois's story about the scars on her face:

> My husband did this to me, you know. If I didn't want to have sex with him. Even if I did, it didn't seem to matter. He would take out his knife and he would cut marks in my skin with it. He would tie me whenever we had sex to a bed or a chair or whatever. . . . He ripped my rectum so many times that the doctors in the emergency room used to laugh when I'd walk in. . . . He would stick all kinds of things in my vagina, like the crucifix with the picture of Jesus on it. (1979: 121)

This bizarre and frightening story illustrates the horrors that activists suggest are typical of domestic violence in general.

In addition to sexual abuse, advocates have also presented stories of intense emotional battering, degrading treatment, and mental manipulation. NiCarthy documents Janice's story of emotional and physical abuse by her husband Raul:

> I was emotionally trapped. . . . He'd say he couldn't stand me, he didn't want anything to do with me, except to have sex. And that was a big emotional thing to me, because he was so hateful and nasty to me. I hated it! . . . I hated everything about him. . . . The worst thing he did was to call me a whore and say I was nothing to him, that I'd never be anything to anybody else, because after a while he said it so much that I believed him. . . . I was always afraid. . . . I thought if I left him he would always come looking for me. I knew I'd never be through with this man. Still today I'm not through with him. (1987: 175–176)

NiCarthy's story of Janice personalizes the claim that emotional abuse can have long-lasting and terrible effects.

In presenting such stories, advocates have suggested that extreme physical violence and severe emotional abuse are representative of domestic violence in the United States. Because these cases contain few moral ambiguities, movement activists have needed to provide little commentary or interpretation to convince their audience that these women are in need of sympathy and support. The depravity and injustice inflicted on these victims speaks for itself. Shock and disgust are the only appropriate moral responses, public intervention and substantive assistance the only appropriate policy responses. And, indeed, these are precisely the responses the movement from the beginning has sought to elicit. Consequently, victim narratives of extreme brutality and abuse have the greatest public impact and have best served the movement and its goals.

Trapped and Isolated

Movement advocates have not only typified battered women as severely mistreated, they have also focused on how victims are trapped into staying with their husbands or partners. Battering is more than a single beating or abusive incident; it is a pattern of mistreatment over a period—usually a long period—of time. The ongoing nature of the violence and abuse raises the question of why battered women do not simply end the relationship rather than continue in it. The question of staying, as Gelles observes, "derives from the elementary assumption that any reasonable individual, having been beaten and battered by another person, would avoid being victimized again (or at least avoid the attacker)" (1987: 108). In part as a response to this question, movement activists have argued that victimization effectively leaves battered women with little or no option but to stay and endure the battering. For victims, continuing in an abusive relationship is not a matter of choice. They are trapped, and without outside help, they have few—if any—avenues of escape.

Movement advocates have provided four general interconnected reasons why victimization traps battered women and have presented corresponding victim narratives that illustrate this captivity. According to advocates, the primary reason battered women stay with their abusers is because they fear further violence toward themselves or their children if they attempt to leave. This fear is both implicitly and explicitly indicated in the many stories of severe violence and abuse that advocates have employed. Nicole's story serves as a prototypical example of this claim in NiCarthy's book of stories of women who eventually left their abusers. After having had been beaten for three and a half hours with a coat hanger and having had a fireplace poker shoved into her face, Nicole pressed charges against her husband. In explaining why she had not done so earlier, she contrasts this point with an earlier one in her relationship:

"I had dropped the charges once before when he had said that he had been working for the Mafia and they would come and kill me and the kids. I believed him" (1987: 271). This threat of harm to herself and her children paralyzed Nicole into remaining with a man whom she already knew was truly dangerous.

A second reason victims stay, advocates have argued, is because the institutions that should be of assistance have traditionally ignored their plight. This "system" of official help sources includes law enforcement, government agencies, the criminal justice system, the medical and mental health professions, and religious organizations. Through selected narratives, advocates have demonstrated how battered women are neither protected nor helped by these institutions. In the prototypical victim's narrative quoted earlier from Martin's book, for example, the woman describes seeking aid from a clergyman, doctor, friend, professional family guidance agency, and the police. None gave her assistance to get free of her husband's domination or to help her in preventing further abuse. Instead, her experience was downplayed and effectively dismissed in every case. She wanted to leave, but without help, she had "nowhere to go."

The psychological effects of domestic violence on the victim are a third reason proffered by advocates for victims' entrapment. According to movement activists, battered women face a "slow but certain destruction, psychologically and physically" (Gibbs 1993: 41). Psychologically, battering and the terror that goes with it cause a wide variety of debilitating problems, including depression, anxiety, low self-esteem, psychological paralysis, shock reactions, identity loss, posttraumatic stress disorder, helplessness, denial, and guilt. Advocates have argued that these problems, individually or in combination, erode the capacity of victims to act independently or assert themselves, and selected victim stories provide testimony to this progressive incapacitation. NiCarthy relates Sandy's story of having been beaten for long periods of time but prevented from leaving because of emotional difficulties:

> I don't know why I stayed . . . but I think it was still fear. My self-esteem, from not being allowed to talk to people, was just as low as it has ever been. I was afraid of everything, and I didn't feel well most of the time, which lowered my energy. I just wasn't ready, yet. It was almost as though I was physically paralyzed and I wanted to [leave], but I couldn't. . . . The worst of the emotional abuse was accepting his opinion of me, his devaluing what I

know are my considerable skills. "You're a rotten person, a
lousy fuck, a rotten cook, a rotten lover, a rotten musician, you
don't know anything." (1987: 95)

Women are thus "paralyzed" into remaining, such stories relate, because
of these degrading physical and emotional experiences.

A final reason battered women stay with abusive partners, according
to advocates, concerns the disadvantages of being a woman living in a
patriarchal society. One form of this argument holds that women are
socialized into gender roles that lead them to believe that they have no
choice but to be a victim. They stay because they were taught to stay. In
another form, advocates have argued that "society" places stigmas on
women who leave their husbands or admit to being battered. As
NiCarthy's example of Janine illustrates: "I was convinced that I was a
loser, that my parents had had a bad marriage, I had a bad marriage, that
this was the way it was. I had heard that from my husband and my
mother. 'This is the way it is. You stick it out'" (1987: 175). NiCarthy also
cites Edith's story in which both her counselor and minister advised her:
"Don't put those kids through a divorce'" (71). Both Janine and Edith,
according to NiCarthy, rethought their plans because of the disapproval
they felt from others when they considered leaving their abusive husbands.
At the same time, advocates have maintained, society both directly and
indirectly condones the use of violence and the right of men to hit women.
The prototypical story quoted by Martin, cited earlier, exemplifies this
point. After detailing her rejection by each of those she approached for
help, the woman observes: "Everyone I have gone to for help has somehow
wanted to blame me and vindicate my husband" (1981: 3).

From the inception of the movement, activists have stressed the multiple vulnerabilities that women—particularly those who do not work outside the home—face in a patriarchal society. These vulnerabilities include
social isolation, financial dependence, child-care responsibilities, unemployment, and a lack of educational opportunities, access to transporta-
tion, and/or housing. According to advocates, such vulnerabilities and
dependencies often leave victims without the opportunity or wherewithal
to break away and start over. Martin uses the following story from a
woman who feels her liability acutely:

I know that I have to get out. But when you have nowhere to go,
you know that you must go on your own and expect no support.

I have to be ready for that. I have to be ready to support myself and the children completely, and still provide a decent environment for them. I pray that I can do that before I am murdered in my own home. . . . [E]ach night I dread the final blow that will kill me and leave my children motherless. I hope I can hang on until I complete my education, get a good job, and become self-sufficient enough to care for my children on my own. (1981: 3–5)

In these cases, activists have argued, the disadvantages of being a woman in American society are amplified by the horrors of abuse.

By using victim stories that describe a kind of captivity, movement advocates have sought to show that domestic violence victims never stay in abusive relationships by choice. Demonstrating such entrapment is essential to the movement. Commenting on the movement's need to construct "staying" in a way that does not undermine its claims about domestic violence, Loseke notes: "if a woman stays because violence is not 'that bad,' if she stays because she does not mind the abuse, indeed, if she stays because she *chooses* to stay for any reason, then claims about the content of this public problem are challenged" (1992: 21; emphasis in original). This challenge is rooted in the movement's general claim that domestic violence is not the problem of individual women, but is instead a *social* problem. Introducing the notion of personal choice into the picture weakens that overarching claim. But if battered women are trapped and isolated, effectively held against their will, then public action is obvious and necessary. Public intervention and remedies have been the movement's goals; stories of captivity, like stories of extreme violence and abuse, make these responses both concrete and urgent.

Rich and Poor, But Especially Rich

Movement activists have gone beyond arguing that battered women are severely beaten and abused, trapped and isolated. Advocates have also typified the domestic violence victim as unmarked by any distinguishing feature or class location, arguing that domestic violence is as serious a problem for the middle and upper classes as it is for the lower. Claims about the prevalence of domestic violence are not typically put directly into narrative form; statistics rather than stories are the preferred mode of discourse. Walker's 1984 study, for example, involved primarily

"intelligent, well-educated, competent people who held responsible jobs,"
with about 25 percent of the participants holding professional occupa-
tions (1984: 10). In her first book, Walker asserts that

> most battered women are from middle-class and higher-income
> homes where the power of their wealth is in the hands of their
> husbands. . . . Battered women are found in all age groups, races,
> ethnic and religious groups, educational levels, and socioeco-
> nomic groups. *Who are the battered women? If you are a
> woman, there is a 50 percent chance it could be you!* (1979: 19;
> emphasis added)

By claiming that one-half of all women are victims of domestic violence,
Walker hopes the public—and women especially—will personally feel
threatened by the "epidemic" of domestic violence and thus be more willing to take the issue seriously.

Individual stories have been important, however, in showing that
domestic violence really does happen to "strong," well-off women—
women who should have options. Martin's prototypical story of Anne,
cited earlier, begins by noting that the abuser is a college graduate living
in a middle-class home. Both batterer and victim are "attractive and, for
the most part, respected and well-liked" (1981: 1). Pagelow also cites
numerous stories of middle- and upper-class women who were victims of
domestic violence. The following are a few examples:

> [One] example was Doris, a college graduate . . . who lived in
> one of the most expensive areas in Southern California, whose
> husband raped her and caused her severe pain by driving his car
> erratically. Other women living in palatial homes with highly
> educated husbands in high income brackets also were living with
> men who kept tight control of all incomes and expenditures and
> watched their movements carefully. Some arrived at shelters with
> no money or credit cards, or access to a checking or savings
> account. One woman, the wife of a multinational corporation
> chief executive and member of the church board of directors,
> finally drove off one day in the family camper. She claimed that
> all her telephone calls were screened and the rooms of her home
> "bugged." . . . [One woman] disclosed that beatings by her psy-
> chiatrist husband, who had an income in excess of $200,000 per
> year, had caused spontaneous abortions twice. Because of his

medical background, she said, her husband administered necessary care to her at home which avoided public records and
incriminating evidence. She related . . . that her husband inserted
a hot hair curling iron into her vagina on the same day she was
awarded the "Outstanding Woman of the Year" award by the
regional YWCA. (1981: 86)

These stories, related one after another, serve as evidence of the prevalence of domestic violence in well-off families. Having money or being
famous does not prevent women from being victimized and can, advocates
claim, make situations even more dire than having no money at all. Perhaps out of concern that the attention would shift too far in the other
direction, one *New York Times* editorial reminds its readers that "women
are battered not just in the glamorous climes of Hollywood but in every
town" (Stapels 1995: D14). Although it is unlikely that such a reminder is
necessary, this quote is emblematic of the attempts of advocates to refocus
the problem of domestic violence away from the poor.

By linking the social problem with prominent names and frequently
relying on the individual stories of famous, well-off, and professional
women, advocates have attempted to take the stigma away from the
image of the battered woman. For those they are most trying to convince—the middle and upper classes—it has been important that activists
convey the urgency of the social problem by demonstrating that domestic
violence is a problem for people "just like them." By eliminating stereo-
types and prejudices, activists have hoped to make domestic violence victims more sympathetic, "worthy," and relatable to an audience that could
otherwise be dismissive of a problem that "only affects the poor." Horrific stories of extreme abuse experienced by powerful women also
strongly demonstrate how abusers and the conditions surrounding domestic violence provide even upper-class battered women no options to leave.
Knowing that the public continues to ask "Why do they stay?," activists
realize that hearing that even women "with money" stay substantiates
their claim that abused women have few options to leave.

This emphasis on the prevalence of battering—particularly in the
middle and upper classes—has led advocates to make contradictory claims
about the nature and pervasiveness of domestic violence. By featuring narratives that almost exclusively focus on extreme and brutal assault, they
have portrayed domestic violence in terms of only the most severe cases.
But by suggesting that domestic violence is everywhere—that as many as

50 percent of all women are battered (Walker 1979)—advocates have defined "battered women" inclusively. Advocates have thus been left to argue simultaneously for an inclusive and exclusive definition of domestic violence, where the violence is exceptionally brutal and extreme, but at the same time, exceptionally widespread. This has resulted in a tension between the different frames that structure the battered women's movement and the realities of domestic violence in American homes.

CONFORMING COMPLEX EXPERIENCES

As with all aspects of social life, the causes, experiences, and manifestations of domestic violence are complex and multilayered. In seeking to change public perceptions of domestic violence victims and to win public support for movement-sponsored remedies, early battered women's advocates framed the category of battered women around selected cases, which have in turn come to represent what it means to be a victim of domestic violence. Presenting such stories as representative of the experiences of all victims in many ways has obscured the complexities of domestic violence as a social problem. In contrasting the movement's prototypical narrative themes with the findings of the domestic violence research literature, the tensions between these themes and the complexities of domestic violence become more apparent.

Perhaps most striking in considering the narratives put forward by the battered women's movement has been the nearly exclusive presentation of men as abusers and women as victims. The tendency of the movement has been to see the problem of domestic violence in entirely gendered terms. Empirical data at the time the movement emerged, however, suggests a different reality. Nationwide surveys have concluded that both women and men are at times perpetrators and victims of violence (Straus and Gelles 1986; Straus, Gelles, and Steinmetz 1980). One study found that in 49 percent of all reported instances of marital violence, both partners were involved in the assaults. In the remainder of cases, 27 percent were situations in which the husbands alone were violent and 24 percent were cases in which only the wives were abusive. As far as specific violent acts were concerned, women, on the one hand, were almost twice as likely to throw something at their husbands and they were also more likely to kick or hit with an object. Men, on the other hand, more frequently pushed, shoved, slapped, beat up, and/or used weapons (knives or guns). Concerning frequencies of beatings, the researchers concluded (to their own surprise) that rates of wives assaulting their husbands were slightly higher than those of husbands assaulting their wives (Straus, Gelles, and Steinmetz 1980: 37–40). While these findings do not mean that women inflict the same level of harm as men, they are striking because they suggest that women, too, are perpetrators of domestic violence. Movement activists' portrayal of women alone as victims has thus simplified what may be a more complicated relationship between men, women, and violence in intimate relationships.

In selecting those women's stories that illustrate the most extreme and horrific forms of abuse, early advocates also presented an image of domestic violence that diverged from the everyday realities of physical assaults in American families at the time. The majority of violence, as Straus, Gelles, and Steinmetz (1980) suggest, may not be nearly as brutal as the selected narratives suggest, but instead is much more likely to involve pushing, grabbing, and shoving than assaults with knives, guns, or other objects. These findings do not deny the existence of the more extreme forms of domestic violence, but they do make it apparent just how extreme such forms of violence are. By excluding stories that involve less threatening and less violent forms of physical assault, advocates paint a picture of domestic violence in the United States that is at odds with the empirical portrait found in surveys and studies.

Movement activists have also recounted personal stories from professional and upper-class women to make the case that domestic violence knows no socioeconomic boundaries. With these stories, advocates have sidestepped the complex interaction between poverty and domestic violence. Evidence suggests that domestic violence, like other manifestations of marital troubles, is more prevalent in poorer families due to economic stress (Stark and Flitcraft 1988). In an attempt to make the social problem relevant to the middle and upper classes, advocates may have ignored one of the primary correlates to family violence.

By presenting stories whose point is to illustrate how battered women are trapped in abusive relationships against their will, advocates have also diverted attention away from the many women who do leave abusive relationships or who actively choose to stay. Ferraro (1998) contends that women attempt to leave on average between five and seven times before doing so permanently—but that many do ultimately leave. This statistic suggests that the process of leaving an abuser is a complicated one in which women have the agency to leave but have difficulty establishing independent lives due to external, and possibly internal (psychological), obstacles. This task can be so daunting that many women choose to return because they find these difficulties insurmountable. Narratives that suggest women have virtually no options for leaving have thus ignored the often difficult and lengthy process of extricating oneself from an abusive relationship.

Further, this selectivity tends to obscure important differences in the experiences and alternative opportunities for poor and well-off women. Christina's story, presented by Walker is a case of "how economics can trap someone who has her own professional career, yet is bound to a battering husband who earns over $150,000 per year":

> I finally decided to leave him. . . . Though I was fearing another incident which I felt impending, I filed divorce papers. Within a short time, the Internal Revenue Service filed a claim with my attorney charging me $35,000 in taxes that represented my share of the income Russell was earning. . . . On my $18,000 salary per year, I simply couldn't afford it. So Russell and I decided to try to live together again. What a mistake. Before the year was out, I had almost killed him in defending myself from another brutal beating. (1979: 128)

Walker (1979) also recounts the story of a woman, Julia, who tried unsuccessfully to leave her abusive husband, after having put him through school by working as a secretary. While she had still been with him, she had collaborated on his professional papers, serving as the ghostwriter. Although Julia wanted to leave her husband, she did not because she did not want to lose other aspects of her life. She asks: "How could I be a secretary again when I had been doing all those other exciting things? It wasn't enough for me then. It still isn't enough for me" (138). Julia made a decision to remain with her battering husband because her alternative life would not be as "exciting." Christina returned to her husband because she did not want to live on $18,000 annually. Although there is little doubt that their situations were indeed difficult, the decisions that Julia and Christina chose to make are often not available to lower-class women who face very different prospects. By downplaying class differences, advocates have perhaps inadvertently minimized the exceptionally difficult obstacles poor battered women experience.

Advocates also have not recounted stories in which battered women actively choose to remain with their abusers on the basis of love. In both the domestic violence literature and in media articles, these kinds of narratives are rare. In my survey of domestic violence narratives, I found only one such autobiographical story told by the daughter of a battered woman. Andrea Todd writes: "My mother stayed with my father for many reasons, not all of them noble and none that others would consider reasonable given the risks we faced" (1995: 32). She notes that

> Forgiveness used to be a virtue, the stuff saints were made of. No more. Take someone back, someone who makes the same mistake again and again—particularly after a show of remorse and a promise to repent—and you are a fool, sick. Perhaps you enjoy the pain you experience. Perhaps you deserve it. (32)

Nonetheless, Todd and her mother chose to "love and trust, despite pain and risk" and ended up being "lucky. My dad came through for us" (32). This narrative is told by a woman who is not associated with the battered women's movement. The story and tone serve as a striking contrast to stories told by activists in which women do not choose to stay, but are instead trapped into remaining.

Taken together, the realities of domestic violence in American life have often posed a problem for battered women's advocates. The prototypical narrative and the framing of the movement have not always correlated with these realities. Women, like men, are at times violent and contribute to incidents of domestic violence. The poor do appear to be disproportionately affected by family violence. And women, despite victimization, often do find the means to leave and assert their own agency. Others choose to remain despite viable alternatives because of emotional or financial bonds. These scenarios, however, do not align well with the prototypical narrative. Advocates have thus been left with the task of rectifying such discrepancies.

CONFORMING STORIES

For the most part, of course, advocates have not recounted stories that deviate from the prototypical narrative, choosing instead to provide individual accounts that illustrate the movement's framing of domestic

violence. These selected narratives have tended to be unambiguous and
thus do not represent the complexities of social life. However, advocates
have occasionally presented and interpreted less clear-cut stories of
domestic violence. These stories are noteworthy, for they have the potential to challenge the claims of advocates. Yet the stories are often interpreted in such a manner as to be brought within the boundaries of the
movement's discourse.

Walker, for example, tells the story of how one woman, Donna, in
response to her husband Paul's coming home late from work, threw a
glass that hit his head and then shoved a chair into his knee. In retaliation,
Paul beat her. In Walker's analysis of the problem, she writes that

> it is difficult to sort out how much the battered woman entered
> into her own victimization. In Donna's case, it is clear that there
> was a good deal of provocation. However, it is also clear from
> the rest of her story that *Paul had been battering her by ignoring
> her and by working late,* in order to move up the corporate
> ladder, for the entire five years of their marriage; although this
> one incident alone might have been Donna's provocation, it
> could have been retaliatory, too. (1979: 98; emphasis added)

In this example, Walker interprets the story in such a way as to remove
most blame from Donna and excuse the instigation. She takes what could
conceivably be interpreted as a complex situation in regard to blame and
interpretively aligns it with the movement's discourse.

In another such example, NiCarthy describes Barb's first experience
with domestic violence:

> Five weeks into the marriage [my husband] hit me. My family
> always had this big thing about birthdays, so I assumed he should
> have the same feelings. But on my birthday I visited his grand-
> mother, while he went to the football game and went out with the
> guys. He picked me up and I was expounding on how hurt I was,
> and nagging on and on, and he started getting really, really angry.
> I stopped the car and said, "Get out and walk home," because I
> can't stand arguments. . . . [H]e said he wasn't going to get out so
> I did, and started walking down the driveway. He came after me
> and threw me back in the car and there was a lot of violence. My
> brain clicked and said, "If you don't quit fighting, you're going to

die." I just went limp, it was instinctual, and as soon as I did, the blows stopped. (1987: 44–45)

Barb's first encounter with physical violence from her husband was one in which both partners reacted physically. There was, as she notes, "a lot of violence" that stopped only when she too stopped fighting. What is noteworthy here, for the purposes of narrative analysis, is how Barb's role in either instigating or contributing to the violence is played down. This is especially apparent in the sentence construction about there being "a lot of violence"—a more passive construction than simply stating that "we fought." By phrasing the encounter in this manner, Barb's agency is downplayed so that her story aligns better with the movement's discourse. Although it is Barb herself who minimizes her role in the fight, advocate NiCarthy selects this narrative for publication as an illustration of a battered woman with few alternatives. In her analysis of Barb's case, NiCarthy never mentions Barb's role in the violent incident and instead emphasizes the beatings she received "for no discernible reason" (45).

Allie's story, also quoted in NiCarthy, is a further demonstration of the reluctance of advocates to recognize women as abusive. Allie, in a lesbian relationship with Jane, was the victim of domestic violence:

When I tried to get help I encountered homophobia. I called a hotline and I would not mention the gender at first, and if they would say "he" I would just continue saying "he." Jane might as well have been a "he," so, why not? Other times they would kind of clam up a bit after I mentioned it was a woman. I knew that the rhythm had broken, that something had shifted. I would sense the change in how they were perceiving me and I just got off the phone." (62)

The advocates with whom Allie spoke were unprepared for her story of abuse to include a woman as batterer. Indeed, even Allie contributes to this assumption by suggesting that Jane "might as well" have been a man for her violent actions. This narrative about a lesbian batterer, selected for publication by NiCarthy, helps to perpetuate the notion that only men batter by equating an abusive lesbian with a violent man. Thus, even in the case of a battering woman, the story is recounted in such a manner that men are still understood as the typical abusers.

Exceptionally rare are stories of battered women who are aware that their children are also being abused. Such narratives, movement activists fear, threaten the ability of the audience to sympathize with a woman who does not protect her children. NiCarthy tells the story of Dee, a woman routinely and often savagely beaten by her husband. Dee knew that her children were also being abused; one was left with a permanently deformed leg because her husband refused to get medical treatment for his son's broken kneecap. Dee also tells how her husband denied medical help for his sick daughter until after her appendix had burst, and that he also let the dogs "'die out of neglect.'" NiCarthy attempts to play down Dee's potential compliance, arguing that although "Dee often stopped the overt violence against the children[,] she couldn't always protect them." NiCarthy suggests that Dee had to accept the violence toward her children because she "didn't see how she could take care of them if she left" (140). With this explanation, NiCarthy interprets Dee's story in light of the movement's discourse, emphasizing Dee's innocence and helplessness. Stories like Dee's are very rarely told. Advocates assume—probably rightly—that audiences are uncomfortable with the idea of women knowingly allowing their children to be harmed.

Stories in which women choose to remain with abusers for any reason have also been interpreted in such a manner as to play down the woman's agency. In a story cited earlier, Julia remains with her abusive husband because her other alternative would be to work as a secretary. She explains: "How could I be a secretary again when I had been doing all those other exciting things? It wasn't enough for me then. It still isn't enough for me" (Walker 1979: 138). Although this could conceivably be interpreted as Julia's own decision to remain with her abuser, Walker discourages such a view by arguing that "the use of economic deprivation as a coercive technique" leaves a woman with "virtually no freedom" (139). Walker minimizes Julia's potential agency in an effort to align her experience with the claim that all battered women are trapped.

Given the potential discrepancies between the kinds of stories advocates recount and the complex nature of domestic violence in the United States, it is not surprising that advocates have occasionally told stories that do not fit the prototype. Because there are so many such stories, advocates have periodically had to recognize and deal with individual cases that do not easily align with the movement's claims. Thus, stories like those of Donna, Barb, Allie, and Julia are recounted and interpreted in a manner that conforms their experiences to the framing of the movement.

CONCLUSION

The telling of battered women's stories has been crucial to the movement. Individual narratives concretize and personalize an otherwise abstract and socially invisible issue. Narratives make the problem "real," substantiating movement frames and demonstrating that the issue is as advocates claim it to be. Moreover, narratives provide the evidence that calls forth and justifies the specific remedies that the movement advocates. Without such individual narratives and the ongoing identification of new cases, the person category of the "battered woman" would arguably never have been established or continue to carry the public meaning it has.

But as I have sought to show, not just any personal stories of domestic violence tell the story the movement wants told. Rather, from the welter of lived experiences of violence, movement activists have carefully selected and interpreted stories so as to transform a complex phenomenon into a simplified and morally unambiguous one. This is not to argue that domestic violence is any less of a problem than we perceive it to be today. There are many terrible cases, like the ones cited by advocates, of women who are routinely beaten by their partners and who have few avenues of escape. But as the empirical research indicates, the causes, manifestations, and experiences of domestic violence are complex. By sidestepping such complexity through narrative selection, advocates depict domestic violence as without moral ambiguities or gray areas. At the same time, and as an unintended consequence of this selection, they exclude certain types of people from the category of "domestic violence victim." Stories that do not more or less easily align with the prototypical narrative cannot be recognized as "belonging" to the movement.

Ultimately, public resources and sympathy are made available to those individuals who demonstrate that they fit into the category of the "battered woman." Those outside the boundaries of the movement—including men, battered women who themselves use physical violence, or women who choose to stay—are denied such support. In an effort to gain these resources, women themselves may learn to tell their personal story in a manner that aligns with the discourse of the movement. Loseke provides a telling example from a battered women's shelter. She notes that shelter workers make decisions about who is "battered," and therefore worthy of admitting, based on both space availability and their evaluation of a potential client's story. In one instance, a woman seeking admittance to the shelter and the worker in charge of making the decision reconstruct

the woman's story over several phone calls. The following entries come
from the log book prepared by the shelter worker:

> Woman called, staying in motel and can't afford it for too much
> longer. Told her we were full and suggested [another shelter].

> Susan (motel woman) called back and she is really desperate. She
> has four children (4, 3, 2, 1) and no transportation. She said she
> would stay in motel but cannot afford it.

> 8:30 P.M. Susan called. Needs shelter badly, has four children,
> husband searching for her. She's been battered and is fright-
> ened—requires shelter till she can relocate. Called [another
> worker] and we think we should pick her up. (1992: 85)

In this example, both Susan, seeking admittance, and the worker making
the decision retell her story, recasting it from a woman needing alternative
housing to a battered woman in need of emergency shelter and protection.
The example cited earlier of Allie, an abused woman in a lesbian relationship, is another such illustration. Allie admits she would avoid mentioning
the gender of her batterer when calling a battered women's hotline for
fear that the hotline workers would be less willing to help her. Barb's
story, also cited earlier, of an incident in which there was "a lot of violence" that only stopped when she no longer fought back, suggests that
women downplay situations in which they too rely on physical violence.
By conforming their own stories, women are able to receive crucial
resources and support that come with being a member of the battered
woman category. Yet they also inadvertently help to reproduce the very
image of the domestic violence victim that neither represents the complexities of their own lives nor the realities of domestic violence in general.

Conforming or simplifying the messiness of human experience
through narrative is not unique to the battered women's movement. Many
movements select stories on the basis of having common themes that support the movement's frames and evoke the appropriate emotional
responses from targeted audiences—like outrage and sympathy in the case
of domestic violence. Narratives that could be deemed morally question-
able or considered to fall into a gray area are either never recounted or are
interpreted in a manner that allows the experience to be brought within
the boundaries of the movement. Of course, this process is always unfinished since nonconforming stories—stories that do not fit movement

frames—always remain a potential threat. But in general, by preventing ambiguous cases from being incorporated and recognized, activists help solidify discourse by centering social movements around simplified stories of right and wrong.

ACKNOWLEDGMENT

The author wishes to thank Karin Peterson and Joseph Davis for comments on earlier drafts.

PART THREE

Conclusion

TEN

The Storied Group

Social Movements as "Bundles of Narratives"

GARY ALAN FINE

One cannot predict when one's claims will hit a nerve. This book represents a reflex to a casual, if insistent, tap. As a scholar whose work explored the areas of small groups (Fine 1979, 1982), folk narrative (Fine 1992), organizational culture (Fine 1984), and collective behavior (Rosnow and Fine 1976; Fine and Stoecker 1985), I had been interested in the intersection of these largely distinct scholarly realms. The invitation to present a paper to the Workshop of the American Sociological Association's Section on Social Movements and Collective Behavior in San Diego in June 1992 provided an opportunity to explore this intellectual nexus.

Thinking about what a social psychologist interested in group culture could contribute to such a gathering, I chose to emphasize the reality that in most groups—and in social movements in particular—participants share accounts of their lives and activities within the movement organization. These discursive practices are shaped in light of the goals of the group and the characteristics of members (Boje 1991; Martin et al. 1983; Wilkins 1979). Stories, along with behaviors and material objects, come to characterize the group and constitute the group culture or "idioculture." I argued that social movements consist of a "bundle of narratives" (Fine 1995: 128). Some scholars even claim that all forms of human communication are essentially "stories" (Fisher 1987: ix). Although it is surely true—as many of these preceding chapters demonstrate—that not all embedded talk is characterized by "emplotment," many accounts of events are. Narrative is often present explicitly or implicitly, detailed or telegraphed. Talk that is structured by sequence is effective for communication.

All ideas have a "life cycle"; it was an unplanned, but welcomed, happenstance that this argument, emphasizing the centrality of group narratives, captured the interest of a set of social movement scholars who, given the concern with the effects of frames of meaning, were ready to incorporate this interest in group culture and narrative in their own projects.[1] This argument proved to be well-timed with a sense that the decade of the 1990s represents "narrative's moment" in the social sciences (Maines 1993). While I cannot claim any priority of innovation for any individual piece of the discussion, the combination proved fruitful, at least as evident in these analyses of social movements.

With the publication of this volume, the approach that treats social movements as bundles of stories has entered a broader scholarly discourse. In this volume these ideas and claims are being refined, expanded, and challenged as the understanding of the role of discourse in collective action matures. In time the movement narrative perspective, just now beginning to yield fruit, will be defined as old-fashioned, with the most useful aspects incorporated into other, developing models. Understanding social movements through the stories of participants is not a totalistic attempt to explain all aspects of collective action: "group narrative" does not replace "frame analysis," "resource mobilization," "neo-institutionalism," or "rational choice" as explanations, but stands beside them. Social movements do not consist only of waves of talk, as behavior, cognition, resources, and responses of others matter, but narrative is central to group identity. Talk helps people process the material conditions of their existence and comprehend their place within the social order by creating verbal representations of society (Maynard and Whalen 1995; Goffman 1981). Without shared and communicated culture, sustained collective action is impossible. Discourse shapes identity and action.

In emphasizing the power of narrative, I do not deny the reality of organizations or their obdurate, consequential character. One can say whatever one wishes, but consequences exist for these actions, as groups fighting against powerful opponents can attest. As Tom Lehrer once sarcastically sang about the defeat of the Loyalists in the Spanish Civil War: "They won all the battles, but we had all the good songs" (see Eyerman and Jamison 1998). In the short run, bullets have an obdurate character that ballads lack, even if over time, ballads can sometimes tip the balance in sedimented historical memory. As neo-institutionists recognize (Powell and DiMaggio 1991), group structures emerge from interaction, while simultaneously and recursively action is embedded in these social structures. The structure channels the discourse that is seen as appropriate, just as discourse sets the terms for the creation and alteration of structure (Sewell 1992).

In this concluding chapter I address several themes raised by the preceding chapters. I begin by discussing the relationship of frame analysis and the understanding of narrative. I then examine the concept of idioculture, and how that concept provides a framework for the analysis of social movements, drawing insight from the analysis of organizational cultures. Following from this, I examine how participants think—and sometimes do not think—about the narratives that they spread, and describe the variability of narrative among social movements. I emphasize that each of the currently disparate analytic approaches to social movements contributes to our understanding of collective action. This volume should not be read as a call to anoint narration as the sole explanation of identity or movement success.

FRAMES AND NARRATIVES

Over the past two decades, the idea of "frame alignment" in social movement research has become increasingly popular (Gamson, Rytina, and Fireman 1982; Snow and Benford 1992; Snow et al. 1986). Narrative analysis both builds on the understanding of frames, as used in social movement research, and specifies it by referring to concrete examples of discourse in interaction.

The original sociological impulse for the examination of frames derived from Erving Goffman (1974; see Bateson 1972). For Goffman, a frame consists of a strategy of understanding reality. The frame is a form of mental organization that organizes perception and interpretation (Johnston 1995: 217). Our "natural" view of the world consists, in Goffman's view, of our "primary framework." However, this primary framework can be undercut, altered, or manipulated by others. These alterations then changing the proper interpretation of what is happening, Goffman (1974: 43–44) refers to as a "key" or "the set of conventions by which a given activity, one already meaningful in terms of some primary framework, is transformed into something patterned on this activity but seen by the participants to be something quite else." For instance, a "con game" or a "psychological experiment" belongs to a different framework than does ordinary experience.

Although the impact of Goffman's analysis has been modest in much of sociology (Fine and Manning 2000), social movement scholars have found the metaphor of "frame alignment" compelling, particularly deriving from the research of William Gamson and David Snow. Gamson and his colleagues attempted to explain social movement activity in light of the set of core interpretive schemas of the participants (Gamson 1992)—attempting to create a social psychology for resource mobilization theory (Gamson, Fireman, and Rytina 1982: 9)—what they describe as "an intellectual porridge of Tilly and Goffman" (x). They speak, for instance, of an "injustice frame" in which activities of one's opponents would be "read" as constituting oppression or injustice, whereas others observing the same actions would find no inherent injustice at all. For Gamson, encounters with unjust authority have keying characteristics that most routine interaction lacks, as the recognized injustice impels participants to define actions in special ways that might not be recognized in circumstances of legitimacy.

In contrast, Snow and his colleagues (1986) shifted the focus significantly away from the cognitive interpretations that Goffman and Gamson emphasized. While this produced a quite useful approach, it was one that built less on Goffman's insights than on the rudiments of an emerging cultural sociology that emphasized a rhetorical analysis of movement claims. A social movement's frame became another way of addressing its "theme." They asked from what discursive elements does the social movement draw. Such an approach is essentially a macrolevel content or textual analysis, rather than a phenomenology. Snow and Benford (1992: 136–37; see Snow and Benford 1988) explicitly explained their emphasis on frames as an attempt to recapture the significance of beliefs and ideology in the study of social movements; for them frame represents signification, involving "the amplification and extension of extant meanings, the transformation of old meanings, and the generation of new meanings" (Snow and Benford 1992: 136).

Ultimately, narrative analysis of social movements is closer to the Snow rhetorical version of "frame alignment" as signification than to a Goffmanian phenomenological version in which the very nature of interaction is being explored. Narrative analysis presents detailed stories and, from this data, emphasizes the analysis of the discourse that Snow's approach has traditionally taken for granted. Following from Goffman's insight, we address what are the conditions and circumstances in which discourse is interpreted. Put another way, what is the "illocutionary force" of the narrative (Austin 1975): that is, what is the narrator trying to do through the text and how does the audience interpret that doing as a category of action?

IDIOCULTURE AND GROUP NARRATIVE

The sociology of culture has expanded profoundly over the past two decades as it became evident that the meanings shared by social actors affect the conditions of group life and of social order. Having been trained within the group dynamics tradition (see, for example, Bales 1970; Hare 1962), I believe that the small group is a rich locus in which to analyze how social life is organized. In particular, the shared meanings of members of the group determine patterns of behavior. I emphasize the centrality of group culture—or idioculture—as a local culture that comes to characterize every interacting group (Fine 1979, 1982; Wiley 1991). I define an idioculture as a system of knowledge, beliefs, behaviors, and customs shared by members of an interacting group to which members can refer and which they can employ as the basis of further interaction. While this group culture includes many genres of discourse, narratives with their explicit plot lines and morals are often particularly central. For this reason it is possible, as noted above, to treat social movements as bundles of narratives.

Idiocultures are themselves structured through group interaction. The content of a group culture does not emanate "randomly," but emerges in light of the structure of the group. The specific content of the group culture results from cultural elements that are known, usable, functional, appropriate, and triggered (Fine 1979).

Known Culture

By known culture, I refer to the reality that culture does not emerge *de novo* (Hebb 1974), but in contrast is built on a novel combination of previously familiar elements. Thus, the stories told within a social movement are limited and constrained by the previous experience of participants, and the stories in turn, as they become shared, serve to increase the likelihood that certain participants will decide to join and that others will exit or become inactive. The existence of pools of knowledge based on demography and social networks (Degh and Vazsonyi 1975; Shibutani 1955) implies that despite the sincere desires of leaders to create a movement that transcends social categories, the creation of a broadly based movement culture proves to be very difficult in practice. A movement with impoverished blacks and well-educated whites, with distinct and often nonoverlapping information pools and racialized narrative structures (Maines 1999; Turner 1993), tends to be unstable. Strains based on pools of knowledge are too great to produce trust. Similarly, movements that transcend social class, ethnicity, and religion often are filled with tension and mistrust, a problem that communist labor organizers often discovered and that their opponents were often able to exploit. Stories do not appeal to everyone. The background knowledge among participants is too often not shared, making casual narrative problematic.

Usable Culture

A second, related issue is that for a narrative or other culture element to be incorporated into group culture it must be seen as "usable" in group interaction. Some information—sexual discourse, for instance—may be unusable in some settings, and treasured in others. Sacred talk similarly may have distinct patterns of usability. Again, differences in cultural usability may strain group culture and movement cohesion. The differences in cultural usability is one feature of interaction that separates men and women, making each gender uncomfortable in the presence of the other. There are "male" stories and "female" stories. Similarly, "God-talk" has variable usability, destabilizing movements shared by Christians, Jews, and secular humanists. Most narratives are usable, but the reality that some tendentious and salient topics (politics, religion, sex) cause problems may make it seem that movement participants lack ideology (Eliasoph 1998).

Functional Culture

The first two elements relate to the characteristics, attitudes, and cultural capital of the members that they bring to the social movement. The other three elements are linked to the way that narratives depend on the group interaction itself. First, does the group cultural element serve some need of the group: Is it functional for the survival and achieving the goals of the group? Those stories that help (or are believed to help) social movements alter their environment in desirable ways are likely to continue and are likely to be culturally central. Changes in the environment can involve positive changes in group process (increasing the size of the group or increasing the internal satisfaction of members) or can involve effects that are external to the group (changing law, shifting policy, influencing other groups, or acquiring additional resources). While it may be difficult to specify how cultural elements contribute directly to group survival, analyses of organizational culture in management (Martin 1992; Ouchi and Wilkins 1985) strongly suggest a linkage between the content of an organizational culture and its effectiveness. In fact, the domain of the social sciences in which the group culture metaphor has been most influential is in organizational analysis (Smircich 1983)—in this domain the analysis of organizational stories, sagas, and histories (Boje 1991; Clark 1972; Martin et al. 1983) is central. From the early 1980s, scholars have argued that the "culture" of an organization has a considerable influence on its effectiveness. The claim by those in management is that organizational culture is functional in its ability to affect the bottom line (Deal and Kennedy 1982; Peters and Waterman 1982)—a plausible-sounding claim, even if supportive evidence has been thin and even if it is impossible to ascertain how the organization might fare in the absence of a particular cultural tradition. Others suggest that a strong and effective organizational culture is functional in that it ties the employee to the company, reducing alienation (Ouchi 1981; Rohlen 1973). As a consequence, effective leaders are conscious of the expressive and symbolic content of their statements—and, in the process, engage in what Jeffrey Pfeffer (1981) speaks of as "management as symbolic action." In sum, stories should matter in how group members define their identities and define the set of behaviors that are legitimate within a group context.

Appropriate Culture

Cultural traditions, and stories in particular, are connected to particular group members. To be effective and to become incorporated into a group's idioculture, the images of the *dramatis personae* of the stories must be consistent with the personal status of those individuals within the group (Whyte 1943). Cultural traditions must be appropriate in light of the established status system of the group. This is often dramatically evident in the nicknames that are judged appropriate. But such appropriateness is no less evident in narrative. The heroes of stories should have high status in the group, storied incompetence is linked to low status, and villainy is tied to belonging outside the moral boundary of the group. Stories often provide a mirror of the group's social structure. The appropriateness of actors in collective stories applies not only to participants in the life of the group, but also to those who stand outside of the organizational boundaries. In "war stories," for instance, one's opponents are detailed as are one's allies. For a story to "work," the characters must make sense in light of the position of the images of those characters.

Triggering Mechanism

These four components of group culture—that it is known, usable, functional, and appropriate—permits any number of possible narratives to become part of group lore. For a story to become part of a group's idioculture, it must be triggered by some event. Some happening—a behavior, a comment, a natural phenomenon—serves as a spark that creates an idea or image that eventually becomes part of the lore or the behavioral repertoire of the group. This serves as a "triggering mechanism" for culture. The reality that culture springs from interactional events means that it is difficult to predict the creation of specific narratives, although *post hoc* explanations are, as always, far more explicable. In this sense, culture is fundamentally situational and emergent, despite the characteristics of the group and of its members.

The existence of group culture is central to all organized social interaction (Dundes 1977). As indicated in the definition of an idioculture, numerous cultural forms may be incorporated into the group traditions. While writers in this volume emphasize a single aspect of culture—that of narrative—narratives are only one domain of the way that collective action is shaped by culture. Narratives, however, are particularly effective for cementing group allegiance in that they are performances that convey in verbal form a recognizable sequence of events, typically chronological, which encourages identification with the protagonist of the story (seeing the world through his or her eyes). When colleagues see the world together, they are likely to share the same understandings of that world.

METANARRATIVE

While narrative is in itself important for the analysis of movement concerns, the importance of narrative also relates to the fact that it is shared and is capable of being referred to. Group discourse often directs attention to events and occasions that have been encountered by the group or previously recounted, and, as a result, can be broadly referred to as narrative, even if on any particular occasion the plot is implicit and obliquely referred to. Established members are familiar with the stories that are being told, and only need a gentle reminder to recognize the references inherent in the account. New members become socialized to the narratives of the group, which occurs between friends or on certain set ritual occasions (and, of course, some groups keep written records that cement texts). It has been claimed that one truly experiences group membership when one is able to gossip with members (Fine and Rosnow 1978; Haviland 1977); this claim is based on the recognition that to gossip means that one has been exposed to a significant share of the stories of the group, understands the set of implicit morals, and one feels a part of the narrative community. Exposure to narrative permits participants to refer to these narratives without having to repeat them.

Given the existence of "sociological poetics" (Brown 1977) and in particular "genre contact" (Bakhtin 1963, 1985; Olick 1999) in which one genre performance refers back to and is grounded on others, it is often difficult to achieve a sharp distinction between "plotted stories" and opinions, evaluations, and explanations, as is evident in many of the chapters. Attitudes and accounts are often grounded on stories, and participants, when questioned, may refer to a story to justify their position. In other words, these apparently "unplotted" discursive forms point back to stories of which listeners are aware. Suitable audiences either are aware of the references intended or would question the speaker to clarify the obscure references. Although narrative theorists often conceptualize discourse as flowing from teller to listeners, in practice a process of collaboration occurs (Georges 1969).

Unplotted discursive forms that refer implicitly to narratives can be conceptualized as metanarratives. Consider the following example from a Santa Fe channeler:

> I've learned, very much the hard way and through personal experience, that channeled information isn't all valid. I need to run it through *me* and see what fits for *me*. (see Brown, chapter 5)

This account, like many others, does not itself contain a plot or explicit characters, yet it refers to stories that were likely shared on other occasions. In other words, it involves discourse about stories—a metanarrative: the kind of talk that is common in groups in which members know each other and talk in "storied shorthand," much like the long-term prisoners in the classic anecdote who refer to jokes by number. In practice we provide these references whenever we present a claim about the world: frequently we can provide stories to support that claim, although in less intimate circumstances such stories are not requested, but are taken for granted.

STORIES AND IDEOLOGY

Stories bind individuals to each other as they recognize that they have common experiences that shape their identity and their linked futures. As a result, this perspective is both retrospective and prospective. Stories—and discourse in general—represent a processing of a shared past (Katovich and Couch 1992) and through this creation of a shared past, coordination of action emerges (Couch 1984). Yet to conceptualize collective discourse as only looking backward would be misleading. Stories contain explicit or implicit morals that are to be taken as guides for actions. Although narratives are a *mirror* that show the group its defining characteristics, they can also be a *lamp* that directs group action (Schwartz 1996).

However, the claim that narrative can serve to direct action and define the past seems to make individuals highly self-conscious. Many studies of social action (Eliasoph 1998; Sclafani 1979) have demonstrated that individuals frequently act—sometimes with considerable courage and facing considerable cost—without having a clearly developed or recognized sense of the justifications for their action. Although this applies to the conditions of much natural behavior, in the case of participants in social movements, such a belief must be modified to some degree. As social movements are voluntaristic organizations, many participants have elected to join because of a general, if imperfect, agreement with the goals, perspectives, or ideology of the group. The extent to which individuals are aware of the details and implications of these beliefs varies, as does the extent to which the group has a self-conscious and well-developed ideology. Many groups have only an inchoate set of beliefs, whereas groups that have a more explicit ideology that members take seriously often find themselves torn asunder because of differing views; divisions over ideology may take the place of battles with those outside of the formal boundaries of the group. In fact, ideology seems more closely linked to identification than to cognitive consistency.

Perhaps more common than formal narratives is a set of beliefs that serves as a general orientation for joining and that may be referred to on ritual occasions. On more mundane occasions, the ideology of the group remains in the unspoken background. Just as ministry students do not talk about their beliefs in God—scornfully referred to as "God-talk" (Kleinman 1984)—assuming that others share their perspective and that such discourse is a form of bragging ("being holier than thou"), so activists assume that their ideologies are shared and that explicit discussion might be seen as patronizing. I was struck while observing political party volunteers (in this case, local Republicans) with how infrequently these committed workers referred to those beliefs that caused them to select this party and to devote considerable time, energy, and money to the group. Within a group of Republicans it was *assumed* that all shared the same belief system, and so reference was unnecessary and might even be seen as a form of showing off ("I'm more conservative than you"). However, just as with the ministry students, discussions with the participants revealed that there was considerably more disagreement about both particular issues and general partisan orientation than participants suspected, and a free and continual expression of these beliefs could easily undermine the assumption of unity within the group. Focusing on the technical tasks of electing candidates and other party-building activities outweighed the divisions that remained largely unrecognized in the daily rounds of group members. As a result, narratives serve to carry ideology in forms where the focus is not on the details of belief, but is linked to characters with whom the audience shares identification. Sociability trumps theory.

Narrative permits the expression of an implicit ideology that even the parties to the discourse may not fully realize is present. Following Schudson (1989), this suggests that culture is not something that is imposed on the person, but rather comes to constitute the person. Activities are made from meanings, even if these meanings are not explicitly recognized (Geertz 1973).

NARRATIVE VARIATIONS

As the authors of these selections emphasize, social movements vary in the importance of stories. Although all groups—all social movements—have a set of stories, the prominence and type of stories differ. Given that the analysis of movement narrative is still developing, comparative research is essential to examine how groups differ in their narrative use.

Schudson (1989) emphasizes, congruent with the literature on organizational culture, that sometimes culture "works" and sometimes it doesn't. He posits a set of five dimensions that when present, contribute to the potency or influence of cultural products: retrievability, rhetorical force, resonance, retention, and resolution.

Retrievability refers to the degree to which a cultural object is known by or is available to a relevant audience. To what extent are members of a movement aware of a narrative? Is the narrative part of the culture of the movement, or in contrast, only shared by particular dyads? Stories in self-help movements are likely to be more localized, told primarily by their "owner," in contrast to stories from the civil rights groups that recount the "adventures" of the collective when facing opponents.

Rhetorical Force refers to the effectiveness or impact of the narrative on its audience. Does the story move its listeners, leading to greater commitment or activism? The most effective "war stories" cause the audience to want to support the movement. These narratives "manipulate" their audience emotionally and cognitively, just as is true for great literature.

Resonance relates to the extent to which one set of symbols fits with other symbols in the culture. Is the set of narratives in a social movement thematically linked? Does one narrative draw on others? For instance, for narratives in a "self-help" group to be effective, they need to be making the same kind of argument. Second stories need to build on those that have gone before (Arminen 1998; Denzin 1987; Sacks 1992). As is said colloquially, everyone must be "on the same page." Even with forceful and known stories, a group will not be cohesive unless the meanings of those stories are interconnected.

Retention speaks to the extent to which stories are "sedimented" in the culture of a group (Busch 1980, 1982). Many stories are told, but few are recalled. Story-based movements need institutional or collective memories to preserve stories. Written documents or ritual events often provide spaces that build in institutional retention. For some evanescent social movements the need for institutional retention can be a problem, as the movement has not been institutionalized itself, and stories fade, given an absence of long-time members or collective memory.

Resolution refers to the extent to which cultural symbolism produces action. Within social movements little could be more important. Stories have the potential to spark activism. The story should ideally produce a means by which the wrong that has been depicted can be corrected. A story that depicts an insoluble horror is likely to be ineffective for movement building; the horror must be sufficiently great, while simultaneously there needs to be an opportunity for effective correction and change.

Together these constructs provide a means by which the effectiveness of narratives can be evaluated. While Schudson's model, based on the examination of a society, is not perfectly adapted to the study of social movements, it properly emphasizes both the continuities and discontinuities of narrative discourse.

Further, movements vary on several dimensions in their use of narrative, including the *elaboration* of narrative; the extent to which narratives reveal *ownership* by individuals, as opposed to the larger movement; the *stance* of the narrative; the focus on group process as opposed to boundary issues; the *assessment* of the events depicted in narrative as positive, neutral or negative; the *saturation* of narratives throughout the movement; and the *target* of the stories—directed to primarily internal or external audiences.

Elaboration

Some movements are relatively "storied," whereas others have a more attenuated narrative culture. Among the elements that can be expected to increase narrative elaboration is the amount of "time" in which uninterrupted discourse can occur and the narrative skills within the culture from which members are drawn. Just as some cultures emphasize the performance of narrative as a central aspect of the expressive culture of the group (cultures with epic singers represent an archetypal example), so do some movements, such as self-help movements. In some cases the processing of narrative can be seen as the primary purpose of the movement (Denzin 1987).

Ownership

Are narratives treated as personally "owned," as opposed to belonging to the movement? New movements and identity movements are known for their focus on personal narratives of individual development, whereas more traditional political social movements are likely to submerge the identity of the individual in the goals of the collectivity. One is unlikely to find a movement narrative in a twelve-step self-help group, where the movement is structured to help the individual. In labor or civil rights groups, such collective narratives are more likely to be evident as group activity is more central.

Stance

Does the content of the narrative focus on issues within the group or between the group and its publics? Does the theme of the narrative involve group process or boundary work? Some narratives explore issues of internal dynamics—the experiences that members have shared together without references to confrontations—while other narratives emphasize contacts with those outside of the group and in which "conflict" or "contrast" is central. Movements that collectively confront countermovements or hostile agents of the state are likely to develop a set of stories about boundary confrontations, whereas movements arrayed against social problems that lack supporters (drunk driving, drug use, family abuse) are likely to emphasize group process.

Assessment

Some narratives recount triumphs to be savored, while others emphasize failures to be overcome. Some narratives reflect collective successes, whereas others reflect defeats and frustrations. While some differences between movement narratives may be a function of their objective successes or failures or their subjective evaluations of these experiences, the differential presence of these stories may be a consequence of strategies of how best to motivate continued commitment. In most cases, a mix of stories provokes the belief that success is possible, though not assured.

Saturation

Some movements emphasize stories that are known to all or most members of the group, whereas other movements are more heavily reticulated (Gerlach and Hine 1970), at least as measured in their narratives—in this case, stories may be spread among only a subset of members. One might hypothesize that the more homogeneous the membership, the more stories are widely shared, although heavily heterogeneous movements may make a special effort to develop a set of narratives that transcend social and demographic boundaries.

Target

Some stories serve as publicity for the movement to recruit potential supporters. A goal of any movement is rhetorical. Action and narrative both have a common goal: persuasion. Whether one persuades through identification, threats, discomfort, or moral suasion, one wants opponents to agree with one's demands, through ideological conversion, shifts in identity, or compliance in the face of consequences. Some stories are designed to achieve persuasion and recruitment beyond group boundaries. Other stories—many of those described in this volume—are directed at members to increase their commitment: to bolster identification in the face of personal costs.

These variables remind us that most movements traffic in a diverse set of stories but the amount of stories or the proportion of stories of different types may vary. As narrative analysis is deepened, the conditions under which particular types of stories are most common will surely become better specified.

MOVEMENT NARRATIVES

As the chapters in this volume demonstrate, analyzing social movement "discourse" can expand our analysis of the dynamics of collective action.

Stories have the power to produce identification with narrators and characters (Goffman 1974; Burke 1969). Several chapters in this volume (see chapters 1 and 5) are explicit in emphasizing the centrality of "community-building" through narrative. Further, for certain institutional structures—courts, for example (chapters 7 and 8)—storytelling skills determine organizational effectiveness.

Movement narratives are both cognitive and emotional. As Polletta argues in chapter 2, through the strength of identification stories can produce "mobilizing emotions." Certain stories—horror stories, war stories—may provoke disgust or anger, leading to increased commitment and the desire for action. As Martin (1992) has argued in discussing organizational cultures, examples often have power that either ideological claims or statistics lack, stressing why stories are so powerful for encouraging and controlling collective action. By setting emotional boundaries, stories not only encourage action but also serve as a mechanism of social control (see chapter 3). The cognitive component of stories—their analytical structure—allows audiences to generalize from their emotions to the worldview that the narrator is promoting implicitly or explicitly and to make explicit the boundaries that are otherwise implicit through the placements of heroes and villains in the narratives.

Narratives do matter. By making concrete the theoretical, stories cement individuals into group life emotionally, intellectually, and behaviorally. If you consider those social movements about which you feel most strongly, you are likely to discover that you joined because of some profound narrative account, you ignored the costs involved in not being a free rider because of other narratives, and you claim that the movement represents who you "truly" are because of still other narratives.

Ultimately this volume suggests that, although there are numerous effective ways of seeing the organization and dynamics of collective action, narrative analysis has compelling benefits for appreciating social movements as "bundles of stories."

NOTE

1. As folklorists have pointed out, numerous genres of narrative exist. Without being exhaustive, narratives can include jokes, gossip, personal experience stories, accounts of media productions ("media narraforms"), secondary accounts of the personal experiences of others,

anecdotes, ballads, folktales, epic poetry, legends, and mythology. While the mix of narrative types varies by groups, contemporary social movements are awash in jokes, gossip, personal experience stories, and accounts of others' experiences. Narrative may be proclaimed to be fictional or factual, and may be recognized as either by tellers and audience. Jokes, for instance, are typically not recounted as "true" stories and personal experiences are to be "taken" as true (even if a close accounting would recognize considerable embroidery and exaggeration). In stable groups, narrative becomes traditional, with family stories (Zeitlin, Kotkin, and Cutting-Baker 1977) exemplifying this process. Through the process of traditionalization the narrative comes to represent both the teller and the group. Although behaviors (such as rituals) and objects (such as totems) have traditional elements, stories, by virtue of their often explicit meaning and their ability to be collaboratively narrated, may be particularly effective in demonstrating the existence of a shared perspective in a discursive community.

Bibliography

Ahmad, Jalal Al-I. 1984. *Occidentosis: A Plague from the West.* Berkeley, CA: Mizan Press.

Albanese, Catherine L. 1990. *Nature Religion in America: From the Algonkian Indians to the New Age.* Chicago: University of Chicago Press.

Ammerman, Nancy. 1991. "North American Protestant Fundamentalism." In *Fundamentalisms Observed,* edited by M. Marty and R. S. Appleby, 1–65. Chicago: The University of Chicago Press.

Aran, Gideon. 1991. "Jewish Zionist Fundamentalism: The Bloc of the Faithful in Israel (Gush Emunim)." In *Fundamentalisms Observed,* edited by M. Marty and R. S. Appleby, 265–344. Chicago: University of Chicago Press.

Aries, Philippe. 1981. *The Hour of Our Death.* New York: Alfred A. Knopf.

Aristotle. 1926. *The "Art" of Rhetoric.* Trans. J. H. Freese. Cambridge, MA: Harvard University Press.

Arminen, Ilkka. 1998. "Sharing Experiences: Doing Therapy with the Help of Mutual References in the Meetings of Alcoholics Anonymous." *The Sociological Quarterly* 39: 491–515.

Ash, Roberta. 1972. *Social Movements in America.* Chicago: Markham.

Austin, J. L. 1975. *How to Do Things with Words.* Cambridge, MA: Oxford University Press.

Bakhtin, Mikhail. 1963. *Problems of Dostoevsky's Poetics.* Ed. and trans. C. Emerson. Minneapolis: University of Minnesota Press.

———. 1985. *The Dialogic Imagination.* Trans. C. Emerson and M. Holquist. Austin: University of Texas Press.

Bales, Robert Freed. 1970. *Personality and Interpersonal Relations.* New York: Holt, Rinehart and Winston.

Baram, Amatzia. 1994. "Two Roads to Revolutionary Shi'ite Fundamentalism in Iraq." In *Accounting for Fundamentalisms,* edited by M. Marty and R. S. Appleby, 531–588. Chicago: University of Chicago Press.

Barker, Colin. Forthcoming. "Fear, Laughter, and Collective Power: Transforming Emotions at the Lenin Shipyard, Gdansk, August 1980." In *Passions and Politics: Emotions in Social Movements,* edited by J. Goodwin, J. Jasper, and F. Polletta. Chicago: University of Chicago Press.

Bateson, Gregory. 1972. *Towards an Ecology of Mind.* New York: Ballantine.

Battin, Margaret. 1994. *The Least Worst Death: Essays in Bioethics on the End of Life.* New York: Oxford University Press.

Beattie, Melody. 1987. *Codependent No More: How to Stop Controlling Others and Start Caring for Yourself.* New York: Harper/Hazelden.

Beckford, James A. 1981. "Cults, Controversy, and Control: A Comparative Analysis of the Problems Posed by New Religious Movements in the Federal Republic of Germany and France." *Sociological Analysis* 42: 249–263.

Bell, Daniel. 1978. *The Cultural Contradictions of Capitalism.* New York: Basic Books.

Bellah, Robert N., Richard Madsen, William M. Sullivan, Ann Swidler, and Steven M. Tipton. 1985. *Habits of the Heart: Individualism and Commitment in American Life.* New York: Harper and Row.

Benford, Robert D. 1987. "Framing Activity, Meaning, and Social Movement Participation: The Nuclear Disarmament Movement." Ph.D. dissertation, University of Texas-Austin.

———. 1993a. "Frame Disputes within the Nuclear Disarmament Movement." *Social Forces* 71 (3): 677–701.

———. 1993b. "'You Could Be the Hundredth Monkey': Collective Action Frames and Vocabularies of Motive within the Nuclear Disarmament Movement." *The Sociological Quarterly* 34 (2): 195–216.

———. 1996. "Whose War Memories Shall Be Preserved?" *Peace Review* 8: 189–194.

———. 1997. "An Insider's Critique of the Social Movement Framing Perspective." *Sociological Inquiry* 67: 409–430.

Benford, Robert, and Scott Hunt. 1992a. "Dramaturgy and Social Movements: The Social Construction and Communication of Power." *Sociological Inquiry* 62 (1): 36–55.

———. 1992b. "Social Movement Myths and Taboos: Sacred Frames within the U.S. Peace Movement, 1982–1991." Paper presented at the First European Conference on Social Movements, Berlin, October.

Benford, Robert D., and David A. Snow. 2000. "Framing Processes and Social Movements: An Overview and Assessment." *Annual Review of Sociology* 26: 611–639.

Bennett, Lerone, Jr. 1960. "What Sit-Downs Mean to America." *Ebony* 15: 35–43.

Bere, Marge, and Suhdari T. K. Ravindran. 1996. "Fundamentalism, Women's Empowerment, and Reproductive Rights." *Reproductive Health Matters* (8 November).

Berger, Peter L. 1963. *Invitation to Sociology*. Garden City, NY: Doubleday.

Berger, Peter L., and Thomas Luckmann. 1966. *The Social Construction of Reality: A Treatise in the Sociology of Knowledge*. Garden City, NY: Doubleday.

Bethune, John. 1990. "Pens and Needles." *Publisher's Weekly* (20 July).

Biale, David. 1985. "The Messianic Connection: Zionism, Politics, and Settlement in Israel." *The Center Magazine* 18 (5): 35–45.

Boje, David M. 1991. "The Storytelling Organization: A Study of Story Performance in an Office-Supply Firm." *Administrative Science Quarterly* 36: 106–126.

Booth, Wayne C. 1988. *The Company We Keep: An Ethics of Fiction*. Berkeley: University of California Press.

Bowen, William M., Jr. 1984. *Globalism: America's Demise*. New York: Hunting House.

Boyers, Robert, ed. 1975. *Psychological Man*. New York: Harper and Row.

Bradshaw, John. 1988. *Bradshaw On: The Family*. Deerfield Beach, FL: Health Communications.

———. 1989. *Healing the Shame that Binds You*. Deerfield Beach, FL: Health Communications.

Bromley, David G. 1997. "Remembering the Future: A Sociological Narrative of Crisis Episodes, Collective Action, Culture Workers, and Countermovements." *Sociology of Religion* 58 (2): 105–140.

Bromley, David G., and Anson Shupe. 1990. "Rebottling the Elixir: The Gospel of Prosperity in America's Religioeconomic Corporations." In *In Gods We Trust: New Patterns of Religious Pluralism in America,* 2d ed., edited by T. Robbins and D. Anthony, 233–254. New Brunswick, NJ: Transaction Publishers.

Bromley, David G., Anson D. Shupe, Jr., and Joseph C. Ventimiglia. 1979. "Atrocity Tales, the Unification Church, and the Social Construction of Evil." *Journal of Communication* 29: 42–53.

Brooks, Peter. 1985. *Reading for the Plot: Design and Intention in Narrative.* New York: Vintage.

———. 1996. "The Law as Narrative and Rhetoric." In *Law's Stories: Narrative and Rhetoric in Law,* edited by P. Brooks and P. Gewirtz, 14–22. New Haven, CT: Yale University Press.

Brooks, Peter, and Paul Gewirtz, eds. 1996. *Law's Stories: Narrative and Rhetoric in Law.* New Haven, CT: Yale University Press.

Brown, Michael F. 1997. *The Channeling Zone: American Spirituality in an Anxious Age.* Cambridge, MA: Harvard University Press.

———. 1999. "The New Alienists: Healing Shattered Selves at Century's End." In *Paranoia within Reason,* edited by G. E. Marcus, 137–156. Chicago: University of Chicago Press.

Brown, Richard. 1977. *A Poetic for Sociology.* Cambridge: Cambridge University Press.

Brulle, Robert J. 1995. "Environmentalism and Human Emancipation." In *Social Movements: Critiques, Concepts, Case-Studies,* edited by S. M. Lyman, 309–328. New York: New York University Press.

Bruner, Jerome. 1986. *Actual Minds, Possible Worlds.* Cambridge, MA: Harvard University Press.

———. 1987. "Life as Narrative." *Social Research* 54: 11–32.

Buechler, Steven M. 1990. *Women's Movements in the United States.* New Brunswick, NJ: Rutgers University Press.

———. 1993. "Beyond Resource Mobilization Theory? Emerging Trends in Social Movement Theory." *The Sociological Quarterly* 34: 217–235.

———. 2000. *Social Movements in Advanced Capitalism.* New York: Oxford University Press.

Buhle, Paul. 1987. *Marxism in the United States: Remapping the History of the American Left.* London: Verso.

Burke, Kenneth. 1969. *A Rhetoric of Motives.* Berkeley: University of California Press.

Burns, Stewart. 1990. *Social Movements of the 1960's: Searching for Democracy.* Boston: Twayne Publishers.

Burston, Daniel. 1996. *The Wing of Madness: The Life and Work of R. D. Laing.* Cambridge, MA: Harvard University Press.

Busch, Lawrence. 1980. "Structure and Negotiation in the Agricultural Sciences." *Rural Sociology* 45: 26–48.

———. 1982. "History, Negotiation and Structure in Agricultural Research." *Urban Life* 11: 368–384.

Callahan, Daniel. 1993. *The Troubled Dream of Life: Living with Mortality.* New York: Simon & Schuster.

Cameron, David R. 1974. "Toward a Theory of Political Mobilization." *Journal of Politics* 36: 138–171.

Čapek, Stella M. 1993. "The 'Environmental Justice' Frame: A Conceptual Discussion and Application." *Social Problems* 40: 5–24.

Carr, David. 1986. *Time, Narrative, and History.* Bloomington: Indiana University Press.

Carson, Clayborne. 1981. *In Struggle: SNCC and the Black Awakening of the 1960's.* Cambridge, MA: Harvard University Press.

———, ed. 1990. *The Student Voice.* Westport: Meckler.

Chafe, William H. 1980. *Civilities and Civil Rights: Greensboro, North Carolina, and the Black Struggle for Freedom.* New York: Oxford University Press.

Clark, Burton R. 1972. "The Organizational Saga in Higher Education." *Administrative Science Quarterly* 17: 178–184.

Clinton, W. Terry. 1993. *Broward County Drug Court: A Preliminary Report.*

Collier, Peter, and David Horowitz. 1989. *Destructive Generation: Second Thoughts about the Sixties.* New York: Summit Books.

Cooley, Charles Horton. 1964. *Human Nature and the Social Order.* New York: Scribner's.

Couch, Carl. 1984. "Symbolic Interaction and Generic Sociological Principles." *Symbolic Interaction* 8: 1–13.

Couto, Richard A. 1993. "Narrative, Free Space, and Political Leadership in Social Movements." *The Journal of Politics* 55: 57–79.

Currie, Mark. 1998. *Postmodern Narrative Theory.* New York: St. Martin's Press.

Dalton, Harlon L. 1996. "Storytelling on Its Own Terms." In *Law's Stories: Narrative and Rhetoric in Law,* edited by P. Brooks and P. Gewirtz, 57–59. New Haven, CT: Yale University Press.

Danto, Arthur C. 1968. *Analytical Philosophy of History.* London: Cambridge University Press.

Davis, Joseph E. 2000a. "Accounts of False Memory Syndrome: Parents, 'Retractors,' and the Role of Institutions in Account Making." *Qualitative Sociology* 23: 29–56.

———. 2000b. "Introduction: Social Change and the Problem of Identity." In *Identity and Social Change,* edited by J. E. Davis, 1–10. New Brunswick, NJ: Transaction.

Deal, Terrence E., and A. Kennedy. 1982. *Corporate Cultures: The Rites and Rituals of Corporate Life.* Reading, MA: Addison-Wesley.

Degh, Linda, and Andrew Vazsonyi. 1975. "The Hypothesis of Multi-Conduit Transmission in Folklore." In *Folklore: Performance and Communication,* edited by D. Ben-Amos and K. Golstein, 207–251. The Hague: Mouton.

Delgado, Richard. 1989. "Storytelling for Oppositionists and Others: A Plea for Narrative," *Michigan Law Review* 87: 2411–2441.

De Man, Paul. 1979. *Allegories of Reading: Figural Language in Rousseau, Nietzsche, Rilke, and Proust.* New Haven, CT: Yale University Press.

Denzin, Norman K. 1987. *The Recovering Alcoholic.* Newbury Park, CA: Sage.

———. 1990. "Presidential Address On *The Sociological Imagination* Revisited." *Sociological Quarterly* 30: 1–22.

Dershowitz, Alan. 1996. "Life Is Not a Dramatic Narrative." In *Law's Stories: Narrative and Rhetoric in Law,* edited by P. Brooks and P. Gewirtz, 99–105. New Haven, CT: Yale University Press.

Diani, Mario. 1992. "The Concept of Social Movement." *The Sociological Review* 40: 1–25.

Drug Strategies. 1997. *Cutting Crime: Drug Courts in Action.*

Dundes, Alan. 1976. "Myth." In *Encyclopedia of Anthropology,* edited by D. E. Hunter and P. Whitter, 279–281. New York: Harper and Row.

———. 1977. "Who Are the Folk?" In *Frontiers of Folklore,* edited by W. Bascom, 17–35. Boulder, CO: Westview.

Durkheim, Emile. 1965. *Elementary Forms of the Religious Life.* New York: Free Press.

Dykeman, Wilma, and James Stokely. 1960. "Sit Down Chillun, Sit Down!" *Progressive* (June 24): 8–13.

Eliasoph, Nina. 1998. *Avoiding Politics: How Americans Produce Apathy in Everyday Life.* Cambridge: Cambridge University Press.

Elshtain, Jean Bethke. 1986. *Meditations on Modern Political Thought.* New York: Praeger Publishers.

Embree, Ainslie T. 1994. "The Function of the Rashtriya Swayamsevak Sangh." In *Accounting for Fundamentalisms,* edited by M. Marty and R. S. Appleby, 617–652. Chicago: University of Chicago Press.

Esposito, John L. 1991. *Islam: The Straight Path.* New York: Oxford University Press.

Ewick, Patricia, and Susan S. Silbey. 1995. "Subversive Stories and Hegemonic Tales: Toward a Sociology of Narrative." *Law and Society Review* 29: 197–226.

Eyerman, Ron, and Andrew Jamison. 1998. *Music and Social Movements: Mobilizing Traditions in the Twentieth Century.* Cambridge: Cambridge University Press.

Ezzy, Douglas. 1998. "Theorizing Narrative Identity: Symbolic Interactionism and Hermeneutics." *The Sociological Quarterly* 39: 239–259.

Farber, Daniel A., and Suzanna Sherry. 1996. "Legal Storytelling and Constitutional Law: The Medium and the Message." In *Law's Stories: Narrative and Rhetoric in Law,* edited by P. Brooks and P. Gewirtz, 37–53. New Haven, CT: Yale University Press.

Ferguson, Tim W., and Josephine Lee. 1996. "Coin of the New Age." *Forbes* (September 9).

Ferraro, Kathleen. 1998. "Battered Women: Strategies for Survival." In *Public and Private Families: A Reader,* edited by A. J. Cherlin, 243–256 New York: McGraw Hill.

Filene, Peter G. 1998. *In the Arms of Others: A Cultural History of the Right-to-Die in America.* Chicago: Ivan R. Dee.

Fine, Gary Alan. 1979. "Small Groups and Cultural Creation: The Idioculture of Little League Baseball Teams." *American Sociological Review* 44: 733–745.

———. 1982. "The Manson Family as a Folk Group: Small Groups and Folklore." *Journal of the Folklore Institute* 19: 47–60.

———. 1984. "Negotiated Orders and Organizational Cultures." *Annual Review of Sociology* 10: 239–262.

———. 1992. *Manufacturing Tales: Sex and Money in Contemporary Legends.* Knoxville: University of Tennessee Press.

———. 1995. "Public Narration and Group Culture: Discerning Discourse in Social Movements." In *Social Movements and Culture,* edited by H. Johnston and B. Klandermans, 127–143. Minneapolis: University of Minnesota Press.

Fine, Gary Alan, and Philip Manning. 2000. "Erving Goffman." In *Blackwell Companion to Major Social Theorists,* edited by G. Ritzer, 457–485. Oxford: Blackwell.

Fine, Gary Alan, and Ralph L. Rosnow. 1978. "Gossip, Gossipers, Gossiping." *Personality and Social Psychology Bulletin* 4: 161–168.

Fine, Gary Alan, and Randy Stoecker. 1985. "Can the Circle Be Unbroken?: Small Groups and Social Movements." *Advances in Group Processes* 2: 1–28.

Finke, Roger, and Rodney Stark. 1992. *The Churching of America, 1776–1990: Winners and Losers in Our Religious Economy.* New Brunswick, NJ: Rutgers University Press.

Fisher, Walter R. 1984. "Narration as a Human Communication Paradigm: The Case of Public Moral Argument." *Communication Monographs* 51: 1–22.

———. 1987. *Human Communication as Narration: Toward a Philosophy of Reason, Value, and Action.* Columbia: University of South Carolina Press.

Foucault, Michel. 1972. *The Archaeology of Knowledge.* New York: Vintage.

Fox, Elaine, Jeffrey J. Kamakahi, and Stella M. Ĉapek. 1999. *Come Lovely and Soothing Death: The Right to Die Movement in the United States.* New York: Twayne Publishers.

Frank, Jerome. 1961. *Persuasion and Healing: A Comparative Study of Psychotherapy.* New York: Schocken.

Fredman, Lynn P. 1996. "The Challenge of Fundamentalisms." *Reproductive Health Matters* (8 November).

Freeman, Jo. 1975. *The Politics of Women's Liberation.* New York: David McKay.

———. 1979. "Resource Mobilization and Strategy: A Model for Analyzing Social Movement Organization Actions." In *The Dynamics of Social Movements,* edited by J. McCarthy and M. Zald, 167–190. Cambridge, MA: Winthrop.

Fuller, Helen. 1960. "We Are All So Very Happy." *The New Republic* (April 25).

Gagne, Patricia. 1998. *Battered Women's Justice: The Movement for Clemency and the Politics of Self-Defense.* New York: Twayne Publishers.

Gamson, William A. 1988. "Political Discourse and Collective Action." *International Social Movement Research* 1: 219–244.

———. 1992. *Talking Politics.* Cambridge: Cambridge University Press.

———. 1995. "Constructing Social Protest." In *Social Movements and Culture,* edited by H. Johnston and B. Klandermans, 85–106. Minneapolis: University of Minnesota Press.

Gamson, William A., Bruce Fireman, and Steven Rytina. 1982. *Encounters with Unjust Authority.* Homewood, IL: Dorsey Press

Garland, David. 1990. *Punishment and Modern Society.* Chicago: The University of Chicago Press.

Garrow, David. 1988. *Bearing the Cross.* New York: Vintage Books.

Geertz, Clifford. 1973. *The Interpretation of Cultures.* New York: Basic Books.

Gelles, Richard J. 1987. "Abused Wives: Why Do They Stay?" In *Family Violence,* 108–125. Newbury Park, CA: Sage Publications.

Georges, Robert. 1969. "Toward an Understanding of Storytelling Events." *Journal of American Folklore* 82: 313–328.

Gergen, Kenneth J. 1991. *The Saturated Self: Dilemmas of Identity in Contemporary Life.* New York: Basic Books.

———. 1994. *Realities and Relationships: Soundings in Social Construction.* Cambridge, MA: Harvard University Press.

Gerlach, Luther P., and Virginia H. Hine. 1970. *People, Power, Change: Movements of Social Transformation.* Indianapolis, IN: Bobbs-Merrill.

Gewirtz, Paul. 1996. "Narrative and Rhetoric in Law." In *Law's Stories: Narrative and Rhetoric in Law,* edited by P. Brooks and P. Gewirtz, 135–161. New Haven, CT: Yale University Press.

Gibbs, Jack P. 1989. *Control: Sociology's Central Notion.* Urbana: University of Illinois Press.

Gibbs, Nancy. 1993. "Fighting Back." *Time* (18 January).

Giddens, Anthony. 1991. *Modernity and Self-Identity: Self and Society in the Late Modern Age.* Stanford, CA: Stanford University Press.

Gitlin, Todd. 1980. *The Whole World Is Watching*. Berkeley: University of California Press.

————. 1987. *The Sixties: Years of Hope, Days of Rage*. New York: Bantam Books.

Goffman, Erving. 1959. *The Presentation of Self in Everyday Life*. New York: Anchor Books.

————. 1974. *Frame Analysis: An Essay on the Organization of Experience*. Cambridge, MA: Harvard University Press.

————. 1981. *Forms of Talk*. Philadelphia: University of Pennsylvania Press.

Goldkamp, John S., and Doris Weiland. 1993. *Assessing the Impact of Dade County's Felony Drug Court—Final Report*. National Institute of Justice Report.

Goldman, Ari L. 1991. "Portrait of Religion in U.S. Holds Dozens of Surprises." *New York Times* (April 10).

Gomez, Carlos F. 1991. *Regulating Death: Euthanasia and the Case of the Netherlands*. New York: Free Press.

Goodman, Nelson. 1978. *Ways of Worldmaking*. Indianapolis: Hackett.

Goodwin, Jeff, James M. Jasper, and Francesca Polletta. Forthcoming. "The Return of the Repressed: Several Generations of Scholarship on Emotions in Social Movements." *Mobilization* 5 (1): 65–84.

Greenberg, Gary. 1994. *The Self on the Shelf: Recovery Books and the Good Life*. Albany: State University of New York Press.

Griffin, Larry J. 1993. "Narrative, Event-Structure Analysis, and Causal Interpretation in Historical Sociology." *American Journal of Sociology* 98: 1094–1133.

Gross, Martin. 1978. *The Psychological Society*. New York: Random House.

Gusfield, Joseph. 1994. "The Reflexivity of Social Movements: Collective Behavior and Mass Society Theory Revisited." In *New Social Movements: From Ideology to Identity*, edited by E. Laraña, H. Johnston, and J. R. Gusfield, 58–78. Philadelphia, PA: Temple University Press.

Haber, Robert Alan. 1966. "From Protest to Radicalism: An Appraisal of the Student Movement." In *The New Student Left*, edited by M. Cohen and D. Hale, 34–42. Boston: Beacon Press.

Haines, Herbert. 1988. *Black Radicals and the Civil Rights Mainstream, 1954–1970*. Knoxville: University of Tennessee Press.

Halbwachs, Maurice. 1980. *The Collective Memory.* Trans. F. J. Ditter, Jr., and V. Y. Ditter. New York: Harper Colophon Books.

Halliday, Fred. 1995. "Fundamentalism and the Contemporary World." *Contention: Debates in Society, Culture, and Science* 4 (2): 41–58.

Halton, Eugene. 1992. "The Cultic Roots of Culture." In *Theory of Culture,* edited by R. Munch and N. Smelser, 29–63. Berkeley: University of California Press.

Harding, Susan. 1994. "Imagining the Last Days: The Politics of Apocalyptic Language." In *Accounting for Fundamentalisms,* edited by M. Marty and R. S. Appleby, 57–78. Chicago: University of Chicago Press.

Hare, A. Paul. 1962. *Handbook of Small Group Research.* New York: Free Press.

Harrell, Adele, and Shannon Cavanaugh. 1996. "Drug Test Results during the Month before Sentencing: Preliminary Results from the Evaluation of the D.C. Superior Court Drug Intervention Program for Drug Felony Defendants." Paper presented at the National Association of Drug Court Professionals Conference, 10 May, Washington, D.C.

Harrell, Adele, and Barbara Smith. 1996. "Evaluation of the District of Columbia Superior Court Drug Intervention Program: Focus Group Interviews." Research supported by the National Institute of Justice.

Haviland, John B. 1977. *Gossip, Reputation, and Knowledge in Zinacantan.* Chicago: University of Chicago Press.

Hebb, Donald O. 1974. "What Psychology Is About." *American Psychologist* 29: 71–87.

Heelas, Paul. 1996. *The New Age Movement: The Celebration of Self and the Sacralization of Modernity.* Oxford: Blackwell.

Heirich, Max. 1971. *The Spiral of Conflict: Berkeley.* New York: Columbia University Press.

Herrnstein Smith, Barbara. 1980. "Narrative Versions, Narrative Theories." In *On Narrative,* edited by W. J. T. Mitchell, 209–232. Chicago: University of Chicago Press.

Hess, David J. 1993. *Science in the New Age: The Paranormal, Its Defenders and Debunkers, and American Culture.* Madison: University of Wisconsin Press.

Highlander Papers. State Historical Society of Wisconsin, Madison.

Hinchman, Lewis P., and Sandra K. Hinchman, eds. 1997. *Memory, Identity, Community: The Idea of Narrative in the Human Sciences.* Albany: State University of New York Press.

Hochschild, Arlie. 1979. "Emotion Work, Feeling Rules, and Social Structure." *American Journal of Sociology* 85: 551–575.

———. 1983. *The Managed Heart: Commercialization of Human Feelings.* Berkeley: University of California Press.

Hodgson, Marshall G. S. 1974. *The Venture of Islam: Conscience and History in a World of Civilization.* 3 vols. Chicago: University of Chicago Press.

Hoefler, James M., and Brian E. Kamoie. 1994. *Deathright: Culture, Medicine, Politics, and the Right to Die.* Boulder, CO: Westview Press.

Horowitz, David. 1996. "Rethinking Betty Friedan and The Feminine Mystique: Labor Union Radicalism and Feminism in Cold War America." *American Quarterly* 48 (1): 1–42.

Horton, Aimee. 1989. *The Highlander Folk School: A History of Its Major Programs, 1932-1961.* Brooklyn, NY: Carlson Publishers.

Hosenball, Mark. 1995. "The Guru and the FAA." *Newsweek* (March 6).

Hunt, Lynn. 1984. *Politics, Culture, and Class in the French Revolution.* Berkeley: University of California Press.

———. 1988. "The Sacred and the French Revolution." In *Durkheimian Sociology: Cultural Studies,* edited by J. Alexander, 25–43. New York: Cambridge University Press.

Hunt, Scott A. 1991. "Constructing Collective Identity in a Peace Movement Organization." Ph.D. dissertation, University of Nebraska-Lincoln.

Hunt, Scott A., and Robert D. Benford. 1994. "Identity Talk in the Peace and Justice Movement." *Journal of Contemporary Ethnography* 22 (4): 488–517.

Hunt, Scott A., Robert D. Benford, and David A. Snow. 1994. "Identity Fields: Framing Processes and the Social Construction of Movement Identities." In *New Social Movements: From Ideology to Identity,* edited by E. Laraña, H. Johnston, and J. R. Gusfield, 185–208. Philadelphia, PA: Temple University Press.

Hunter, James Davison. 1987. *Evangelicalism: The Coming Generation.* Chicago: University of Chicago Press.

———. 1991. *Culture Wars: The Struggle to Define America.* New York: Basic Books.

————. 1994. *Before the Shooting Begins: Searching for Democracy in America's Culture War*. New York: Free Press.

Inglehart, Ronald. 1991. *Culture Shift in Advanced Industrial Societies*. Princeton: Princeton University Press.

Iser, Wolfgang. 1972. "The Reading Process: A Phenomenological Approach." *New Literary History* 3 (2): 279–299.

Jasper, James M. 1997. *The Art of Moral Protest: Culture, Biography, and Creativity in Social Movements*. Chicago: University of Chicago Press.

————. 1998. "The Emotions of Protest: Affective and Reactive Emotions in and around Social Movements." *Sociological Forum* 13: 397–424.

Jasper, James M., and Dorothy Nelkin. 1992. *The Animal Rights Crusade: The Growth of a Moral Protest*. New York: Free Press.

Johnston, Hank. 1995. "A Methodology for Frame Analysis: From Discourse to Cognitive Schemata." In *Social Movements and Culture*, edited by H. Johnston and B. Klandermans, 217–247. Minneapolis: University of Minnesota Press.

Johnston, Hank, and Bert Klandermans, eds. 1995a. *Social Movements and Culture*. Minneapolis: University of Minnesota Press.

————. 1995b. "The Cultural Analysis of Social Movements." In *Social Movements and Culture*, edited by H. Johnston and B. Klandermans, 3–24. Minneapolis: University of Minnesota Press.

Johnston, Hank, Enrique Laraña, and Joseph R. Gusfield. 1994. "Identities, Grievances, and New Social Movements." In *New Social Movements: From Ideology to Identity*, edited by E. Laraña, H. Johnston, and J. R. Gusfield, 3–35. Philadelphia, PA: Temple University Press.

Kaminer, Wendy. 1992. *I'm Dysfunctional, You're Dysfunctional: The Recovery Movement and Other Self-Help Fashions*. Reading, MA: Addison-Wesley.

————. 1999. *Sleeping with Extra-Terrestrials: The Rise of Irrationalism and the Perils of Piety*. New York: Pantheon.

Kanter, Rosabeth Moss. 1968. "Commitment and Social Organization: A Study of Commitment Mechanisms in Utopian Communities." *American Sociological Review* 33: 499–517.

Katovich, Michael, and Carl Couch. 1992. "The Nature of Social Pasts and Their Use as Foundations for Situated Action." *Symbolic Interaction* 15: 25–47.

Kaye, Judith S. 1998. "Lawyering for a New Age," *Fordham Law Review* 67: 1–12.

Kennedy, D. James. 1998. "Foreward," *For Such a Time as This: Twenty-Seven Christian Leaders on Reclaiming America for Christ.* Fort Lauderdale, FL: Coral Ridge Ministries.

Kerby, Paul Anthony. 1991. *Narrative and the Self.* Bloomington: Indiana University Press.

Kevorkian, Jack. 1991. *Prescription-Medicide: The Goodness of Planned Death.* Buffalo, NY: Prometheus Books.

Khomeini, Ayatollah. 1980. *Sayings of the Ayatollah Khomeini: Political, Philosophical, Social, and Religious.* New York: Bantam Books.

Killian, Lewis M. 1984. "Organization, Rationality and Spontaneity in the Civil Rights Movement." *American Sociological Review* 49: 770–783.

King, Katie. 1986. "The Situation of Lesbianism as Feminism's Magic Sign: Contests for Meaning and the U.S. Women's Movement, 1968-1972." *Communication* 9: 65–91.

Klandermans, Bert. 1988. "The Formation and Mobilization of Consensus." *International Social Movement Research: Comparing Movement Participation Across Cultures* 1: 173–197.

———. 1992. "The Social Construction of Protest and Multiorganizational Fields." In *Frontiers in Social Movement Theory,* edited by A. Morris and C. Mueller, 77–103. New Haven, CT: Yale University Press.

Klandermans, Bert, Hanspeter Kriesi, and Sidney Tarrow, eds. 1988. *International Social Movement Research: From Structure to Action: Comparing Movement Participation Across Cultures.* Greenwich, CT: JAI Press.

Kleidman, Robert. 1993. *Organizing for Peace: Neutrality, The Test Ban, and the Freeze.* Syracuse, NY: Syracuse University Press.

Kleinman, Sherryl. 1984. *Equals Before God.* Chicago: University of Chicago Press.

Kohl, Herbert. 1995. *Should We Burn Babar? Essays on Children's Literature and the Power of Stories.* New York: New Press.

Kosmin, Barry A., and Seymour P. Lachman. 1993. *One Nation Under God: Religion in Contemporary American Society.* New York: Crown.

Kronman, Anthony. 1996. "Leontius' Tale." In *Law's Stories: Narrative and Rhetoric in Law,* edited by P. Brooks and P. Gewirtz, 54–56. New Haven, CT: Yale University Press.

Kumar, Krishan. 1995. *From Post-Industrial to Post-Modern Society: New Theories of the Contemporary World.* New York: Blackwell.

LaHaye, Tim. 1980. *The Battle for the Mind.* Old Tappan, NJ: Fleming H. Revell Company.

Laing, R. D. 1967. *The Politics of Experience.* New York: Pantheon.

Laraña, Enrique, Hank Johnston, and Joseph R. Gusfield, eds. 1994. *New Social Movements: From Ideology to Identity.* Philadelphia, PA: Temple University Press.

Lasch, Christopher. 1965. *The New Radicalism in America, 1889-1963: The Intellectual as a Social Type.* New York: Knopf.

———. 1978. *The Culture of Narcissism.* New York: W. W. Norton and Company.

Lawrence, Bruce B. 1989. *Defenders of God: The Fundamentalist Revolt Against the Modern Age.* New York: Harper and Row Publishers.

Layman, Geoffrey C. 1997. "Religion and Political Behavior in the United States: The Impact of Beliefs, Affiliations, and Commitment from 1980–1994." *Public Opinion Quarterly* 61 (2): 288–316.

Leitch, Thomas M. 1986. *What Stories Are: Narrative Theory and Interpretation.* University Park: Pennsylvania State University Press.

Lewis, J. M. 1972. "A Study of the Kent State Incident Using Smelser's Theory of Collective Behavior." *Sociological Inquiry* 42: 87–96.

Lewis, James R., and J. Gordon Melton, eds. 1992. *Perspectives on the New Age.* Albany: State University of New York Press.

———. 1994. *The Church Universal and Triumphant: In Scholarly Perspective. Special Issue of Syzygy.* Stanford, CA: Center for Academic Publication.

Lifton, Robert. 1961. *Chinese Thought Reform and the Psychology of Totalism.* New York: Norton.

Lofland, John. 1966. *Doomsday Cult: A Study of Conversion, Proselytization, and Maintenance of Faith.* Englewood Cliffs, NJ: Prentice-Hall.

———. 1985. *Protest: Studies of Collective Behavior and Social Movements.* New Brunswick, NJ: Transaction Books.

Loseke, Donileen R. 1992. *The Battered Woman and Shelters.* Albany: State University of New York Press.

Luhrmann, T. M. 1993. "The Resurgence of Romanticism: Contemporary Neopaganism, Feminist Spirituality, and the Divinity of Nature." In *Environmentalism: The View from Anthropology,* edited by K. Milton, 219–232. London: Routledge.

Luker, Kristin. 1984. *Abortion and the Politics of Motherhood.* Berkeley: University of California Press.

Lustick, Ian S. 1987. "Israel's Dangerous Fundamentalists." *Foreign Policy* (68): 118–39.

———. 1993. "Jewish Fundamentalism and the Israeli-Palestinian Impasse." In *Jewish Fundamentalism in Comparative Perspective: Religion, Ideology, and the Crisis of Modernity,* edited by L. J. Silberstein, 104–116. New York: New York University Press.

Lynd, Staughton. 1966. "On White Power." *New Left Notes* (August 24).

Lyotard, Jean-Francois. 1984. *The Post-Modern Condition: A Report on Knowledge.* Minneapolis: University of Minnesota Press.

MacIntyre, Alasdair. 1981. *After Virtue: A Study in Moral Theory.* Notre Dame, IN: University of Notre Dame Press.

———. 1984. *After Virtue,* 2d ed. Notre Dame, IN: University of Notre Dame Press.

MacKinnon, Catherine. 1996. "Law's Stories as Reality and Politics." In *Law's Stories: Narrative and Rhetoric in Law,* edited by P. Brooks and P. Gewirtz, 232–237. New Haven, CT: Yale University Press.

Maines, David R. 1993. "Narrative's Moment and Sociology's Phenomena: Toward a Narrative Sociology." *The Sociological Quarterly* 34: 17–38.

———. 1999. "Information Pools and Racialized Narrative Structures." *The Sociological Quarterly* 40: 317–326.

Malkani, K. R. 1980. *The RSS Story.* New Delhi: Impex India.

Martin, Bernice. 1981. *A Sociology of Contemporary Cultural Change.* New York: St. Martin's.

Martin, Del. 1981. *Battered Wives.* San Francisco: Volcano Press.

Martin, Joanne. 1992. *Cultures in Organizations.* New York: Oxford University Press.

Martin, Joanne, M. S. Feldman, M. S. Hatch, Sim B. Sitkin. 1983. "The Uniqueness Paradox in Organizational Stories." *Administrative Science Quarterly* 28: 438–453.

Martin, Wallace. 1986. *Recent Theories of Narrative.* Ithaca, NY: Cornell University Press.

Marty, Martin, and R. Scott Appleby, eds. 1994. *Accounting for Fundamentalisms*. Chicago: University of Chicago Press.

Marzen, Thomas J., Mary K. O'Dowd, Daniel Crone, and Thomas J. Balch. 1985. "Suicide: A Constitutional Right?" *Duquesne Law Review* 24: 1–242.

Maslow, Abraham. 1964. *Religions, Values, and Peak-Experiences*. Columbus: Ohio State University Press.

———. 1968. *Toward a Psychology of Being*. Princeton, NJ: Van Nostrand Reinhold.

———. 1970. *Motivation and Personality*, 2d ed. Princeton, NJ: Van Nostrand Reinhold.

Massaro, Toni M. 1989. "Empathy, Legal Storytelling, and the Rule of Law: New Words, Old Wounds?" *Michigan Law Review* 87: 2099–2127.

Matthews, Donald, and James Prothro. 1966. *Negroes and the New Southern Politics*. New York: Harcourt, Brace, and World.

Matthiez, Albert. 1904. *Les Origines des Cultes Revolutionnaires, 1789–1792*. Paris: G. Bellais.

Maynard, Douglas, and Marilyn Whalen. 1995. "Language, Action, and Social Interaction." In *Sociological Perspectives on Social Psychology*, edited by K. S. Cook, G. A. Fine, and J. S. House, 149–175. Boston: Allyn and Bacon.

McAdam, Doug. 1982. *Political Process and the Development of Black Insurgency, 1930–1970*. Chicago: University of Chicago Press.

———. 1988. *Freedom Summer*. New York: Oxford University Press.

———. 1994. "Culture and Social Movements." In *New Social Movements: From Ideology to Identity*, edited by E. Laraña, H. Johnston, and J. R. Gusfield, 36–57. Philadelphia, PA: Temple University Press.

McCarthy, John D., and Mayer N. Zald. 1973. *The Trend of Social Movements in America: Professionalization and Resource Mobilization*. Morristown, NJ: General Learning Press.

McDew, Charles. 1966. "Spiritual and Moral Aspects of the Student Nonviolent Struggle in the South." Pp. 51–57 in *The New Student Left*, ed. M. Cohen and D. Hale. Boston: Beacon.

Mead, George Herbert. 1934. *Mind, Self, and Society*, ed. C. W. Morris. Chicago: University of Chicago Press.

———. 1978. *On Social Psychology*, ed. A. Strauss. Chicago: University of Chicago Press.

Melucci, Alberto. 1989. *Nomads of the Present: Social Movements and Individual Needs in Contemporary Society.* Philadelphia, PA: Temple University Press.

Mendel-Reyes, Meta. 1995. *Reclaiming Democracy: The Sixties in Politics and Memory.* New York: Routledge.

Meyer, David S. 1990. *A Winter of Discontent: The Nuclear Freeze and American Politics.* New York: Praeger.

Meyer, David S., and Suzanne Staggenborg. 1996. "Movements, Countermovements, and the Structure of Political Opportunity." *American Journal of Sociology* 101: 1628–1660.

Meyer, John W., and Brian Rowan. 1977. "Institutionalized Organizations: Formal Structure as Myth and Ceremony." *American Journal of Sociology* 83: 340–363.

Miller, J. Hillis. 1990. "Narrative." In *Critical Terms for Literary Study,* edited by F. Lentricchia and T. McLaughlin, 66–79. Chicago: University of Chicago Press.

Miller, James. 1987. *Democracy Is in the Streets: From Port Huron to the Siege of Chicago.* New York: Simon and Schuster.

Mills, C. Wright. 1940. "Situated Actions and Vocabularies of Motive." *American Sociological Review* 5: 404–413.

———. 1959. *The Sociological Imagination.* New York: Oxford University Press.

Mishra, Dina Nath. 1980. *RSS: Myth and Reality.* New Delhi: Vikas Publishing House.

Mitchell, W. J. T. 1981. *On Narrative.* Chicago: University of Chicago Press.

Morris, Aldon. 1984. *The Origins of the Civil Rights Movement: Black Communities Organizing for Change.* New York: Free Press.

Morris, Aldon, and Carol McClurg Mueller, eds. 1992. *Frontiers in Social Movement Theory.* New Haven, CT: Yale University Press.

Nelkin, Dorothy, and Michael Pollak. 1981. *The Atom Beseiged.* Cambridge, MA: MIT Press.

NiCarthy, Ginny. 1987. *The Ones Who Got Away: Women Who Left Abusive Partners.* Seattle, WA: The Seal Press.

Nielsen, Niels, Jr. 1993. *Fundamentalism, Mythos, and World Religions.* Albany: State University of New York Press.

Nolan, James L., Jr. 1996. "Contrasting Styles of Political Discourse in America's Past and Present Culture Wars." In *The American Cul-*

ture Wars: Current Contests and Future Prospects, edited by J. L. Nolan, Jr., 155–188. Charlottesville: University Press of Virginia.

————. 1998. *The Therapeutic State: Political Legitimation at Century's End.* New York: New York University Press.

Nuland, Sherwin B. 1995. *How We Die: Reflections on Life's Final Chapter.* New York: Random House.

Oberschall, Anthony. 1989. "The 1960 Sit-Ins: Protest Diffusion and Movement Take-Off." *Research in Social Movements, Conflict and Change* 11: 31–53.

Olick, Jeffrey. 1999. "Genre Memories and Memory Genres: A Dialogical Analysis of May 8, 1945 Commemoration in the Federal Republic of Germany." *American Sociological Review* 64 (3): 382–403.

Olick, Jeffrey, and Joyce Robbins. 1998. "Social Memory Studies: From 'Collective Memory' to the Historical Sociology of Mnemonic Practices." *Annual Review of Sociology* 24: 105–140.

Oppenheimer, Martin. 1989. *The Sit-In Movement of 1960.* Brooklyn, NY: Carlson.

Ouchi, William G. 1981. *Theory Z.* Reading, MA: Addison-Wesley.

Ouchi, William G., and Alan L. Wilkins. 1985. "Organizational Culture." *Annual Review of Sociology* 11: 457–483.

Pagelow, Mildred Daley. 1981. *Woman-Battering: Victims and Their Experiences.* Beverly Hills: Sage Publications.

Peters, Thomas J., and R. H. Waterman, Jr. 1982. *In Search of Excellence.* New York: Harper and Row.

Pfeffer, Jeffrey. 1981. "Management as Symbolic Action: The Creation and Maintenance of Organizational Paradigms." In *Research in Organizational Behavior,* vol. 3, edited by L. L. Cummings, 1–52. Greenwich, CT: JAI Press.

Pichardo, Nelson A. 1997. "New Social Movements: A Critical Review." *Annual Review of Sociology* 23: 411–430.

Pingry, Patricia. 1980. *Jerry Falwell: Man of Vision.* Milwaukee, WI: Ideals Publishing.

Polkinghorne, Donald E. 1988. *Narrative Knowing and the Human Sciences.* Albany: State University of New York Press.

Polletta, Francesca. 1997. "Culture and Its Discontents: Recent Theorizing on the Cultural Dimensions of Protest." *Sociological Inquiry* 67 (4): 431–450.

————. 1998a. "'It Was Like a Fever . . .' : Narrative and Identity in Social Protest." *Social Problems* 45 (2): 137–159.

————. 1998b. "Contending Stories: Narrative in Social Movements." *Qualitative Sociology* 21 (4): 419–446.

————. 1998c. "Legacies and Liabilities of an Insurgent Past: Remembering Martin Luther King, Jr. on the House and Senate Floors." *Social Science History* 22 (4): 479–512.

Powell, W. W., and Paul DiMaggio, eds. 1991. *The New Institutionalism in Organizational Analysis*. Chicago: University of Chicago Press.

Pratt, Mary Louise. 1977. *Toward a Speech Act Theory of Literary Discourse*. Bloomington: Indiana University Press.

Price, Jerome. 1982. *The Antinuclear Movement*. Boston: Twayne Publishers.

Quill, Timothy E. 1996. *A Midwife through the Dying Process: Stories of Healing and Hard Choices at the End of Life*. Baltimore, MD: Johns Hopkins University Press.

Rappaport, Roy A. 1979. *Ecology, Meaning, and Religion*. Richmond, CA: North Atlantic Books.

Red River Peace Network. 1985. *Pantex Pilgrimage 85 Peace Camp Handbook*.

Rice, John S. 1992. "A Disease of One's Own: Psychotherapy, Addiction, and the Emergence of Co-Dependency." Ph.D. dissertation, University of Virginia.

————. 1994. "The Therapeutic God: Transcendence and Identity in Two Twelve-Step Quasi-Religions." In *Religion and the Social Order*, vol. 4, edited by A. L. Greil and T. Robbins, 151–164. Greenwich, CT: JAI Press.

————. 1996. *A Disease of One's Own: Psychotherapy, Addiction, and the Emergence of Co-Dependency*. New Brunswick, NJ: Transaction Publishers.

Richardson, J. T. 1983. "New Religious Movements in the United States: A Review." *Sociological Compass* 30: 85–110.

Richardson, Laurel. 1990. "Narrative and Sociology." *Journal of Contemporary Ethnography* 19: 116–35.

Ricoeur, Paul. 1984. *Time and Narrative*, vol. 1, trans. K. McLaughlin and D. Pellauer. Chicago: University of Chicago Press.

————. 1988. *Time and Narrative*, vol. 3, trans. K. Blamey and D. Pellauer. Chicago: University of Chicago Press.

Rieff, Philip. 1966. *The Triumph of the Therapeutic: Uses of Faith After Freud*. New York: Harper and Row.

Robbins, Thomas. 1979. "Cults and the Therapeutic State." *Social Policy* 10: 42–46.

———. 1984. "Constructing Cultist 'Mind Control.'" *Sociological Analysis* 45: 241–256.

Robbins, Thomas, and Dick Anthony. 1978. "New Religions, Families, and Brainwashing." *Society* 15: 77–83.

———. 1982. "Deprogramming, Brainwashing, and the Medicalization of Deviant Religious Groups." *Social Problems* 29: 283–297.

Rochberg-Halton, Eugene. 1986. *Meaning and Modernity: Social Theory in the Pragmatic Attitude*. Chicago: University of Chicago Press.

Rohlen, Thomas P. 1973. "Spiritual Education in a Japanese Bank." *American Anthropologist* 75: 1542–1562.

Roof, Wade Clark. 1993. *A Generation of Seekers: The Spiritual Journeys of the Baby Boom Generation*. San Francisco: HarperSanFrancisco.

Rose, Vicki McNickle. 1977. "Rape as a Social Problem: A Byproduct of the Feminist Movement." *Social Problems* 25: 75–89.

Rosnow, Ralph, and Gary Alan Fine. 1976. *Rumor and Gossip: The Social Psychology of Hearsay*. New York: Elsevier.

Rossman, Michael. 1979. *New Age Blues: On the Politics of Consciousness*. New York: E. P. Dutton.

Roucek, Joseph S. 1978. "Ideology." In *Social Control for the 1980's*, edited by J. S. Roucek, 150–160. Westport, CT: Greenwood Press.

Rupert, Glenn A. 1992. "Employing the New Age: Training Seminars." In *Perspectives on the New Age*, edited by J. R. Lewis and J. G. Melton, 127–135. Albany: State University of New York Press.

Russell, Cheryl. 1993. *The Master Trend: How the Baby Boom Generation Is Remaking America*. New York: Plenum.

Sacks, Harvey. 1992. *Lectures on Conversations*. Cambridge: Blackwell.

Sale, Kirkpatrick. 1973. *SDS*. New York: Random House.

Sarbin, Theodore. 1986. *Narrative Psychology: The Storied Nature of Human Conduct*. New York: Praeger.

———. 1995. "Emotional Life, Rhetoric, and Roles." *Journal of Narrative and Life History* 5 (3): 213–220.

Sargent, William. 1957. *Battle of the Mind*. Garden City, NY: Doubleday.

Schaef, Anne Wilson. 1986. *Co-Dependence: Misunderstood—Mistreated*. New York: Harper and Row.

Schechter, Susan. 1982. *Women and Male Violence: The Visions and Struggles of the Battered Women's Movement*. Boston: South End Press.

Scheff, Thomas. 1994. *Bloody Revenge: Emotions, Nationalism, and War*. Boulder, CO: Westview Press.

Schein, Edgar, I. Schneir, and C. H. Barker. 1961. *Coercive Persuasion*. New York: Norton.

Scheppele, Kim Lane. 1989. "Foreword: Telling Stories," *Michigan Law Review* 87: 2073–2098.

Schudson, Michael. 1989. "How Culture Works: Perspectives from Media Studies on the Efficiency of Symbols." *Theory and Society* 18: 153–180.

———. 1992. *Watergate in American Memory: How We Remember, Forget, and Reconstruct the Past*. New York: Basic Books.

Schur, Edwin. 1976. *The Awareness Trap: Self-Absorption Instead of Social Change*. New York: McGraw-Hill.

Schwartz, Barry. 1991. "Social Change and Collective Memory: The Democratization of George Washington." *American Sociological Review* 56: 221–236.

———. 1996. "Memory as a Cultural System: Abraham Lincoln in World War II." *American Sociological Review* 61: 908–927.

Schwartz, Lita, and Natalie Isser. 1981. "Some Involuntary Conversion Techniques." *Jewish Social Studies* 43: 1–10.

Sclafani, Richard J. 1979. "Artworks, Art Theory, and the Artworld." *Theoria* 39: 18–34.

Seliktar, Ofira. 1983. "The New Zionism." *Foreign Policy* 51: 118–138.

Sennett, Richard. 1976. *The Fall of Public Man: The Social Psychology of Capitalism*. New York: Vintage.

Sewell, William. 1992. "A Theory of Structure: Duality, Agency, and Transformation." *American Journal of Sociology* 98: 1–29.

Shibutani, Tamotsu. 1955. "Reference Groups as Perspectives." *American Journal of Sociology* 60: 562–569.

Shupe, Anson D., Jr., and David G. Bromley. 1980. *The New Vigilantes: Deprogrammers, Anticultists, and the New Religions*. Beverly Hills: Sage.

———. 1983. "Apostates and Atrocity Stories: Some Parameters in the Dynamics of Deprogramming." Pp. 179–215 in *The Social Impact of New Religious Movements*, ed. B. Wilson. New York: Rose of Sharon.

Silverstein, Michael, and Greg Urban. 1996. "The Natural History of Discourse." In *Natural Histories of Discourse*, edited by M. Silverstein and G. Urban, 1–17. Chicago: University of Chicago Press.

Sivan, Emmanuel. 1985. *Radical Islam, Medieval Theology, and Modern Politics.* New Haven: Yale University Press.

Smelser, Neil. 1962. *Theory of Collective Behavior.* New York: Free Press.

Smircich, Linda. 1983. "Concepts of Culture and Organizational Analysis." *Administrative Science Quarterly* 28: 339–358.

Snow, David A., and Robert D. Benford. 1988. "Ideology, Frame Resonance, and Participant Mobilization." In *International Social Movement Research: From Structure to Action,* edited by B. Klandermans, H. Kriesi, and S. Tarrow, 197–217. Greenwich, CT: JAI Press.

———. 1992. "Master Frames and Cycles of Protest." In *Frontiers in Social Movement Theory,* edited by A. Morris and C. Mueller, 133–155. New Haven, CT: Yale University Press.

Snow, David A., E. Burke Rochford, Jr., Steven K. Worden, and Robert D. Benford. 1986. "Frame Alignment Processes, Micromobilization, and Movement Participation." *American Sociological Review* 51: 464–481.

Snow, David A., Louis A. Zurcher, and Robert Peters. 1981. "Victory Celebrations as Theater: A Dramaturgical Approach to Crowd Behavior." *Symbolic Interaction* 4: 21–41.

Somers, Margaret R. 1994. "The Narrative Constitution of Identity: A Relational and Network Approach." *Theory and Society* 23: 605–649.

Sprinzak, Ehud. 1993. "The Politics, Institutions, and Culture of the Gush Emunim." In *Jewish Fundamentalism in Comparative Perspective: Religion, Ideology and the Crisis of Modernity,* edited by L. J. Silberstein, 117–147. New York: New York University Press.

Stapels, Brent. 1995. "Learning to Batter Women." *New York Times* (12 January).

Stark, Evan, and Anne Flitcraft. 1988. "Violence among Intimates." In *Handbook of Family Violence,* edited by V. B. Van Hasselt, 293–317. New York: Plenum Press.

Steinmetz, George. 1992. "Reflections on the Role of Social Narratives in Working-Class Formation: Narrative Theory in the Social Sciences." *Social Science History* 16: 489–516.

Stewart, Charles J., Craig Allen Smith, and Robert E. Denton, Jr. 1994. *Persuasion and Social Movements,* 3rd ed. Prospect Heights, IL: Waveland Press.

Stoecker, Randy. 1995. "Community, Movement, Organization: The Problem of Identity Convergence in Collective Action." *The Sociological Quarterly* 36 (1): 111–130.

Stoper, Emily. 1989. *The Student Nonviolent Coordinating Committee: The Growth of Radicalism in a Civil Rights Organization.* Brooklyn, NY: Carlson.

Straus, Murray A., and Richard J. Gelles. 1986. "Societal Change and Change in Family Violence from 1975 to 1985 as Revealed by Two National Surveys." *Journal of Marriage and the Family* 48: 465–479.

Straus, Murray A., Richard J. Gelles, and Suzanne K. Steinmetz. 1980. "The Marriage License as a Hitting License." In *Behind Closed Doors: Violence in the American Family,* 31–50. New York: Anchor Books.

Student Nonviolent Coordinating Committee (SNCC) Papers Microfilm, 1959–1972. Sanford, NC: Microfilming Corporation of America.

Swidler, Ann, and Jorge Arditi. 1994. "The New Sociology of Knowledge." *Annual Review of Sociology* 20: 305–329.

Tarrow, Sidney. 1998. *Power in Movement,* 2d ed. Ithaca, NY: Cornell University Press.

Tauber, Jeffrey. 1993. "A Judicial Primer." Unpublished paper (20 August).

Taylor, Charles. 1989. *Sources of the Self: The Making of the Modern Identity.* Cambridge, MA: Harvard University Press.

Taylor, Verta. 1989. "Social Movement Continuity: The Women's Movement in Abeyance." *American Sociological Review* 54 (5): 761–775.

———. 1996. *Rock-A-By Baby: Feminism, Self-Help and Postpartum Depression.* New York: Routledge.

Taylor, Verta, and Nancy Whittier. 1992. "Collective Identity in Social Movement Communities: Lesbian Feminist Mobilization." In *Frontiers of Social Movement Theory,* edited by A. Morris and C. Mueller, 104–129. New Haven, CT: Yale University Press.

Thoits, Peggy. 1989. "The Sociology of Emotions." *Annual Review of Sociology* 15: 317–342.

Tibi, Bassam. 1988. *The Crisis of Modern Islam: A Preindustrial Culture in the Scientific Technological Age.* Salt Lake City: University of Utah Press.

Tierney, Kathleen J. 1982. "The Battered Women Movement and the Creation of the Wife Beating Problem." *Social Problems* 29: 207–219.

Tilly, Charles. 1978. *From Mobilization to Revolution.* Reading, MA: Addison-Wesley.

Todd, Andrea. 1995. "When He Was Good." *New York Times Magazine* (21 May).

Trilling, Lionel. 1980. *Sincerity and Authenticity.* New York: Harcourt Brace Jovanovich.

Turner, Patricia. 1993. *I Heard It Through the Grapevine.* Berkeley: University of California Press.

Turner, Ralph H., and Lewis M. Killian. 1987. *Collective Behavior,* 3d ed. Englewood Cliffs, NJ: Prentice Hall.

Turner, Victor. 1967. *The Ritual Process.* Ithaca, NY: Cornell University Press.

———. 1974. *Dramas, Fields, and Metaphors: Symbolic Action in Human Society.* Ithaca, NY: Cornell University Press.

Veroff, Joseph, Elizabeth Douvan, and Richard A. Kulka. 1981. *The Inner American: A Self-Portrait From 1957 to 1976.* New York: Basic Books.

Voll, John. 1991. "Fundamentalism in the Sunni Arab World: Egypt and the Sudan." In *Fundamentalisms Observed,* edited by M. Marty and R. S. Appleby, 345–402. Chicago: University of Chicago Press.

Voss, Kim. 1996. "Defeat 'Frames' and Solidarity: Researching the Impact of Social Movement Culture." Paper presented at the American Sociological Association Annual Meeting.

Walker, Lenore. 1979. *The Battered Woman.* New York: Harper and Row.

———. 1984. *The Battered Woman Syndrome.* New York: Springer Publishing Company.

Walsh, Edward J. 1981. "Resource Mobilization and Citizen Protest in Communities around Three Mile Island." *Social Problems* 29: 1–21.

Walzer, Michael. 1960. "A Cup of Coffee and a Seat." *Dissent* 7 (Spring): 111–120.

Weisberg, Robert. 1996. "Proclaiming Trials as Narratives: Premises and Pretenses." In *Law's Stories: Narrative and Rhetoric in the Law,* edited by P. Brooks and P. Gewirtz, 61–83. New Haven, CT: Yale University Press.

Weisburd, David. 1989. *Jewish Settler Violence: Deviance as Social Reaction.* University Park: Pennsylvania State University Press.

White, Hayden. 1981. "The Value of Narrativity in the Representation of Reality." In *On Narrative,* edited by W. J. T. Mitchell, 1–23. Chicago: University of Chicago Press.

Whitfield, Charles. 1986. *Healing the Child Within.* Baltimore, MD: The Resource Group.

Whyte, William Foote. 1943. *Street Corner Society.* Chicago: University of Chicago Press.

Wiley, Juniper. 1991. "A Refracted Reality of Everyday Life: The Constructed Culture of a Therapeutic Community." *Symbolic Interaction* 14: 139–163.

Wilkins, Alan L. 1979. *Organizational Stories as an Expression of Management Philosophy.* Ph.D. dissertation, Stanford University.

Williams, Raymond. 1961. *The Long Revolution.* New York: Columbia University Press.

Williams, Rhys H. 1994. "Movement Dynamics and Social Change: Transforming Fundamentalist Ideology and Organizations." In *Accounting for Fundamentalisms,* eds. M. Marty and R. S. Appleby, 785–833. Chicago: University of Chicago Press.

Wuthnow, Robert. 1987. *Meaning and Moral Order: Explorations in Cultural Analysis.* Berkeley: University of California Press.

Wuthnow, Robert, and Matthew R. Lawson. 1994. "Sources of Christian Fundamentalism in the United States." In *Accounting for Fundamentalisms,* edited by M. Marty and R. S. Appleby, 18–56. Chicago: University of Chicago Press.

Yankelovich, Daniel. 1982. *New Rules: Searching for Self-Fulfillment in a World Turned Upside Down.* New York: Bantam.

York, Michael. 1995. *The Emerging Network: A Sociology of the New Age and Neo-Pagan Movements.* Lanham, MD: Rowman & Littlefield.

Zeitlin, Steven J., Amy J. Kotkin, and Holly Cutting-Baker. 1982. *Celebration of American Family Folklore.* New York: Pantheon.

Zilbergeld, Bernie. 1983. *The Shrinking of America.* Boston: Little, Brown.

Zinn, Howard. 1964. *SNCC: The New Abolitionists.* Boston: Beacon.

Zurcher, Louis A. 1982. "The Staging of Emotions: A Dramaturgical Analysis." *Symbolic Interaction* 5: 1–22.

———. 1985. "The War Game: Organizational Scripting and the Expression of Emotion." *Symbolic Interaction* 8: 191–206.

Zurcher, Louis A., Jr., and R. George Kirkpatrick. 1976. *Citizens for Decency: Antipornography Crusades as Status Defense.* Austin: University of Texas Press.

Zurcher, Louis A., Jr., and David A. Snow. 1981. "Collective Behavior: Social Movements." In *Social Psychology: Sociological Perspectives,* edited by M. Rosenberg and R. H. Turner, 447–482. New York: Basic Books.

Contributors

ROBERT D. BENFORD is professor and chair of the Department of Sociology at Southern Illinois University. His published works on framing processes and other social constructionist issues associated with social movements, nuclear politics, war museums, and environmental controversies have appeared in journals such as the *Annual Review of Sociology, American Sociological Review, Social Forces, The Sociological Quarterly, Sociological Inquiry, Peace Review,* and *Mobilization.* He serves as editor of the *Journal of Contemporary Ethnography* and Twayne Publishers' "Social Movements Past and Present" series.

MICHAEL F. BROWN is the James N. Lambert professor of anthropology and Latin American Studies at Williams College. He is the author, most recently, of *The Channeling Zone: American Spirituality in an Anxious Age* (Harvard 1997). His earlier books include *War of Shadows: The Struggle for Utopia in the Peruvian Amazon* (with Eduardo Fernández) (California, 1991), and *Tsewa's Gift: Magic and Meaning in an Amazonian Society* (Smithsonian Institution, 1986).

JOSEPH E. DAVIS is program director of the Institute for Advanced Studies in Culture and research assistant professor of sociology at the University of Virginia. His articles have appeared in academic journals such as *Qualitative Sociology, Journal of Policy History,* and *The Hedgehog Review,* as well as in more popular publications. He is author of a book on the theoretical foundations of anticultism and editor of *Identity and Social Change* (Transaction 2000).

275

GARY ALAN FINE is professor of sociology at Northwestern University. He is the author of many books, including *Rumor and Gossip: The Social Psychology of Hearsay* (with Ralph Rosnow; Elsevier 1976) and *Manufacturing Tales: Sex and Money in Contemporary Legends* (Tennessee 1992). His recent work on racial rumors appears in *Rumor in Black and White* (with Patricia Turner; California 1998). His most recent work on reputations is *Difficult Reputations: How We Remember the Evil, the Inept, and the Controversial* (Chicago 2001).

JAMES DAVISON HUNTER is the William R. Kenan professor of sociology and director of the Institute for Advanced Studies in Culture at the University of Virginia. He is the author of many books, including *The Death of Character: Moral Education in an Age Without Good or Evil* (Basic Books 2000), *Before the Shooting Begins: Searching for Democracy in America's Culture War* (Free Press 1994), *Culture Wars: The Struggle to Define America* (Basic Books 1991), and *Evangelicalism: The Coming Generation* (Chicago 1987). His numerous articles have appeared in a wide variety of academic and opinion journals.

JAMES L. NOLAN JR. is assistant professor of sociology at Williams College. He is the author of *The Therapeutic State: Justifying Government at Century's End* (NYU Press 1998), and *Reinventing Justice: The American Drug Court Movement* (Princeton University Press 2001). He is also the editor of *The American Culture Wars: Current Contests and Future Prospects* (Virginia 1996)

FRANCESCA POLLETTA is assistant professor of sociology at Columbia University. Her articles on culture and social movements have appeared in *Social Problems, Theory and Society, Sociological Forum, Law and Society Review, Mobilization,* and *Social Text.* She is currently completing *Freedom Is an Endless Meeting: Experiments in Radical Democracy from Pre-War Pacifism to the Present.* With Jeff Goodwin and James Jasper, she is coeditor of a collection of essays entitled *Passions and Politics: Emotions in Social Movements* (Chicago 2001).

JOHN STEADMAN RICE is a sociologist and associate professor in the Watson School of Education at the University of North Carolina, Wilmington. He is the author of *A Disease of One's Own: Psychotherapy, Addiction, and the Emergence of Co-Dependency* (Transaction 1996). His articles have appeared in journals such as *Sociological Quarterly* and *Religion and the Social Order*. He is currently at work on a book on the rise of the therapeutic school.

BESS ROTHENBERG is a doctoral candidate in the department of sociology at the University of Virginia. In addition to her research on the definitional politics of the battered women's movement, she is currently a Fulbright scholar writing a dissertation on cross-cultural understandings of the nation.

JEFFERY D. TATUM, for many years a practicing attorney, is currently a doctoral candidate in the department of sociology at the University of Virginia and an associate fellow of the Institute for Advanced Studies in Culture. His dissertation explores the cultural politics of the right-to-die movement in America.

JOSHUA J. YATES is a doctoral candidate in the department of sociology at the University of Virginia. He is author, with James Davison Hunter, of the U.S. site study for the eleven-nation Cultural Globalization Project, directed by Peter Berger and Samuel Huntington.

Index